ABORIGINAL STUDIES 10

Aboriginal Perspectives

Kainai Board of Education
Métis Nation of Alberta
Northland School Division
Tribal Chiefs Institute of Treaty Six

DUVAL

13 14 15 16   23 22 21 20

Printed and bound in Canada

ISBN 13: 978-1-55220-603-4
ISBN 10: 1-55220-603-3

Duval
Nelson Education Ltd.,
1120 Birchmount Road,
Toronto, Ontario, M1K 5G4
Or you can visit our internet site at
http://www.nelson.com

Library and Archives Canada
Cataloguing in Publication
Aboriginal perspectives / Kainai Board of Education ... [et al.].

(Aboriginal studies; 10)
For Grade 10 aboriginal studies.
ISBN 1–55220–603–3

　　1. Native peoples—Canada—Textbooks.
I. Kainai Board of Education II. Series: Aboriginal studies (Edmonton, Alta.) ; 10.

E78.C2A1495   2004 971.004'97   C2004-903737-4

PUBLISHING PARTNERS
Kainai Board of Education
Métis Nation of Alberta
Northland School Division
Tribal Chiefs Institute of Treaty Six

CONTRIBUTORS
Phyllis Cardinal, *Tribal Chiefs Institute of Treaty Six*
Mary Cardinal Collins, *Northland School Division*
Leo Fox, *Kainai Board of Education*
Gregory King, *Métis Nation of Alberta*
Bernie L'Hirondelle, *Métis educator and consultant*
Bernie Makokis, *Tribal Chiefs Institute of Treaty Six*

We acknowledge the financial support of the Government of Canada through the Book Publishing Industry Development Program (BPIDP) for our publishing activities.

The Aboriginal Perspectives project was an initiative of Alberta Learning. This book could not have been created without Alberta Learning's support of the Aboriginal Studies 10 Program of Studies. We thank all who contributed to the development of the Program of Studies.

VALIDATORS (Aboriginal Studies 10)

Elders and cultural advisors
Mike Beaver, *Bigstone Cree First Nation*
Bob Cardinal, *Enoch Band First Nation*
Theresa Cardinal, *Saddle Lake First Nation*
Brenda Davis, *Cayuga, Six Nations of the Grand River*
Elsie Fabian, *Fort McKay First Nation*
Phyllis Fox, *Kainai First Nation*
Marge Friedel, *Lac Ste Anne, Métis Nation of Alberta*
Elmer Ghostkeeper, *Paddle Prairie Métis Settlement*
Victor Gladue, *Calling Lake, Alberta*
Elmer Gullion, *Métis, Trout Lake, Alberta*
Billy Joe Laboucan, *Little Buffalo, Alberta*
Helen Piper, *Cold Lake First Nation*
Joe Spotted Bull, *Kainai First Nation*
Pauline Three Persons, *Kainai First Nation*
Frank Weasel Head, *Kainai First Nation*

Alberta Learning external review committee
Gabe (Gabriel) Cardinal, *Métis Nation (Zone 2)*
Delia Crosschild, *Treaty 7, Blood Tribe*
Dwayne Donald, *Papascase Cree, Edmonton*
Janette Flett-Jones, *Dene, Fort Chipewyan*
Darrell Fors, *Cree, Treaty 8, Sucker Creek*
Claire Fortier, *Cree, Treaty 8, Lesser Slave Lake*
Jacinta Fox, *Treaty 7, Blood Tribe*
Lillian Gadwa-Crier, *Treaty 6, Kehewin*
Christine Jellet, *Wabasca, Alberta*
Sara Loutitt, *Métis Nation, Fort McMurray*

Alberta Learning internal review team
Barb Esdale	Debbie Mineault
Doris Gladue (Lead)	Noella Steinhauer
Evelyn Goodstriker	Patsy Steinhauer
Bertha Laboucan	Gina Vivone-Vernon
Diane Larkin	

PROJECT TEAM
(Aboriginal Studies 10, 20, 30)

Project managers
Lauri Seidlitz   Kim Doyle Thorsen

Editorial
Shauna Babiuk   Kim Doyle Thorsen
Glenn Rollans   Lynn Zwicky
Lauri Seidlitz

Design and production
Carol Dragich, Dragich Design
Jeff Miles   Leslie Stewart
Elina Rubuliak

Image and rights acquisition
Elina Rubuliak   David Strand

Writers
Mike Bruised Head   Bernie Makokis
Phyllis Cardinal   Dianne Meili
Mary Cardinal Collins   Barry Menary
Bernice Carriere   Laura Okemaw
Marion Dick   Lydia Pungur
Jill Fallis   David Rees
Robert Gardner   Scott Rollans
Jason Gariepy   Shannon Souray
Shane Gauthier   Bonnie Stelmach
Candace Hopkins   Tanya Vanderven
Billy Joe Laboucan   Katherine Walker
André L'Hirondelle   Linda Weasel Head
Bernie L'Hirondelle   Cora Weber-Pillwax
Florence Loyie

Translators
Joseph Allen and Renie Arey, Aklavik, NWT
(Inuktitut/Inuvialuktun)
Cynthia Bearhead, Stoney of Paul Band;
Florence Paul Sr., Elder, Paul First Nation;
Leonard Bearhead, Elder, Paul First Nation
(Nakoda)
Molly Chisaakay, Chateh, Alberta (Dené Tha')
Irene Collins, Métis Nation of Alberta (Michif)
Vera Marie Crowchild, Tsuu T'ina First Nation
(Tsuu T'ina)
Makai'stoo (Leo Fox), Kainai First Nation (Blackfoot)
Nellie Friesen, Dominique Habitant,
Madalin Habitant, High Level, Alberta (Dunne-za)
Billy Joe Laboucan, Little Buffalo, Alberta
(Plains Cree)

Maps
Wendy Johnson, Johnson Cartographics Inc.

Photography
Brad Callihoo, New Visions Photography
Jason Witherspoon, New Visions Photography

Photoshoot coordination
Amiskwaciy Academy
Phyllis Cardinal
Lynn Hamilton

Photoshoot models
Bob Cardinal (Amiskwaciy Academy Elder Advisor)
Marge Friedel (Amiskwaciy Academy Elder Advisor)
Avery Atchooay, Neepin Auger, Felecia Chalifoux,
Natosii Crop Eared Wolf, Jeremy Davis-Taylor,
Raven Delorme, Tamara Goulet, Cody Healy,
Daniel Huntley, Jasmine Mah, Ashley Martel, Levi
McKort, Tamara One-Owl, Brett Rain, Jerome
Shiu, Emily Soder-Duncan, Angela Tran

Cover photo credits
All images are copyright © of their respective
copyright holders, as listed below.

(clockwise from top left to right) Courtesy of
Dianne Meili, Courtesy Terry Lusty; Duval stock
images, PMA Staff/Provincial Museum of Alberta,
Edmonton, Alberta; A. Rafton Canning/National
Archives of Canada/PA-029769; Photo by Bruce
Barrett, Yukon International Storytelling Festival

Photo Credits

Every effort has been made to identify, obtain permission from, and credit all sources. The publisher would appreciate notification of omissions or errors so that they may be corrected. All items are copyright © of their respective copyright holders. Reproduced with permission.

Legend: cw=clockwise t=top r=right l=left b=bottom m=middle
Abbreviations: BCA=British Columbia Archives; CMC=Canadian Museum of Civilization; CP=Canadian Press Photo; ET/EED= Edmonton Tourism/Edmonton Economic Development Corp. GA=Glenbow Archives; LOC=US Library of Congress; NAC=National Archives of Canada; NLC=National Library of Canada; PMA=Provincial Museum of Alberta, Edmonton; T8=Treaty 8 First Nations; RCAP=Royal Commission on Aboriginal Peoples; YISF=Yukon International Storytelling Festival

IMAGE CREDITS

Cover credits: see page iii. Main text 12, 23, 25 (tr), 27 (b), 59, 69, 70 (all), 75, 77, 78 (l), 80, 83, 91, 98, 129, 148 (b), 177, 222 (bl), 227, 228 Courtesy of Terry Lusty **53 (l), 84, 112 (all), 211 (b)** Courtesy of Fred Cattroll **42, 203** Courtesy of Leo Fox, from *Kipaitapiiwahsinnooni: Alcohol and Drug Abuse Education Program* **67, 183, 204 (t), 206** Courtesy of Blood Tribe **120, 188** Windspeaker, Canada's National Aboriginal News Service **13 (all), 135, 144, 150** by Charles William Jefferys **57, 78 (r)** Courtesy of Kim Doyle Thorsen **17 (bunchberries), 33, 60, 61, 200 (b), 201** Courtesy of Carol Dragich **117 (r), 174** Courtesy of Elina Rubuliak **44, 70** Courtesy of David Strand
3 Courtesy of Ernie Whitford, Calgary **9** George M. Dawson/NAC/ PA-037756 **10** BCA G-00754 **11** A. Rafton Canning/NAC/PA-029769 **15 (b)** GA NA-1727-67 **(t)** Image courtesy of Canadian Tourism Commission **16** ET/EED **19** LOC LC USZ62-133896 [P] **21** NAC/ C-038948 **24** NAC/C-000403/Gift of Mrs. J.B. Jardine **25 (tl)** LOC LC-USZ62-123167 [P&P] **(br)** NAC/ PA-017947 **26** GA NA-1315-22 **27 (t)** Glenbow-Alberta Institute **28** (bison) ET/EED (canoe) NAC/Accession No. 1989-401-2/C-002774 **29** Bernie Makokis **34** BCA D-08249 **35** Courtesy of Kelvin Scheuer **37** by Arnold Aron Jacobs, Ohsweken. Acrylic background, oil on masonite. Photo by Martin Bomberry **38** CP(Kevin Frayer) **39** Leah Fontaine **40** Terry Garvin **41** ©Lindsay Hebberd/CORBIS/MAGMA **43** Courtesy of T8/Lynn Muskwa **45** Monty Sloan/Wolf Park © 2000 **46** Royal Saskatchewan Museum, sculpture by Lloyd Pinay **47 (t)** Robin Karpan **(b)** Okotoks Erratic/Ondrej Tlach **50** Royal Saskatchewan Museum, painting by Dale Stonechild **51** © Bruce Barrett, from YISF **52 (l)** Photograph: Michel Goedart **53** Linda Kershaw **56** Courtesy of PMA/PMA Staff **65** Rocky Barstad **67** Myron Fox, Blood Tribe **68** Emily and Bill Sewepagaham **69** (both) Jill Fallis **71** NASA; JSC AS17-148-22727; GRIN GPN-2000-001138 **73** Courtesy of Treaty 8 First Nation/Kathy Cheecham **79** (all) Courtesy of Pimee Well Servicing Ltd. **87** Rocky Barstad **88** Amiskwaciy Academy, Edmonton Public Schools **89** Courtesy of PMA/PMA Staff **90** K. McGuire **92** Courtesy of Linda Kershaw **96** Molly Chisaakay **97** INAC/Allen Sapp **98** Courtesy of Anna Chief **99 (t)** Courtesy of Anna Chief **(b)** Shirley Hill **100 (t)**Courtesy of Anna Chief **(bl)** Warren Bird **(br)** Kevin Buffalo **101** Jackie Soppit **102** The Workun Garrick Partnership Architecture and Interior Design **105** Zoey Wood-Salomon **107** GA NB-6-7 **109** Les Buckskin Jr. **110** NLC C-142559 **111** Evelyn Goodstriker/Alberta Learning **115** Courtesy Blood Tribe Police Service **121** O.B. Buell/NAC/C-001871 **122 (t)** Alex Redcrow/Confederacy of Treaty 6 **123** Dorothy McDonald **124** NAC/C-033643 **126** LOC LC-USZ62-88073 [P] **127** GA NC-1-189 **130** GA NA-2770-4 **133** Courtesy of Ron Noganosh **134** Provincial Archives of Newfoundland **136** NAC/NLC C-017159 **138** NLC **139** Hudson's Bay Company Archives, Archives of Manitoba, P-228 (N8317 c.) **140** NAC/C-141458/ Acquired with the assistance of Hoechst and Celanese Canada and with a grant from the Department of Canadian Heritage under the Cultural Property Export and Import Act **141** NAC/C-002773 **142** LOC LOT 11453-4, no. 27 [P&P] **143** GA NA-667-72 **145** GA NA-949-118 **147** NAC/C-001065/William Henry Edward Napier **148 (t)** © CMC, catalogue no. E-111, photographer Steven Darby **149** GA NA-1406-240 **151** GA NA-1434-32 **152** GA NA-1338-127 **153** GA NA-577-3 **154** Illustration: Head-Smashed-In Buffalo Jump, Alberta Community Development **155** Archives of Manitoba, Currier and Ives, CN178,

"Life on the Prairie - The Buffalo Hunt" **156** Courtesy Dianne Meili **157** NAC/PA-012854 **158** NAC/PA-066544 **160** BCA NA-39553 **164** NAC **165** LOC LC-USZ62-45595 [P&P] **169** Art by Jane Ash Poitras, RCA-Collection of the Indian Art Centre **171** GA NA-1406-40 **172** GA NA-870-7 **175** GA NC-1-1170-f **178** Courtesy © Katelin Peltier/Métis National Council of Canada **180** Patricia Russell **182** Métis Settlements General Council **185** Anne Marie Auger, Lesser Slave Lake Indian Regional Council **186** GA NA-73-1 **187** Steinhauer Family **191** CP/Calgary Herald(Zoran Bozicevic) **192** Government of Nunavut **195** © CMC, by Lawrence Paul Yuxweluptun, 1990, photo Harry Foster, no. S97-10761 **196** CP(Andrew Vaughan) **197** Courtesy of Wanda McCaslin, Native Law Centre of Canada. Thanks to Shaune Kaye, Kelly Feargue, Paula Robinson, Kim Hamm, Carol Bird, Glen Larlviere, Robert Rooke, Sandra Primeau, Ken Nelson, Alwyn Aubichon, Doug Moran. **202** Courtesy Peace Hills Trust **203** Bernie Makokis **204 (b)** Courtesy of Sawridge Inn and Conference Centre **205 (l)** Courtesy Brenda Holder **(r)** George Halfe, Goodfish Lake Development Corporation **209** Courtesy of Aboriginal Cuisine, Inc. **211 (t)** Photo by Jasper Studios © 2004 Rex Smallboy **212** © CMC, catalogue no. V-B-8 a-b **213** Courtesy of Anna Chief **214** NAC/C-0018739 **217** CP/Associated Press (M. Spencer Green) **218** H85.1067.T/PMA/Brad Callihoo **219** Courtesy Pat Bruderer Half Moon **220** (all) Courtesy of Margaret Cardinal **221** © Bruce Barrett, from YISF **222 (t)** Courtesy of Dale Auger **223 (t)** Photo courtesy of Grande Prairie Regional College **(b)** Courtesy of Alberta Filmworks Inc. **224 (l)** Kent Goetz/Cornell University, Schwartz Center **(r)** © Igloolik Isuma Productions **226** CBC Still Photo Collection/Chris Large **229** Courtesy of Drew Hayden Taylor **230** Don Denton Photo **232** CP/Winnipeg Free Press **235** Courtesy of Priscilla Morin

TEXT CREDITS

Most text credits appear in the body of the text along with the excerpt.

Excerpts from *Kipaitapiiwahsinnooni: Alcohol and Drug Abuse Education Program* reproduced with permission of Leo Fox.
35, 131 From Freda Ahenakew. *Kôhkominawak Otâcimowiniwâwa (Our Grandmothers' Lives as Told in Their Own Words)*.
44, 47, 54, 75, 130 From Hoffman-Mercredi, Lorraine D. and Philip Coutu. *Inkonze: The Stones of Traditional Knowledge*. Edmonton: Thunderwoman Ethnographics, 1999. Reprinted with permission.
210, 232 "It Crosses My Mind" and "Helen Betty Osborne" from *A Really Good Brown Girl* by Marilyn Dumont, Brick Books, 1996.
152, 160, 167 Dion, Joseph F. *My Tribe the Crees*. Calgary: © Glenbow Museum Publications, 1979. p. 62

2 Used with permission from *Keepers of the Animals* by Michael J. Caduto and Joseph Bruchac. © 1999 Fulcrum Publishing, Inc., Golden, Colorado. All rights reserved. **53** Brass, Eleanor. I *Walk in Two Worlds*. Calgary: © Glenbow Museum Publications, 1987. pp. 65-66 **60** (RCAP excerpt) Canada. RCAP, v. 1, *Looking Forward, Looking Back*, p. 34.
61 Dene Kede excerpt reprinted with permission of the Department of Education, Culture and Employment, GNWT **63** Emma Minde, Saddle Lake First Nation, *kwayask ê-kî-pê-kiskinowapahtihicik: Their Example Showed Me the Way: A Cree Woman's Life Shaped by Two Cultures*, The University of Alberta Press. 1997. **64** Reprinted with permission; © Bernie Makokis **103** Ken Saddleback **168–169** From *The LaFontaine Baldwin Lectures* by John Ralston Saul, Alain Debuc, and Georges Erasmus; edited by Rudyard Griffiths. Copyright © The Dominion Institute, 2002. Reprinted by permission of Penguin Group (Canada) **180** Prepared in consultation with Audrey Poitras **226** T. Curley excerpt courtesy of Tagak Curley, C.M., Rankin Inlet, Nunavut **228** "I Lost My Talk" reprinted with Rita Joe's permission. **228** Keeper excerpt from *Keeper'n Me* by Richard Wagamese. Copyright © 1994 by Richard Wagamese. Reprinted by permission of Doubleday Canada.
229 "heritage" reprinted with Wayne Keon's permission.
229–230 Scofield excerpt from *Thunder Through My Veins*. Published by HarperCollins Publishers Ltd. Copyright © 1999 by Gregory Scofield. All rights reserved. **231** Tallow excerpt reprinted with permission of Robin Melting Tallow. "Four Songs for the Fifth Generation" reprinted with Beth Cuthand's permission. **235** *The Art of the Nehiyawak: Exploring the Arts and Crafts of the Woods Cree*, by Ken Hodgins. Plains Publishing Inc., Edmonton. 1988.

Contents

Acknowledgements

Many people and communities collaborated in completing this textbook. We thank them for their contributions and sincere commitment to creating the best resource possible through their comments, insights, photographs, and moral support.

Special thanks to...

Chiefs of the Tribal Chiefs Institute of Treaty Six: Tommy Houle, Gordon John, Al Lameman, Eddy Makokis, Joyce Metchewais, Morris Monias, and Raymond Quinney

Joyce Goodstriker, Superintendent, Kainai Board of Education

Irene Collins, Director of Métis Governance, Métis Nation of Alberta

Annette Ramrattan, Superintendent, Northland School Division

And to...

Dianne Meili for all her help in writing profiles and sidebars, finding translators and images, and for her creativity

Glenn Rollans, Karen Iversen, and Jean Poulin

David Rees for his research assistance

Jim Parsons for his help organizing activities and questions

Betty Sulikowski and Wanda Whitford, Amiskwaciy Academy guidance counsellors, for their help organizing our photoshoot

The Edmonton Public School Board for allowing the use of Amiskwaciy Academy for our photoshoot.

The photo researchers wish to extend special thanks to all those who made the images and text in this book possible, including: George Blondin, Brenda Carroll (CBC), Fred Cattroll, Margaret Cardinal (Northern Lakes College), Anna Chief, Myron Fox (Kainaiwa), Lil Grubach-Hambrook (Yukon International Storytelling Festival), Pat Bruderer Half Moon, Terry Lusty, Wanda McCaslin (Native Law Centre), Ruth McConnell and staff at the Provincial Museum of Alberta, Frédéric Paradis (Canadian Museum of Civilization), Alex Redcrow (Treaty Six), Debora Steel (Windspeaker), Doreen Vaillancourt (INAC), and staff at the Glenbow Museum.

Publisher's Note to Teachers

Words in many Aboriginal languages appear in this textbook to add to student understanding of particular concepts and to reinforce Aboriginal language programs that students may also be studying. In some languages, correct pronunciation of these words requires sounds that are not easily explained using English letters and accents.

To address this issue, a pronunciation guide and glossary of Aboriginal language words will be included in the teacher guide, where adequate space can be dedicated to explanations. We encourage teachers to familiarize themselves with this guide so that they can assist students, where necessary, in the correct pronunciation, use, and understanding of Aboriginal language words.

To the best of our ability, we have verified the spelling and use of Aboriginal language material with community language specialists and have used published dictionaries, where possible, to aid consistency. The suggested reading list on page 241 includes dictionaries that teachers have recommended as helpful.

Please be aware, however, that individuals and communities may follow different spellings and definitions of words and terms that you will find in this book. We recommend that teachers read all sections of the student resource and all activities in the teacher guide prior to using them with students. Careful consideration should be given to the sensitivities of both the student audience and the community.

We encourage students and teachers defer to local community differences when necessary or appropriate. Aboriginal language speakers, Elders, and cultural advisors are a valuable community resource. Teachers are strongly encouraged to invite them to visit classes to enrich student experience whenever possible. The teacher guide will assist teachers with the correct protocol for issuing these invitations.

How to Use this Book

This textbook helps teach Aboriginal (including First Nations, Métis, and Inuit peoples) history, culture, and issues from the perspectives Aboriginal peoples. We have made every effort to create a resource that reflects the diversity of Aboriginal peoples in Canada. Several features of this textbook will help guide you through the information.

Chapter Openings

Each chapter begins with a story, interview, document, speech, or other written work of significance to Aboriginal peoples in Canada. These readings provide material to reflect upon as you begin and end each chapter.

Chapter Reviews

Each chapter ends with questions and activities to help you remember, reflect upon, apply, and broaden the knowledge and skills that you gained in the chapter. You will also be given the opportunity to further explore topics that caught your interest.

Indigenous Knowledge

[Indigenous or traditional knowledge is] a discrete system of knowledge with its own philosophical and value base. Aboriginal peoples hold the belief that traditional knowledge derives from the Creator and is spiritual in essence. It includes ecological teachings, medical knowledge, common attitudes toward Mother Earth and the Circle of Life, and a sense of kinship with all creatures. — *Report of the Royal Commission on Aboriginal Peoples*

At appropriate points in each chapter, you will be asked to reflect upon what you've read with questions and short activities. This feature will help you make connections between indigenous knowledge, your own ideas, and the topic at hand.

Issues for Investigation

These activities include individual, pair, or group projects that further your knowledge about significant topics or issues. Each investigation encourages you to use a variety of resources for your research, including stories from oral traditions, Elders, and other community members. Each activity helps you to expand your repertoire of skills for learning.

Perspectives

This textbook includes many Aboriginal people's first-hand stories, ideas, viewpoints, and experiences. They appear in the form of quotations that provide you with useful perspectives on the past, present, and future of Aboriginal peoples in Canada. We hope they will help you to shape your own opinions.

Profiles

Profiles showcase contemporary and historical Aboriginal people who have made contributions to local, national, and international communities. These people's life experiences, accomplishments, and ideas make them role models worth exploring further.

Symbolism and Expression

Symbolism and Expression activities encourage you to learn about traditional and contemporary forms of Aboriginal creative expression. You will then have opportunities to express your own ideas using these forms of expression.

Talking Circles

Talking Circle activities are designed for group discussion. They make use of Aboriginal traditions of discussion and consensus-building processes and will help you learn an appropriate protocol for conducting talking circles with your classmates.

Timelines and Maps

Detailed maps and informative timelines illustrate and summarize significant topics. You can use the maps and timelines as study aids and as resources for your activities and projects.

NAMES OF FIRST NATIONS, MÉTIS, AND INUIT PEOPLES

Throughout history, different names may have been used in reference to specific First Nations, Métis, and Inuit peoples. Some of these names were attributed incorrectly or inappropriately. Others may have been correct, but the First Nations or Inuit group has come to prefer a different name, usually derived from their own language. To the best of our ability, we have used names and terms preferred by contemporary First Nations, Métis, and Inuit peoples in this textbook.

When you are conducting research, however, you may find former names in history books and Web sites. The following chart, while by no means a complete listing of the First Nations, Métis, and Inuit peoples of Canada, offers some guidance for the correlation of contemporary and historical names of peoples, particularly those that you might find mentioned in this textbook.

Contemporary Name	Alternate Name(s)	Notes
A'aninin (ah-nin-in)	Gros Ventre, White Clay People, Aaninen	United States nation
Anishinabé (a-nish-na-bay) or Saulteaux (so-tow)	Ojibway, Ojibwa, Anishnaabe, Anishnabe, Bungee	The language is often called Ojibway; in Alberta it is called Saulteaux. Called Chippewa in the United States
Aamskaapipikani	South Peigan, South Piikani, Blackfeet	Refers to United states nation related to Blackfoot Confederacy
Blackfoot Confederacy	Blackfoot	
Cayuga		Member of Six Nations Confederacy
Cree or Nehiyaw	Cris	
Dakota	Sioux	
Dené Tha' (de-nay-thah)	Slavey, Slave, Dene-thah, Dene Dha	
Dene Suliné (de-nay-soong-lin-ay)	Chipewyan, Dene Souline, Denesuline	
Dunne-za (da-nay-za)	Beaver, South Slave	
First Nations	Indian, Tribe, Native	
Gitxsan	Tsimshian, Gitksan	
Gwich'in	Loucheaux, Kutchin, Tukudh	
Haisla	Kitimat	
Heiltsuk	Bella Bella	
Innu	Montahfais, Montagnais-Naskapi	
Inuit	Eskimo	
Inuvialuit	Western Inuit	
Haudenosaunee (how-den-o-show-nee)	Iroquois	Six Nations Confederacy
Kainai	Blood	Member of Blackfoot Confederacy
Kichesiprini	Algonquin	
Kitlinermiut	Copper Inuit	
Ktunaxa (doo-na-ha)	Kutenai, Kootenay	
Kwak'waka'wakw or Oweekeno	Kwakiutl, Kwagiutl, Kwakwuwaw, Kwagiulth	
Lakota	Sioux	
Métis	Half-breed, Country-born, Mixed-blood	

Continued...

Contemporary Name	Alternate Name(s)	Notes
Mi'kmaq	Mi'maq, Micmac, Micmaw	
Mohawk		Member of Six Nations Confederacy
Nakoda	Stoney, Assiniboine, Nakota	The Paul First Nation in Alberta prefers the name *Stoney*
Nakota	Assiniboine, Sioux	
Nisga'a	Nishga, Nisga	
Nlaka'pamux	Thompson	
Nuu-chah-nulth	Nootka	
Nuxaulk	Bella Coola	
Odawa	Ottawa	
Oneida		Member of Six Nations Confederacy
Onondaga		Member of Six Nations Confederacy
Ouendat	Huron, Wendat	
Piikani	Peigan, Pikuni, North Peigan	Member of Blackfoot Confederacy
Secwepemc	Shuswap	
Seneca		Member of Six Nations Confederacy
Siksika	Blackfoot	Member of Blackfoot Confederacy
Stl'atl'imx	Lillooet	
Tłıchǫ	Dogrib	
Tlingit		
Tsilhqot'in	Chilcotin	
Tsuu T'ina	Sarcee, Sarsi	
Tuscarora		Member of Six Nations Confederacy
Wet'suwet'en	Babine Carrier	

In Alberta, the major Aboriginal languages spoken in the province include Blackfoot, two variants of Plains Cree (one sometimes known as Woodland Cree), Dene Sųłiné, Dené Tha', Dunne-za, Métis Cree, Michif, Nakoda, Saulteaux, and Tsuu T'ina. A basic greeting in some of these languages is included in the chart below, along with Inuktitut, the language of the Inuit peoples. Your teacher can help you to pronounce each of these greetings with a pronunciation guide.

Language	Greeting	Translation
Blackfoot	oki	"hello"
Cree	tân'si	"hello"
Dene Sųłiné	edláneté	"how are you?"
Dunne-za	neeah	"welcome"
Inuktitut	atitu	"hello"
Métis Cree	tầ'nisi	"hello"
Michif	tánishi	"hello"
Nakoda	ahawâstet	"good day"
Saulteaux	ânîn	"hello, how are you?"
Tsuu T'ina	da ni t'a da	"how are you?"

CHAPTER ONE
Land and People

AS YOU READ

"How the People Hunted the Moose" is one version of a Cree story that has been passed down through generations of oral storytelling. In Cree, it would be called *mamâhtaw âcimona*, which is a story that includes a miracle or other extraordinary experience. You will learn more about this type of story and others in Chapter Two.

Michael J. Caduto and Joseph Bruchac published "How the People Hunted the Moose" in a collection of stories from the oral tradition of First Nations and Inuit communities across North America. Originally told to them by Elders, the stories in their collection are published in their own words so that they can be used for educational purposes.

As you read this story, think about what makes it educational. What cultural values or traditions does it teach? Why might this story have been told in the past? What might people learn from the story today? Do not worry if you cannot answer these questions yet — this chapter and the ones that follow will give you the background you need to answer these and many more questions.

Before you begin, discuss the Focus Questions below with a partner. On your own, write answers to each one and keep them in your notebook. You will have the chance to look back at them later in the course to see how much your knowledge and understanding of these central ideas has grown.

FOCUS QUESTIONS

As you read this chapter, consider these questions:
△ What does the term *Aboriginal peoples* mean?
△ What differences do Aboriginal cultures across Canada show?
△ How do geographic regions affect First Nations and Inuit cultures in Canada?
△ What traditional ways of life are part of First Nations and Inuit peoples' cultural heritage?
△ What are the main Aboriginal cultural groups in Alberta today?

How the People Hunted the Moose

A Cree story from Canada's Subarctic region, as told by Michael J. Caduto and Joseph Bruchac in *Keepers of the Animals*

Mistahi môswa ispîhtawîhtâkosiw ohci Nehiyawawak kâ sakawipimacihotwâw. Wiya kayâs, môswa ohci e-kî-mîcisotwâw, pahkîkin ohci maskisina, miskotâkaya ekwa mîkiwâhpa ê-osîhcikâtekwâw. Kiyâpic kihteyimâw môswa mistahi Nehiyânâhk.

The moose is highly regarded by Cree people who make their livelihood in the bush. Long ago, the moose provided food and hide for moccasins, coats, and tipis. To this day, the moose is still greatly respected.

O NE NIGHT, A FAMILY OF MOOSE WAS SITTING IN THE LODGE. AS THEY SAT AROUND THE FIRE, A STRANGE THING HAPPENED. A PIPE CAME FLOATING IN through the door. Sweet-smelling smoke came from the long pipe and it circled the lodge, passing close to each of the Moose People. The old bull moose saw the pipe but said nothing, and it passed him by. The cow moose said nothing, and the pipe passed her by also. So it passed by each of the Moose People until it reached the youngest of the young bull moose near the door of the lodge.

"You have come to me," he said to the pipe. Then he reached out and took the pipe and started to smoke it.

Buffalo Spirit, 1992. Soapstone carving by Cree-Métis artist Ernie Whitford.

"My son," the old moose said, "you have killed us. This is a pipe from the human beings. They are smoking the pipe now and asking for success in their hunt. Now, tomorrow, they will find us. Now, because you smoked their pipe, they will be able to get us."

"I am not afraid," said the young bull moose. "I can run faster than any of those people. They cannot catch me."

But the old bull moose said nothing more.

When the morning came, the Moose People left their lodge. They went across the land looking for food. But as soon as they reached the edge of the forest, they caught the scent of the hunters. It was the time of year when there is a thin crust on the snow and the moose found it hard to move quickly.

"These human hunters will catch us," said the old cow moose. "Their feet are feathered like those of the grouse. They can walk on top of the snow."

Then the Moose People began to run as the hunters followed them. The young bull moose who had taken the pipe ran off from the others. He was still sure he could outrun the hunters. But the hunters were on snowshoes, and the young moose's feet sank into the snow. They followed him until he tired, and then they killed him. After they killed him, they thanked him for smoking their pipe and giving himself to them so they could survive. They treated his body with care, and they soothed his spirit.

That night, the young bull moose woke up in his lodge among his people. Next to his bed was a present given to him by the human hunters. He showed it to all of the others.

"You see," he said, "it was not a bad thing for me to accept the long pipe the human people sent to us. Those hunters treated me with respect. It is right for us to allow the human beings to catch us."

And so it is to this day. Those hunters who show respect to the moose are always the ones who are successful when they hunt.

When I find a natural shape in a piece of stone I consider it a gift from the stone. In this piece of stone I found a buffalo, a giver of food, clothing, and shelter. It seems appropriate that the stone, a gift from the earth, depicts the giver, The Buffalo Spirit.

— Ernie Whitford, Calgary

▮ REFLECTION

1. Read Ernie Whitford's statement about his carving. With your partner, discuss the idea of gift-giving and how it is connected to both Whitford's carving and "How the People Hunted the Moose." Consider the ideas of giving and receiving in your answer.
2. Brainstorm ideas for how you might represent the story in a performance or work of visual art. Choose the best idea and prepare your project.

Aboriginal Peoples in Canada

AS YOU READ

Pages 4–7 introduce you to the cultural diversity of contemporary Aboriginal peoples in Canada. Aboriginal languages highlight this diversity. People who study languages classify them into families of languages that show similar characteristics. Did you know that there are more language families among Aboriginal peoples in Canada than there are language families in all of Europe? Within these families are fifty-eight different languages, along with many more variants (often called dialects). What might be some of the positive and negative consequences of this linguistic diversity?

EVERY SOCIETY OR GROUP OF PEOPLE HAS A CULTURE. A CULTURE IS THE COLLECTION OF HEREDITARY BELIEFS, VALUES, AND SHARED KNOWLEDGE OF A GROUP OF PEOPLE. THIS COLLECTION OF IDEAS AND ATTITUDES GIVES individuals a common **perspective** or point of view. This perspective helps shape the customs, routines, roles, and rituals that make that group of people distinct from others. A **cultural group** is a number of physically or historically related people with a common culture.

In its broadest sense, **Aboriginal peoples** refers to all people who are descended from the original inhabitants of North America. International organizations, such as the United Nations, use the term **indigenous peoples** to refer to a land's original people. Aboriginal cultures originate from this land. Their entire cultural history takes place on this landscape.

In 1982, the Canadian constitution recognized three groups of Aboriginal peoples: First Nations, Métis, and Inuit. Each of these groups has a unique history, set of languages and variants, and range of cultural practices.

First Nations has more than one meaning. It often refers to a cultural group or **nation** of indigenous peoples, such as the Kainai, Cree, Anishinabé, or Mi'kmaq. First Nations people were once known by the name **Indians**. However, *Indians* is considered offensive to many people today, partly because the name does not reflect the true position of First Nations as indigenous peoples of Canada. This textbook uses names preferred by Aboriginal groups, unless quoting federal government legislation, where the term *Indian* is still common.

Canada's First Nations are diverse historically, culturally, and linguistically. The term *First Nation* can also refer to the government of a group of First Nations people. There are over 630 First Nations governments today, each representing the interests of a distinct group of people.

Inuit people are from Arctic areas of North America, as well as other countries with polar regions. *Inuit* means "the people" in Inuktitut, the Inuit language. Inuit peoples also have diverse cultural traits that vary across the huge Arctic region. Six variants of Inuktitut are spoken in Canada.

Inuit people are also indigenous to Canada, although they are culturally different from First Nations.

The term *métis* comes from a French word that refers to a person of mixed heritage. It first came into

Inuit

Aboriginal Peoples

First Nations   Métis

Canada's constitution (1982) recognizes three groups of Aboriginal peoples, but each of these groups is diverse, including individuals with many different goals and priorities.

use in the sixteenth century, when the French began to visit North America regularly. **Métis** became a name used to describe the heritage of children born of French fur traders and First Nations women.

As the fur trade developed through the next 300 years, the name Métis gradually became more specific. Métis increasingly referred to a culturally distinct nation of people with First Nations–French ancestry. Many of these people lived in the Red River area of what is now Manitoba.

In the twentieth century, the term became broader, often including people with an English– or Scottish–First Nations heritage who were also from Red River. Today political organizations such as the Métis Nation of Alberta define the **Métis Nation** as a group of individuals who are associated with a recognized Métis family or community and who **self-identify** as Métis people.

SELF-IDENTITY
None of the definitions offered so far will fit all people who consider themselves to be Aboriginal. For example, many individuals of mixed heritage identify themselves as Canadian, or First Nations, or sometimes as more than one group, depending on the situation. How a person self-identifies is a significant part of having an Aboriginal cultural identity.

Despite this simple fact, some people are classified into groups by governments or political organizations, no matter how they self-identify. How this situation came to be has a long history that you will begin to explore in this textbook.

CULTURAL DIVERSITY
The map on page 6 shows the major Aboriginal language families in Canada today. Most of these language families include diverse cultural groups. Indicating that several languages are in the same language family does not mean that the languages are the same. For example, English, Russian, and Hindi are all classified in the same language family — the Indo-European language family. Most people would not consider these languages or cultures to be similar. The same principle applies to Aboriginal languages and cultures.

Language families indicate groups of languages that are distantly related. They may indicate groups of people that were long ago related, living in the same region, or having regular contact with one another.

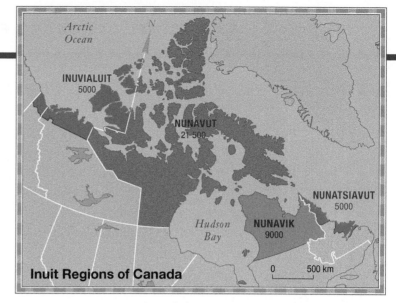

Inuit Regions of Canada

INUVIALUIT 5000

NUNAVUT 21 500

NUNATSIAVUT 5000

NUNAVIK 9000

Hudson Bay

Arctic Ocean

0   500 km

The Inuit Tapiriit Kanatami, a political organization that represents Inuit peoples' interests to the federal government, recognizes four main regions of Inuit peoples. This map shows these regions and their populations.

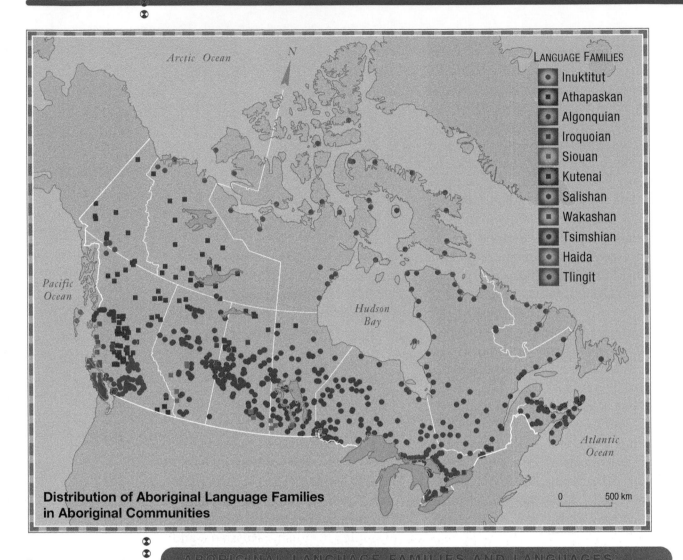

Distribution of Aboriginal Language Families in Aboriginal Communities

LANGUAGE FAMILIES
- Inuktitut
- Athapaskan
- Algonquian
- Iroquoian
- Siouan
- Kutenai
- Salishan
- Wakashan
- Tsimshian
- Haida
- Tlingit

0   500 km

[1] This map and chart give the names Statistics Canada uses in its surveys. Some names are now considered out of date.

[2] Michif, a Métis language that combines French and Cree words, is included in data for the Algonquian language, which is part of the Algonquian Language Family.

[3] The term *isolate* indicates a language for which there are believed to be no other related languages.

ABORIGINAL LANGUAGE FAMILIES AND LANGUAGES[1]

ALGONQUIAN FAMILY	Algonquian[2], Algonquin, Attikamek, Blackfoot, Cree, Malecite, Mi'kmaq, Montagnais-Naskapi, Ojibway, Oji-Cree
ATHAPASKAN FAMILY	Athapaskan, Carrier, Chilcotin, Chipewyan, Dene, Dogrib, Kutchin-Gwitch'in (Loucheux), North Slave (Hare), South Slave
HAIDA (isolate)[3]	
INUKTITUT FAMILY	Inuktitut
IROQUOIAN FAMILY	Iroquoian, Mohawk
KUTENAI (isolate)[3]	
SALISH FAMILY	Salish, Shushwap, Thompson (Ntlakapamux)
SIOUAN FAMILY	Dakoda/Sioux
TLINGIT (isolate)[3]	
TSIMSHIAN FAMILY	Gitksan, Nishga, Tsimshian
WAKASHAN FAMILY	Nootka, Wakashan

Source: Statistics Canada, 1996 Census

Linguistic groups are sometimes more useful in understanding cultural connections. A **linguistic group** is composed of nations who speak the same basic language, although different variations may exist. For example, the Cree linguistic group has five major variants across Canada. One Cree person speaking to another in a different variant could likely make himself or herself understood. However, a Cree person speaking to a Blackfoot speaker will not be understood, even though Cree and Blackfoot are part of the same language family. Blackfoot is its own linguistic group.

Individual communities within one linguistic group can also show many cultural differences from one another.

ABORIGINAL PEOPLES IN CANADA

In the 1996 Census, 799 010 people reported that they were First Nations, Métis, or Inuit. About 6400 people reported that they consider themselves to be a member of more than one Aboriginal group. During this census, Statistics Canada was unable to complete census counts on seventy-seven reserves and settlements. They estimate that approximately 44 000 individuals were therefore not included in their data for 1996. Most of these people are First Nations.

Area	Total Population	First Nations	Métis	Inuit
Canada	28 528 125	554 290	210 190	41 080
Newfoundland	547 160	5430	4685	4265
Prince Edward Island	132 855	825	120	15
Nova Scotia	899 970	11 340	860	210
New Brunswick	729 630	9180	975	120
Quebec	7 045 080	47 600	16 075	8300
Ontario	10 642 790	118 830	22 790	1300
Manitoba	1 100 295	82 990	46 195	360
Saskatchewan	976 615	75 205	36 535	190
Alberta	2 669 195	72 645	50 745	795
British Columbia	3 689 755	113 315	26 750	815
Yukon Territory	30 655	5530	565	110
Northwest Territory	64 120	11 400	3895	24 600

Source: Statistics Canada, 1996 Census

Indigenous Knowledge

In small groups, present some or all of the census information on this page in another format. For example, you might create a pie chart of Aboriginal peoples that shows what percentage of the Aboriginal population each of the three groups composes. Another idea might be a bar graph comparing the Aboriginal population in each province.

LOOKING BACK

This section has introduced you to many new terms and concepts that you will need to understand well before reading the rest of this textbook. Review pages 4–7 and write definitions for each bolded term. Now turn to the glossary at the back of this textbook to read the definitions of each term. Sometimes the glossary presents the term in a slightly different way. Take turns quizzing a partner until you can define each term without referring to your notes.

AS YOU READ

The linguistic diversity described on pages 4–7 is just one aspect of Aboriginal peoples' cultural diversity. Long before European history began in North America, various groups of First Nations and Inuit peoples had developed ways of life to suit every type of geographic environment the continent offered. Pages 8–15 take you back in time to this period before European contact to help you understand the historical connections to the land that underpin today's cultural diversity.

As you read, list general geographic or environmental characteristics (such as the variety of plant life available) that impact the culture of a group of people living in an area. You will use this list for the Issues for Investigation activity on page 14.

THE FIRST PEOPLES WHO LIVED IN NORTH AMERICA LIVED IN HARMONY WITH THE ENVIRONMENT, MAKING LITTLE CHANGE TO THE LANDSCAPE OVER THOUSANDS OF YEARS. WHERE THEY LIVED HAD AN IMPACT ON HOW THEY lived — people in the north had a different lifestyle from those in the south — but all shared a knowledge of and respect for nature that affected every part of their lives.

Where resources were plentiful, people lived in larger groups and developed more structured political, economic, and social lives. Most First Nations and Inuit people, however, lived in small, mobile groups. People travelled in regular seasonal patterns throughout **traditional territories**, which are lands their ancestors had also occupied. Seasonal movements allowed people to make the best possible use of all resources available to them. Their cultures were adapted to this mobility with complex systems of social organization that maintained **kinship** bonds between people who were related, but who lived apart for some or most of the year.

First Nations and Inuit cultures are closely connected to the features of specific environments. Groups living in similar environments often shared many cultural characteristics. For this reason, it is possible to begin a study of First Nations and Inuit peoples in Canada by dividing the country into six geographic environments — the Arctic, Subarctic, Eastern Woodlands, Plains, Plateau, and Pacific

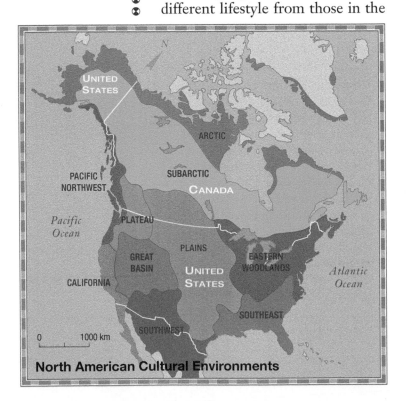

North American Cultural Environments

This map includes the Canada–United States borders to give you reference points, although no such borders existed for most of First Nations and Inuit peoples' history. How are the boundaries between cultural environments shown on the map different from borders between countries?

Northwest. Each environment provides resources and challenges in varying degrees. Each was a **cultural environment** — home to groups of people sharing similar political, economic, and social institutions. **Institutions** are regular, organized patterns of activity within a community.

Keep in mind, however, that differences of language and lifestyle existed even within a cultural group sharing a similar environment. Also remember that although First Nations and Inuit cultures followed **traditional** ways for many centuries, their cultures never stopped evolving (as all cultures do) to suit changing circumstances.

In this textbook, the term *traditional* refers to ways of life that existed before contact with Europeans. It is also used to refer to contemporary ways of life in which people are connected to the spiritual, social, and cultural teachings of their ancestors.

PACIFIC NORTHWEST

Long before the first European visits to North America, First Nations of the Pacific Northwest enjoyed the rich resources of their coastal territory. For these nations, food was almost always plentiful year-round. In this mild, humid climate, dense rainforests covered the land, providing an abundance of edible plants and animals such as deer, bears, and

mountain sheep. Fish filled the many rivers and the ocean, which also provided shellfish, seals, and whales.

This abundance allowed people to live in larger groups and build permanent villages. An estimated 200 000 people lived in this small region around the end of the fifteenth century. Because they had to spend less time on day-to-day tasks, such as finding food, these people had more leisure time. Leisure time allowed them to develop many permanent structures and artistic achievements, such as the large totem poles the region is famous for today.

As some of the world's largest trees grew here, wood was a primary resource. Cedar was used to build large plank houses, bowls, totem poles, toys, sleds, and many other objects. The Tlingit people in the north crafted dugout canoes with projecting knobs to break up ice floes. The Haida were famous for their enormous decorated boats that carried as many as sixty people at a time as they travelled from their islands to fish, hunt, and trade.

This elaborate Haida village at Skidegate in 1878 shows the relatively settled lives for peoples in the Pacific Northwest. What aspects of their surroundings encouraged permanent settlements?

PLATEAU

Traditional ways of life for First Nations from the Plateau region made use of a diverse landscape that varied from desert to forest-covered mountains. First Nations in this region hunted the jackrabbit and antelope that lived on the sagebrush and grasses of the dry flatlands and rolling hills. More game lived in the tall forests — deer, elk, and bear. Various kinds of fish swam in the many rivers and streams. Mountain areas received lots of rain and snow, but little moisture reached the desert land between the ranges.

Many edible plants, such as camas lilies with edible bulbs, wild onions, and wild carrots, grew on the grasslands. Blackberries and huckleberries were harvested from the river valleys. In the fall, salmon filled the rivers, swimming upstream from the ocean to lay eggs.

For most of the year, people lived in temporary wooden lodges. During the winter, they lived in pit-houses in villages along the rivers. Winter was a time for activities such as basket weaving, singing, and storytelling.

Although the many groups of this region spoke different languages, they were often in contact, travelling the rivers to trade.

PLAINS

Life on the land for First Nations from the Plains embraced the wide-open spaces and expansive sky of their grassland home. A few wooded areas dotted the landscape, stands of mostly willow and cottonwoods along river valleys. But the region was mostly grass — kilometres and kilometres of perfect grazing ground for buffalo.

For the people of the Plains, this hefty animal provided a wealth of useful material. As well as food, the buffalo provided material for bedding, clothing, thread, weapons, tools, ceremonial objects, glue, and fuel for fires. Communal buffalo hunts occurred each summer, gathering many independent groups together. These groups were usually connected by kinship bonds or other kinds of partnerships or **alliances**. The large hunts required much organization and cooperation. Smaller hunts occurred during

During winter in the Plateau region, people lived in pithouses. These homes were partially underground; the earth provided insulation against the cold. The pithouse in this 1898 photograph was located in what is now British Columbia's Nicola Valley.

the winter, when individual groups hunted alone.

Buffalo was the staple, but other animals helped vary the diet of Plains dwellers. Pronghorn antelope, mule deer, elk, and prairie birds were plentiful. Hundreds of seasonal plants, such as wild turnip and saskatoon berries, supplemented the diet of all Plains First Nations.

For centuries, First Nations people on the Plains, as in other regions, travelled by foot. Dogs carried supplies and belongings, dragging them on travois made of poles and skins.

In most parts of the Plains, First Nations lived along river valleys, farming and migrating seasonally to hunt. Only a group of nations called the Blackfoot Confederacy in the northern Plains and the Comanches in the south did not grow crops such as corn. Nations of the Blackfoot Confederacy were primarily hunters, sometimes trading with southern groups for agricultural produce. This limited agriculture among Plains First Nations fell off dramatically once the horse became part of their cultures.

EASTERN WOODLANDS

First Nations from the Eastern Woodlands traditionally lived a way of life that was entwined with the rich forest around them. A mixed forest of deciduous and evergreen trees covered the region, providing the

Archaeological discoveries indicate that a prehistoric horse was long ago part of North America's natural ecosystem. However, this animal died out during one of North America's ice ages between 2 000 000 and 10 000 years ago. The modern horse was then introduced to North America by the Spanish in the early sixteenth century.

Beginning in Mexico, where Spanish horses first stepped to shore, the animal was traded from First Nation to First Nation. Horses gradually spread northward through the continent. The first horses appeared on the northern Plains around 1730.

INDIAN TRAVOIS
1910 BY A. RASTON-CHURNING. LETHBRIDGE, ALTA.

Horses transformed Plains First Nations cultures. Suddenly people could travel much farther and transport much more. Territories became broader, trade routes became longer — even tipis became bigger. Plains peoples became expert horse riders, breeders, and traders. Horses became a symbol of status and wealth. Plains cultures shifted and merged as new First Nations on horseback arrived on the Plains to take advantage of the buffalo. Plains First Nations increasingly had hunting, horses, and the buffalo at their core.

When horses appeared on the Plains, the Cree called them mistatim — *"big dog." To the Blackfoot, they were* ponokáómitaa — *"elk dog."*

▯ REFLECTION

Is the horse still an important part of First Nations cultures in Alberta? Explain your answer in a paragraph, or create a painting, drawing, or other work of art to demonstrate the horse's significance in the past or present.

In many parts of the Subarctic, dog teams pulling a toboggan or carryall were an important form of transportation as late as the 1950s and 1960s. Dog races are still a popular sport in many northern communities. Dave Campbell and Margaret Vilbrun are shown here preparing for a race outside Fort Chipewyan, Alberta.

people who lived here with a wide variety of plant foods — berries, nuts, and wild rice — and game, such as bear, deer, rabbit, beaver, otter, fowl, and fish. Summers were longer and hotter than elsewhere in Canada, which provided excellent conditions for growing plants.

The region was rich in resources and was home to First Nations living in year-round settlements. Some villages housed around 1500 people. The Haudenosaunee (Iroquois) and the Ouendat (Huron) were hunters and successful farmers, growing crops such as squash, corn, and beans.

People built permanent homes — wooden longhouses — that housed several families. Sometimes after ten to fifty years, the entire village would move to a different location with fresh soil for growing crops and new supplies of firewood.

SUBARCTIC

First Nations of the Subarctic made use of the extensive forests and many lakes, ponds, sloughs, and rivers of the region. Summers were short and hot, often plagued with mosquitoes; winters were long and cold, usually with deep snow.

The forest provided people with many edible plants and game animals. Most Subarctic people lived in small groups to hunt moose, caribou, muskoxen, deer, and buffalo. Small game included beaver, mink, hare, otter, muskrat, and porcupine. People also ate fish and wildfowl. Hunters preserved their catch by making pemmican — pulverized meat packed with suet and berries. Wild rice fed the Anishinabé people, who helped spread the seeds into new areas.

Houses in the region were portable — tipis, wigwams, or temporary lean-tos made of poles, brush, and leaves. Toboggans and snowshoes made winter travel easier. Birchbark canoes enabled travel along the waterways and were lightweight enough to be easily carried.

Subarctic First Nations often used birchbark to make cooking vessels and containers. Many groups created elaborate designs on clothing, bags, and boxes with dyed porcupine quills and other natural materials.

TECHNOLOGY AND ENVIRONMENT

First Nations and Inuit peoples used a variety of **technologies** that were appropriate for their environment. For example, Haida dugouts were made from massive cedar trees, resulting in huge boats that were perfect for coastal travel. However, such boats would have been impractical in the Subarctic, where travellers frequently had to carry their canoes around rapids or waterfalls.

The illustrations on this page and the photographs throughout this section show some traditional transportation methods and building styles used in different regions of Canada. However, it would be impossible to show all the variations and adaptations of such constructions. For example, the Dené Tha' had a home called a *kwa̧* which is built like a tipi with poles placed in a circle and spruce boughs woven between the poles, and then packed down tightly with tall grass. To keep the *kwa̧* extra warm, sometimes people would place a moose hide over top or just let the snow cover it.

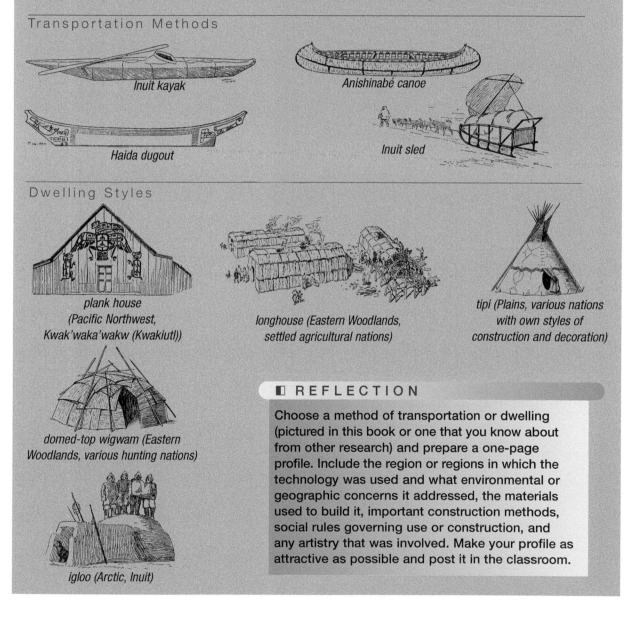

Transportation Methods

Inuit kayak

Anishinabé canoe

Haida dugout

Inuit sled

Dwelling Styles

plank house (Pacific Northwest, Kwak'waka'wakw (Kwakiutl))

longhouse (Eastern Woodlands, settled agricultural nations)

tipi (Plains, various nations with own styles of construction and decoration)

domed-top wigwam (Eastern Woodlands, various hunting nations)

igloo (Arctic, Inuit)

▯ REFLECTION

Choose a method of transportation or dwelling (pictured in this book or one that you know about from other research) and prepare a one-page profile. Include the region or regions in which the technology was used and what environmental or geographic concerns it addressed, the materials used to build it, important construction methods, social rules governing use or construction, and any artistry that was involved. Make your profile as attractive as possible and post it in the classroom.

BECOMING A CULTURAL ENVIRONMENT EXPERT

How do environment and geography affect culture?

WHAT TO DO

1. Divide the class into at least six groups. Your teacher will assign each group one of Canada's geographic environments.

2. As a group, develop a list of geographic or environmental characteristics that may affect the culture of a group of people living in a region. You may have started this list on page 8.

3. Assign each person in your group one of the characteristics. For example, one person might be assigned Significant Water Bodies. If your group's assigned geographic environment is the Arctic, that person would investigate significant water bodies in the Arctic.

4. On your own, research at least two new points of information about your topic.

5. Return to your group and combine all the new information into one group list. Each member of the group should have the same list.

6. Form new groups so that each person has a different list of information.

7. Take turns presenting your information. Add to your notes as your classmates share their research.

ARCTIC

To peoples from the south, the Arctic offers one of the most challenging environments in North America. Here, summers are brief and winters are long with severe blizzards and long periods of darkness. No trees grow on the Arctic tundra, only grasses, lichens, and mosses. The soil beneath the surface remains frozen year-round. The animals of the land — including *tuttu*, which is Inuktitut for "caribou," polar bears, and smaller mammals — are spread over a huge territory. Animals of the rivers and sea are often hidden beneath thick ice.

To Inuit peoples, however, the land was their home and provided all they needed for life. Some Inuit people built winter houses from their most abundant resources — snow and ice. Other Arctic dwellings and tools were made of earth, rock, driftwood, moss, bone, and skins. For protection against extreme cold, Inuit peoples created many specialized articles of clothing. They made insulated waterproof pants and parkas using animal skins and furs, and they lined mukluks (soft boots made of seal skin) and mittens with down and moss for added warmth.

Dog teams pulled sleds, and kayaks with sealed cockpits enabled sea travel. Some umiaks, which are large sealskin boats that can hold up

THE INUKSUK

Some inuksuit were built to warn of danger, to alert others to a good fishing or hunting spot, or to act as a memorial to a loved one. Inuit tradition forbids the destruction of an inuksuk.

One of the most famous symbols of the Arctic is the inuksuk, which means "likeness of a person" in Inuktitut. Inuksuit were made for a variety of reasons. The most well-known reason was to show direction to other travellers. Many places in the Arctic have few natural landmarks to act as trail markers. Inuksuit arms or legs would point direction. The meaning of particular styles of inuksuit varied from place to place. For example, among Baffin Island Inuit, an inuksuk with two arms and legs indicated a valley and that at the end of the valley, one would be able to travel in either direction.

Historically, the most common reason to build an inuksuk was to help in the caribou hunt. Inuit people would build inuksuit in rows along caribou migration routes. Women and children would then stand in their midst to spook the animals towards where the hunters hid. The stone likenesses temporarily added to a small hunting group's strength.

to twelve people, had bone runners on the bottom for travel across ice.

Inuit cultures across the Arctic showed regional variations, just as Subarctic cultures varied across the wide region. For example, the Caribou Inuit lived inland, hunting their namesake animals and fishing in freshwater lakes, and the Kitlinermiut (Copper Inuit) crafted metal tools.

As this 1938 photograph of an Inuit skin tent from Nunavut demonstrates, the igloo was not the only building type in the Arctic. The famous snow structure was used year-round by Inuit living in the central Arctic, but those in the eastern and western regions only used them in the winter for short-term shelter.

LOOKING BACK

Make a map of Canada that shows each of the six geographic regions. Create a legend for the map that describes some characteristics of the traditional lifestyles of the First Nations and Inuit peoples of each region. Why are the Métis peoples not included on this map? Review pages 4–5 if you need help answering this question.

A Life of Movement

AS YOU READ

To European eyes, the windy Arctic tundra and open spaces of the Plains might have seemed empty and inhospitable. However, the people who lived in these places had a thorough understanding of the natural cycles around them. Their lives changed in harmony with the seasons. Even relatively settled groups, such as those of the Pacific Northwest, would move seasonally to take advantage of specific resources, usually during the summer.

It was a life of movement, but it was also a life of predictability. For most First Nations and Inuit peoples, home was not limited to a single spot on the landscape.

For many First Nations and Inuit peoples, permanent (or even long-term) settlement was not an option. The environment contained everything that was needed, but resources were often widely distributed and only seasonally available. The people moved from place to place according to well-defined patterns organized around the availability of resources. Each year, they knew when eggs would hatch, when the buffalo would gather, when to pick plants for medicines, when to tell certain stories, and when it was time to retreat to more sheltered areas for winter. Life for most First Nations followed a **circular seasonal time frame**. In other words, time was measured through natural cycles, such as the movement of the sun and changing appearance or behaviour of plants and animals.

People knew their seasonal patterns of movement, or **migration**, from knowledge passed through oral history from generation to generation. Movements were not aimless or haphazard. Groups always had a purpose and a specific destination within their traditional territory.

Prominent landscape features often acted as landmarks or boundaries. For example, in the nineteenth century, the Blackfoot Confederacy used a territory that was bound in the north by the North Saskatchewan River, in the east by the badlands, and in the west by the Rocky Mountains. Where no natural landmarks existed, people would build them. **Cairns**, mounds of rocks used for this purpose, once dotted the Plains.

> Every time we travelled on Sahtú Dé, we hitched up our dog team, tied a long line to the canoe, and drove the dogs along the shore to pull the canoe up the rapids. The people joked and sang songs. They took time for hunting. There was no hurry to get anywhere; they travelled all over the land, so every place was home.
>
> — George Blondin, Sahtú Dene,
> *When the World Was New: Stories of the Sahtú Dene*

Reaching up to 2.8 metres at the shoulder and weighing up to 900 kilograms, the buffalo once roamed the Plains in enormous herds. Plains First Nations knew buffalo patterns of movement well and used their knowledge to maximize use of this resource.

Traditional calendars were based on the thirteen-month lunar year, although some have now been adapted to coincide with a twelve-month year. This illustration shows examples of twelve-month calendars for Kainai, Plains Cree, and Dene Sųłiné groups. Some groups, such as the Kainai, may have more than one version of this calendar. How might the names of the months be connected to a group's seasonal movements and activities? Create your own illustrated calendar in one of these languages or another Aboriginal language.

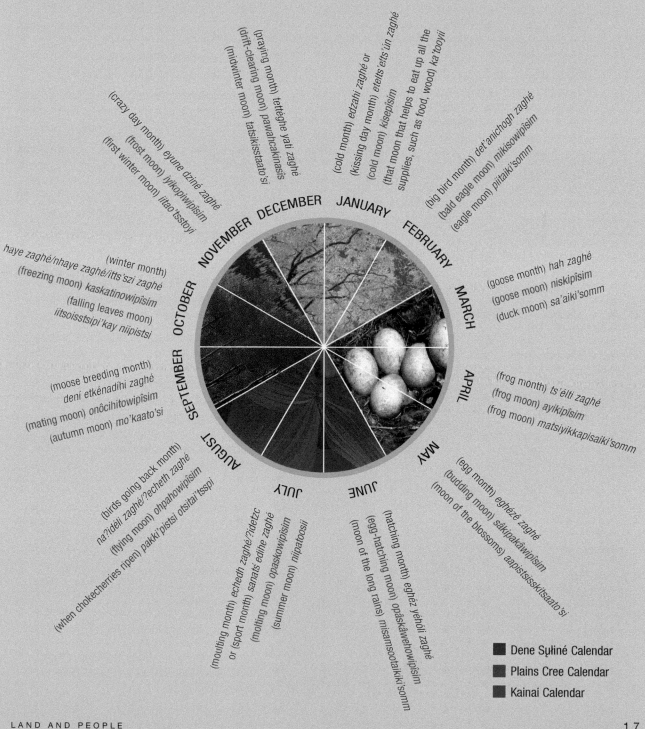

(praying month) tettéghe yati zaghé
(drift-clearing moon) pawahcakinasîs
(midwinter moon) tatsíkisstaato'si

(cold month) edzahi zaghé or
(kissing day month) etelts elts'ín zaghé
(cold moon) kisepîsim
(that moon that helps to eat up all the
supplies, such as food, wood) ka'tooyii

(big bird month) det'anichogh zaghé
(bald eagle moon) mikisowipîsim
(eagle moon) piitaiki'somm

(crazy day month) eyune dziné zaghé
(frost moon) jiyikopîwipîsim
(first winter moon) iitao'tsstoyi

(goose month) hah zaghé
(goose moon) niskipîsim
(duck moon) sa'aiki'somm

(winter month)
haye zaghé/nhaye zaghé/itts'szi zaghé
(freezing moon) kaskatinowipîsim
(falling leaves moon)
iitsoisstsipi'kay niipistsi

(frog month) ts'élti zaghé
(frog moon) ayikipisim
(frog moon) matsiyikkapisaiki'somm

(moose breeding month)
dení etkénadíhi zaghé
(mating moon) onôcihitowipîsim
(autumn moon) mo'kaato'si

(egg month) eghézé zaghé
(budding moon) sâkipakâwipîsim
(moon of the blossoms) aapistsisskitsaato'si

(birds going back month)
na?idéli zaghé/?echeth zaghé
(flying moon) ohpahowipîsim
(when chokecherries ripen) pakki'pistsi otsítai'tsspi

(hatching month) eghéz yéhóli zaghé
(egg-hatching moon) opâskâwehowipîsim
(moon of the long rains) misamsootaikiki'somm

(moulting month) echedh zaghé/?idetzc
or (sport month) sanats'edíne zaghé
(molting moon) opaskowipîsim
(summer moon) niipatoosii

NOVEMBER DECEMBER JANUARY FEBRUARY MARCH APRIL MAY JUNE JULY AUGUST SEPTEMBER OCTOBER

■ Dene Sųłiné Calendar
■ Plains Cree Calendar
■ Kainai Calendar

Seasonal movements through a territory were connected to the use of available resources. The First Nations living in the northern Subarctic knew well the migration trails of the herds of caribou that were a staple of their diet. In places where the trail narrowed or crossed a body of water, the people gathered each year to hunt. In similar fashion, other First Nations followed familiar trails to good hunting or fishing spots, sacred places, and regions where useful plants could be harvested. Such knowledge was gained through generations of experience and observation of the natural world. The following section describes what a typical year might have looked like for a group from the Blackfoot Confederacy centuries ago.

In the spring, after a long, cold winter, the days on the Plains finally began to lengthen. The people were able to spend more time outside. When the weather warmed and the danger of spring snowstorms ended, the people moved their camp from the shelter of the river valleys onto the wide expanses of the grasslands. From there, they travelled as needed, hunting *iiníí* — which is Blackfoot for "buffalo" — and collecting plants. They usually chose camp-sites on high land, near wood and water.

In the summer, when the saskatoon berries ripened, the group travelled to a traditional gathering place. Each group took its traditional spot in a great circle of tipis. Members of the Blackfoot Confederacy called it *Akóka'tssin* —

"the time of all people camping together." It was the only time of the year when the whole confederacy lived in one place.

After *Akóka'tssin*, the large group split up and once again spread out onto the Plains to hunt buffalo and other game, and to gather berries.

In the fall, the group migrated back towards their wintering grounds. They began to prepare a buffalo pound near the *pisskan* — "buffalo jump." At the best hunting sites, several groups might work together in communal hunts.

When the frosty nights arrived, the group moved into a wooded river valley, not far from other wintering groups. The buffalo also preferred to spend the winter in wooded areas, making easy prey for skilled hunters, who tracked them through the snow.

If the group had an adequate supply of firewood and food, it might spend the entire winter — often more than five months — at a single campsite. With the long nights and cold weather, group members spent most of their time in their tipis. It was a time of storytelling, educating, socializing, and ceremonies.

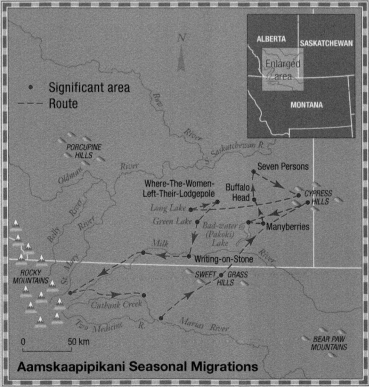

Aamskaapipikani Seasonal Migrations

Significant area •
Route - - -

1. Marias River
2. Sweet Grass Hills
3. Cypress Hills
4. Pakoki Lake
5. Manyberries
6. Buffalo Head
7. Seven Persons
8. Cypress Hills
9. Long Lake
10. Where-the-Women-Left-Their-Lodgepole
11. Green Lake
12. Writing-on-Stone
13. Milk River
14. Cutbank Creek in the foothills
15. Cutbank Creek

This map traces the yearly migration pattern of a clan of Aamskaapipikani (South Piikani) around 1900.

GROUP INTERACTIONS

In addition to allowing First Nations to use the full range of resources that their environment had to offer, regular patterns of migration filled many other significant political, economic, and social needs.

Clans and Kinship

Seasonal migrations helped maintain relationships with clan members. **Clans** are groups of related people who share common ancestry. Clan systems helped maintain strong kinships ties. Clan members were often apart for much of the year so that they could provide for their day-to-day needs, but gathered regularly as part of their seasonal patterns of movement. They would often meet for **ceremonies** and other formal occasions that reaffirmed kinship bonds and cultural values. The regular meetings also allowed people to meet up with friends and relatives to socialize and enjoy themselves.

Relationships Between Nations

Because First Nations lived in traditional territories, they tended to have a long history of interactions with their neighbours. Most nation-to-nation relationships were harmonious, although sometimes **armed conflict** or warfare erupted. Such conflicts were generally because of issues concerning natural resource use between nations that shared boundaries. **Natural resources** are materials existing in nature that are useful or necessary to people, such as forests, minerals, game animals, or water.

As you will learn in Chapter Five, the westward advance of the fur trade caused increased friction among First Nations as groups changed their traditional lifestyles and territories to take advantage of new opportunities. For example, the Plains Cree and Blackfoot nations were traditionally friendly with one another, with a regular trading relationship. However, as competition for horses increased in the late eighteenth century, their relationship became more characterized by antagonism.

Such increased tensions occurred at the same time as European settlement in North America, so Europeans had a distorted view of First Nations history. They often recorded First Nations peoples as warlike, while harmony and peace was traditionally more common.

As was the case with the Blackfoot and Cree nations, sometimes a history of conflict fed more conflict. Young men often gained standing in their nation through acts of bravery in war. Warfare was

The group of Inuit in this photograph, taken sometime in the early twentieth century, was probably comprised of related individuals who were each other's primary living group. How does this group's composition compare to a nuclear family, which consists of a couple and their children?

sometimes not so much about killing other people as about claiming opportunities for valour and acts of courage.

Nations involved in these long-term conflicts included the Inuit and Dene Sų̨liné living west of Hudson Bay, the Dakota and the Anishinabé in the Great Lakes region, the Ouendat and Haudenosaunee, also from the Great Lakes area, and the Blackfoot and Plains Cree in southern Alberta.

Other nations tended to have longstanding friendships and various kinds of trade and political alliances. Sometimes alliances were informal agreements, such as the friendly relations between the Plains Cree and Nakoda (Assiniboine/Stoney).

Other alliances were more formal. Such **confederacies** existed among the Haudenosaunee nations, the Blackfoot nations, and in the east between the Mi'kmaq, Mailiseet, Passamaquoddy, and Penobscot nations. The groups involved in such confederacies tended to live closely together. **Treaties**, which are formal agreements between independent nations, helped them keep peace among themselves and protect their territory from outside groups.

Gift-giving was an essential part of these international relationships. Métis historian Olive Dickason explains in *Canada's First Nations* that treaties needed to be renewed regularly with ceremonies and gifts. Making peace between nations was not an event, but a process that needed regular maintenance.

SIGN LANGUAGE

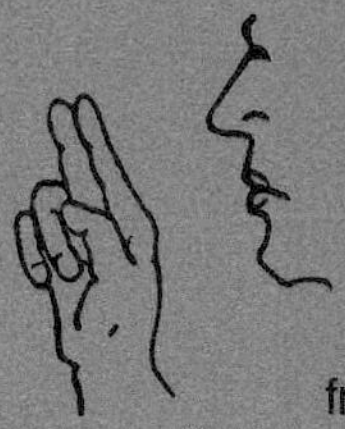

friend

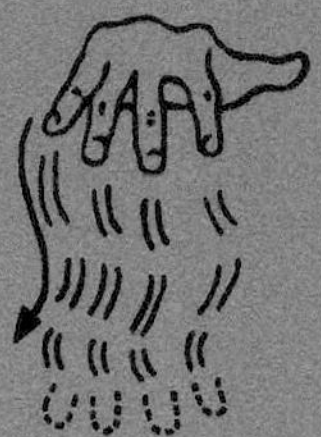

rapids

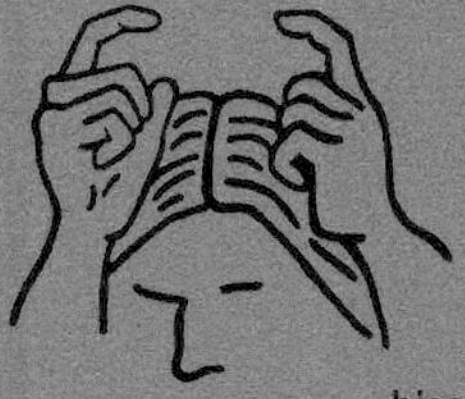

bison

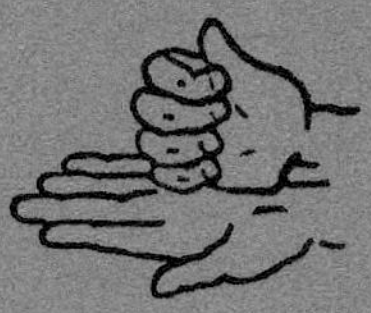

tobacco

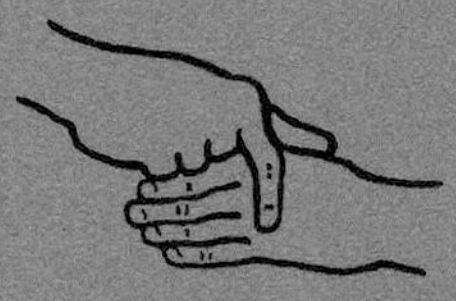

horse

Signs generally meant ideas rather than single words, so listeners needed to be good at interpreting meaning in the context of the situation and other actions of the speaker.

Despite regular encounters, communication was not always easy between different groups, even on the Plains, where different nations shared a similar lifestyle. People with similar cultural features still often spoke unrelated languages. Because of the relative ease of travel on the grasslands, different groups encountered one another more often than they would have in an environment such as the Subarctic. This meant that encounters frequently needed to be managed. The solution was sometimes sign language.

Sign language varied somewhat between groups, but sign speakers generally had no difficulty understanding each other. Most of the signs were logical and easy to recognize and learn. First Nations signs were relatively large compared to, for example, the system of American Sign Language used today. Plains signs rarely depended on the movement of a single finger. Using larger arm movements, the signs could be seen at a much greater distance.

Sign language between different groups was important for diplomacy, trade, and the exchange of news or stories. It was also used between members of the same group for silent communication between hunters.

REFLECTION

Work with a partner to develop signs for words and concepts that you commonly use. Practise them until you can remember them easily. Try to hold a wordless conversation with another pair from your class and see how well you can communicate.

Large gatherings, such as the Blackfoot's *Akóka'tssin*, reinforced ties between affiliated groups. At one time, the Kainai, Piikani, and Siksika belonged to a single group. Regular gatherings and shared ceremonies and customs maintained bonds between this group of affiliated nations that have lasted to contemporary times.

Sometimes political alliances followed from a trading relationship. Other times a trading relationship was a way to achieve a desired political alliance. In both cases, trade and gift-giving ceremonies were crucial methods of maintaining good relationships between nations.

Marriage and adoption were also important methods of forging ties between allied nations. Traditionally, specific kinship ties within an **extended family**, such as that of a father or aunt, carried particular responsibilities. These obligations generally included resource sharing and support in times of trouble. Marriages between families of different nations extended the web of kinship between nations.

Harmony and good relationships were so highly valued among First Nations that, even in cases of nations that experienced many years of conflict, leaders would make periodic attempts to reach peace. On the Plains, for example, a leader would approach the other nation unarmed and carrying a ceremonial pipe, hoping to arrive at an agreement. Such approaches took enormous courage.

Ouendat chief Nicholas Vincent Isawanhonhi is shown in this illustration presenting England's King George IV with a wampum belt in 1825. The belt has an image of a tomahawk which had been given to the Ouendat by King George III.

If matters went well, the groups would sit in a circle and participate in a pipe ceremony. The person who offered the pipe and the person specifically honoured in the ceremony would then become responsible for maintaining peace.

Blackfoot and Cree peace agreements tended to be short-lived in the late eighteenth and early nineteenth centuries. In the mid-nineteenth century, a lasting peace accord was reached at *wetaskiwin spatinow*, which means "the place where peace was made," in Cree. This is how the town of Wetaskiwin, Alberta, got its name.

Eastern Woodland First Nations often recorded their agreements using wampum belts. **Wampum** are shell beads woven into belts or strings. Wampum belts that recorded treaties or other agreements were used as memory aids to clarify misunderstandings. Some treaties between First Nations, as well as between First Nations and European nations, were recorded in this way.

RESEARCHING SETTLEMENT AND MIGRATION PATTERNS

How did traditional First Nations settlement and migration patterns vary from group to group?

WHAT TO DO

1. In pairs, choose a First Nation to research. Brainstorm a list of questions about the seasonal migration of the people you have chosen. Be sure to include the group's reasons for migration, such as geography and environment, kinship relationships, availability of resources, and the life cycles of plants and animals.

2. Organize your questions in preparation for research. You might want to arrange the questions using the Five Ws and One H (who, what, when, where, why, and how) method or another technique suggested by your teacher.

3. Find the answers to your questions using books, the Internet, magazines, or knowledgeable members of your community such as an **Elder**. If approaching an Elder with a request, be sure to use proper **protocol**. A protocol is a set of rules or etiquette that helps maintain harmony and respect between individuals. Your teacher can help you with this.

4. Illustrate your research using a diagram or map. Prepare a short summary to present to the class.

5. As your classmates present, make notes whenever you notice similarities and differences in the way the groups lived in harmony with seasonal change.

Thinking About Your Project
As a class, discuss how landscape and environment affect migration and settlement patterns.

LOOKING BACK

Review pages 16–22 to be sure you can answer the following questions: Why did many First Nations and Inuit peoples move from location to location throughout the year? What political, economic, and social benefits were the result of these movements? Write down each bolded term in this section and look it up in the glossary at the back of the textbook. Write a definition for each concept in your own words.

First Nations and Métis Peoples in Alberta

Alberta includes the northern tip of the Plains geographic region, with most of the province covered by Subarctic terrain. However, within these broad areas are ecological zones that include boreal forest, parkland, foothills, mountains, and grasslands. Each of these zones has different living conditions, with diverse animals, birds, fish, plants, water bodies, weather, and significant landforms.

First Nations communities made the best possible use of all resources in their environment. For example, Plains Cree people who lived in the parkland zone between the Plains grassland and Subarctic forest, hunted woodland animals, such as moose, elk, and deer, for part of the year and buffalo during the summer. Their diet, like that of all First Nations, also relied upon hundreds of edible plants that were available seasonally.

Indigenous Knowledge

Working with a partner, develop a detailed description of the resources and climate for each of the ecological regions in Alberta. Organize your notes using a web or concept map. Use an outline map of Alberta to draw in the boundaries of each region. You can get a map from the National Atlas of Canada Web site at *http://atlas.gc.ca/*.

AS YOU READ

On the previous pages of this chapter, you learned how First Nations and Inuit peoples traditionally lived closely with the natural cycles of the land. Diverse geographic regions across the country meant there were diverse cultural groups, each with well-established political, economic, and social systems. Each nation lived in harmony with the available resources of their environment, migrating seasonally to take advantage of all that was available.

The nations also had long histories of interacting with one another. Many had peace treaties, political and trading alliances, and numerous kinship bonds. When Europeans first arrived in the late fifteenth century, First Nations established relationships with them using the same techniques they used with other First Nations. They established relationships of trade, political alliance, and kinship through marriages of First Nations women to European traders. Eventually these marriages and the further development of the fur trade led to the creation of the Métis Nation. You will learn more about this history in Chapter Five.

Pages 23–33 introduce the First Nations and Métis peoples who are considered indigenous to Alberta. You will learn much more about the early history and contemporary situation of First Nations, Métis, and Inuit peoples in the chapters to come.

Many Alberta First Nations and Métis peoples still practise some elements of the ways of life of their ancestors. Here, moose meat is being smoked at the Treaty Eight centennial celebration at Sucker Creek in 1999.

Understanding the diverse history of the groups and individuals that comprise the Aboriginal population in Alberta can make understanding many current issues easier. The next few pages feature some of the history of the First Nations and Métis groups considered indigenous to Alberta.

Major migrations of First Nations coincided with the beginning of the fur trade on the Hudson Bay. Cree and Nakoda peoples moved farther and farther west in search of fresh trapping areas and western First Nations trading partners. This migration might have been like many others in history, sometimes advancing and sometimes retreating, but this time the Cree had guns from their European trading partners. Unarmed groups could do little to stop them. The Tsuu T'ina and the Blackfoot Confederacy were pushed south and the Dunne-za moved north. These movements in turn impacted the lives and territories of other groups in what is now Alberta.

Some nations, such as the A'aninin (Gros Ventre), the Shoshoni, and the Ktunaxa (Kutenai), once lived in the region, but no longer have territory in Alberta. The A'aninin were allies of the Blackfoot Confederacy, but moved south to the United States in 1861. The Piikani First Nation in Alberta are sometimes considered the North Piikani, with the South Piikani from Montana as the fourth member of the Blackfoot Confederacy.

Another significant cultural group represented in Alberta's population is the Haudenosaunee. During the fur trade era, many Haudenosaunee people came west to work in the trade. Many of their descendants still live in Alberta. You will learn more about this history in Chapter Five.

ANISHINABÉ

The Anishinabé in Alberta are originally from the Eastern Woodlands near what is now Sault Ste Marie. They moved west in the late 1700s to work in the fur trade for the North West Company. The Anishinabé first settled in Manitoba, but then moved farther west and adopted a lifestyle of buffalo-hunting. They were close allies of the Plains Cree.

BLACKFOOT CONFEDERACY
Niitsítapi *(Real People)*

The member nations of the Blackfoot Confederacy were once part of a single group. At some point, they split into three closely allied groups: the Kainai, the Piikani, and the Siksika. Historically, the Blackfoot Confederacy lived in large clan-based groups on the Plains and nearby foothills. According to oral history, they have always lived in this region and their culture was traditionally linked economically and spiritually with the buffalo.

The buffalo was a magnificent resource that attracted many First Nations and Métis peoples to the region that is now Alberta. What features of the buffalo's main habitat made a large hunt such as the one depicted in this painting possible?

Look closely at this photograph. In which of Alberta's ecological regions do you think this Cree man might be? There may be more than one answer.

These Dene Sųłiné people are hunting duck. What characteristics do you notice about their environment? How does this fit with what you learned earlier in this chapter on pages 8–15?

Fort Chipewyan has a clear sense of its community as the historic hub of the fur trade, as well as a sense of humour, as seen in this sign at the Fort Chipewyan airport. Two major trading companies had posts at Fort Chipewyan, leaving a lasting legacy for the community. Many Métis people with names such as Flett, Wylie, Campbell, and Fraser still live in the area.

CREE

Nehiyaw *(Real People)*

Three distinct groups of Cree have a history in this province. The Plains Cree traditionally lived in the east central region of Alberta in the areas of the Battle and North Saskatchewan Rivers. In Cree, their name means "Downstream People," referring to their location farther west from their original territory. They spent part of the year in the woodlands in extended family groups. In the summer, when the buffalo gathered in huge herds on the Plains, Plains Cree joined forces in large groups to hunt the animal.

The Woodland Cree were traditionally expert hunters and trappers. This group of Cree eventually became the backbone of the fur trade as suppliers and traders with other groups. Many Woodland Cree women married fur traders, so many Métis people share elements of the Woodland Cree cultural heritage.

The Rocky Mountain Cree today live in the Grande Cache area. They once lived in more eastern regions of the country, but moved west during the fur trade. They eventually settled along the mountains and foothills.

DENE SUŁINÉ

(the term *Dené* means "person or people" in all Athapaskan languages)

For centuries, the Dene Sųłiné people occupied the boreal forest and waters between Great Slave Lake and Hudson Bay. Their traditional territory encompassed a large triangular area in the Northwest Territories and Nunavut, as well as much of northeastern Alberta. Although their territory reached as far as Hudson Bay and the Arctic Ocean, they normally stayed inland, travelling the extensive water system of rivers, lakes, and muskeg.

Traditionally they lived and migrated in family groups, catching fish and hunting caribou, wood buffalo, and waterfowl. When the Hudson's Bay Company opened in Fort Churchill, the Dene Sųłiné began a trading relationship with the Europeans and expanded their territory even further.

What features do you notice about the surroundings of this 1910 Dunne-za camp near Peace River, Alberta? What do these features suggest about the resources the people of this camp may have relied upon?

DENÉ THA'

The Dené Tha' are the most northerly First Nation in the province. In their own language, Dené Tha' means "simple people." Dené Tha' traditional hunting grounds extend far into the Northwest Territories, but they consider Alberta's Caribou Mountains and Hay River regions part of their homeland. Traditionally they rarely left woodland areas, even if caribou were plentiful on the barren grounds to the north.

DUNNE-ZA

The name Dunne-za means "pure people," but in common usage, the Dunne-za refer to themselves as Chatay, which means "beaver people." The Dunne-za traditionally lived in northern Alberta along the Peace River, which was often known by the Dene Sųłiné name Tsa Des (river of beavers). The Dunne-za lived in small family groups and were expert trappers and hunters in their heavily wooded environment.

■ REFLECTION

Reflect upon the two statements below, one by a Dene person who believes his cultural identity comes from the land, and one by a Plains Cree person who believes language is more significant in her cultural identity. Which statement reflects something about your own sense of cultural identity? If neither, explain the source of your own cultural identity. Answer this question in your journal.

One of my Elders told me a situation. He said we can get rid of all the Dene people in Denendeh, we can all die off for some reason, but if there was another human being that came stumbling along and came to Denendeh, the environment would turn him into a Dene person. It's the environment and the land that makes us Dene people.

— Roy Fabian, Hay River, Northwest Territories, *Report of the Royal Commission on Aboriginal Peoples*

For Plains Cree people, language is the most important gift from the Creator. It shapes our sense of who we are and the values and ceremonies that flow from this identity. The environment, or Mother Earth, is important, too, but today we live with mainstream society. Even our reserves are surrounded and have been changed by non-Aboriginal people.

— Mary Cardinal Collins, Edmonton

MÉTIS PEOPLES

Many Métis peoples in Alberta are the descendants of Métis families who moved west from the Red River area in Manitoba as it became increasingly settled and agricultural. They wanted to live a life based on the buffalo hunt. These Métis were sometimes called the Winter Rovers. Although today Métis people can be found in almost every town and city in Alberta, many live in the **Métis Settlements** that were founded in the 1930s to provide a land base for the Métis peoples in the province. They are the only Métis people in Canada to have a land base.

NAKODA

The Nakoda people were once part of the Yanktonai Sioux, a cultural group of First Nations living between the Mississippi River and Lake Superior. In the early seventeenth century, the Nakoda separated from this group and moved north. By 1670, the Nakoda were a distinct cultural group. They eventually became close Cree allies. Along with the Cree, they moved west along the North Saskatchewan River during the fur trade in pursuit of fresh trapping areas and new trading partners. In time, the Nakoda split into two branches. One continued the woodlands lifestyle that was their heritage. The people of the Paul and Alexis Bands *(Isgabi)* are descendants of these people. The second took up the Plains culture of the buffalo hunt. The people of the Morley Band *(Iyethkabi)* are their descendants.

TSUU T'INA
Tsotli'na *(Earth People)*

The Tsuu T'ina are related to northern Alberta's Dunne-za. They may have split into two groups around the time that the Cree and Nakoda moved west. They have lived apart from the Dunne-za for long enough that their languages are today quite different. Although they once lived mainly in the foothills, the Tsuu T'ina increasingly adapted the Plains life that revolved around the buffalo. They were close allies of the Blackfoot Confederacy and frequently intermarried with them.

This Métis couple is shown in a jumper on their way to Lac La Biche for a New Year's Celebration in 1895.

Traditionally close relationships between members of the Blackfoot Confederacy and the Tsuu T'ina are maintained today. Here you see former Tsuu T'ina Chief Roy Whitney giving a gift to Siksika Elder Tom Crane Bear during the Tsuu T'ina's give-away at a 1998 powwow.

FIRST NATIONS AND MÉTIS LANGUAGES IN ALBERTA

This chart shows the major First Nations and Métis cultural groups considered indigenous to Alberta. Keep in mind, however, that Alberta is also home to many Aboriginal peoples from other regions. These people tend to live in urban centres in family groups.

Review the information on pages 24–27 to find at least two points of information that are reinforced by the information in this chart. For example, you might note that the Tsuu T'ina are in the same language family as the Dunne-za, reinforcing the statement that they were long ago part of the same group.

ALGONQUIAN LANGUAGE FAMILY

Blackfoot Confederacy

Kainai *(Blood)*

Piikani *(Peigan)*

Siksika *(Blackfoot)*

Cree

Plains Cree or *Nehiyaw Paskwaweyiniwak*

Rocky Mountain Cree or *Nehiyaw Asinywaciyiwiyiniwak*

Woodland Cree or *Nehiyaw Sakawiyiniwak*

Anishinabé
(Saulteaux, Western Ojibway)

ATHAPASKAN LANGUAGE FAMILY

Dene Sųłiné *(Chipewyan)*

Dené Tha' *(Slavey)*

Dunne-za *(Beaver)*

Tsuu T'ina *(Sarcee)*

SIOUAN LANGUAGE FAMILY

Nakoda *(Assiniboine/Stoney)*

MÉTIS LANGUAGES

Métis-Cree

Michif

WORDS FROM THE LAND

Language	buffalo	beaver	horse	canoe	dog team	dog sled
Blackfoot	iiníí	ksisskstaki	ponokáómitaa	aahkiohsa'tsis	iimitaohkipistaa	
Cree	paskwâw mostos	amisk	mistatim	cîman	otâpahastimwewin	toboggan*
Dene Sųłiné	ejere	tsá	tjcó	tsi		
Dené Tha'	haikįcho	tsa	k'lįcho	e-lą	k'lįdedeya	
Dunne-za	kaymoe hukgree	cha	klaynchook	ala		klayzha woosloozhy
Métis Cree	pusk'wâw mostos	âmisk	mistâ'tim	oosi		âtimotâpânâsk
Michif	boefloo	kastor	zhwal	canoh		
Nakoda	tatanka**	coba	shortă	wa dah***		shŭga cusnahă
Saulteaux	miskotê-pisihki	amihk	mištâtim			
Tsuu T'ina	hani tii	mi cha di ko di	ist/i			

* *word borrowed from Abenaki language*

** *male buffalo, refers to hump on back*

*** *log carved into boat*

ROBERT SMALLBOY AND LAZARUS ROAN

Ermineskin First Nation and Smallboy Camp

The year was 1968 when Cree visionaries Robert Smallboy and Lazarus Roan led a group of their followers away from the Hobbema reserve into the Rocky Mountain foothills to live on the land.

The two leaders anticipated great challenges ahead for their Ermineskin First Nation. With the First Nation's incoming oil royalties, drugs and alcohol were easily purchased, and an avalanche of social problems assaulted their people. Smallboy believed the only escape from this heartbreak was a return to his ancestors' lifestyle — basic living amidst the beauty of nature. He and Roan, therefore, led a dozen families to camp in the Kootenay Plains, southwest of Nordegg on the David Thompson Highway. Years later, the camp was relocated to an isolated area west of Edson, still in the Rocky Mountain foothills.

"That first year was hell," recalls Dorothy Smallboy, Lazarus Roan's daughter, in a 1988 interview. "We lived in tents and stacked hay bales against the sides for insulation. Still, some of the ladies couldn't hack it, making fire all winter and using the outhouse. They returned to the reserve."

But a hardy group stayed with Smallboy. His people bought some of their supplies, but hunted and fished for much of their food. Visitors were welcome, and many benefited from camp ceremonies and the counsel of Elders.

Robert Smallboy

Smallboy, who was chief of the Ermineskin Band from 1959 to 1968, envisioned a day when his people would return to basic living and a close connection with the Creator and Mother Earth. He brought this message to many European leaders, including the Pope and Queen Elizabeth II. He was honoured many times for his work in preserving traditional and cultural teachings, and he received the Order of Canada in 1980.

Today Smallboy's vision lives on in the families and children who live at the camp. Time is sacred here, and there is a gentle rhythm to life. The pace is slower and the community is attuned to natural cycles, such as preparing for the changing seasons with ceremonies and harvesting and preserving food. Many parents say they gladly uphold Smallboy's vision of living a simple and more rugged way of life in return for their children having the opportunity to live close to the land, participate in traditional ceremonies, and understand exactly who they are.

▌ REFLECTION

In a small group, discuss the actions taken by Smallboy, Roan, and their followers. What would have been some of the challenges faced by their group as they began their new life? If you had lived in Smallboy's community in 1968, do you think you would have joined him? Why or why not?

*The map on page 31 shows the location of the Métis Settlements as well as all First Nations with reserves in Alberta. A **reserve** is land set aside for the use of a First Nation by the federal government. Each First Nation is coded according to its main cultural group. The map guide on this page gives the names of each First Nation and the corresponding number(s) of its reserves on the map. Note that some First Nations have more than one area of land.*

Anishinabé/Cree
O'Chiese 203, 203 A

Blackfoot Confederacy
Kainai 148, 148 A
Piikani 147, 147 B
Siksika 146

Cree
Alexander 134
Beaver Lake 131
Bigstone Cree 166, 166 A–D, 183
Driftpile 150
Duncan's 151 A, 151 K
Enoch 135
Ermineskin 138, 138A
Fort McKay 174, 174 A–B
Fort McMurray 175, 176, 176 A–B
Frog Lake 121, 122
Heart Lake 167
Horse Lake 152 B–C
Kapawe'no 229, 230, 231, 150 B–D

Cree *(continued)*
Kehewin 123
Little Red River 162, 215
Loon River Cree 200
Louis Bull 138 B
Mikisew Cree 217–225
Montana 139
Saddle Lake 125, 128
Samson Cree 137 A
Sawridge 150 G–H
Sturgeon Lake 154, 154 A–B
Sucker Creek 150 A
Sunchild Cree 202
Swan River 150 E–F
Tallcree 163, 163 A–B, 173, 173 A–C
Whitefish Lake 155, 155 A–B
Woodland Cree 226–228

Dene Sųłiné
Athabaskan Chipewyan 201, 201 A–G
Chipewyan Prairie 194, 194 A–B
Cold Lake 149, 149 A–B

Dené Tha'
207, 209–214

Dunne-za
164, 164 A

Nakoda
Alexis 133, 232–234
Paul 133 A–C
Nakoda 142, 142 B, 143, 144, 144 A, 216

Tsuu T'ina
145

Métis Settlements
Buffalo Lake 5
East Prairie 4
Elizabeth 7
Fishing Lake 8
Gift Lake 3
Kikino 6
Paddle Prairie 1
Peavine 2

- *Although each First Nation and reserve has been listed by a single cultural group, many communities include more than one cultural group. For example, while the Heart Lake First Nation is located in the Treaty Eight geographic area, it is considered part of Treaty Six. Heart Lake has many Cree speakers along with its Dene Sųłiné–speaking population.*

- *You will not find the Aseniwuche Winewak Nation, which is Cree for "Rocky Mountain People," on this map. This group lives near Grande Cache and includes an ancestral mix of Cree, Dunne-za, Sekaní, Nakoda, Anishinabé, Haudenosaunee, and Métis people. The nation has six land cooperatives granted by the provincial government. These land holdings are not official reserves, because most members of the Aseniwuche Winewak Nation are **non-Status Indians**, which means they are not registered for benefits under the federal government's **Indian Act**. Learn more about these land cooperatives by visiting www.aseiwuche.com.*

- *One First Nation in Alberta does not have a reserve: the Lubicon Lake Cree. Their **land claim** is still outstanding.*

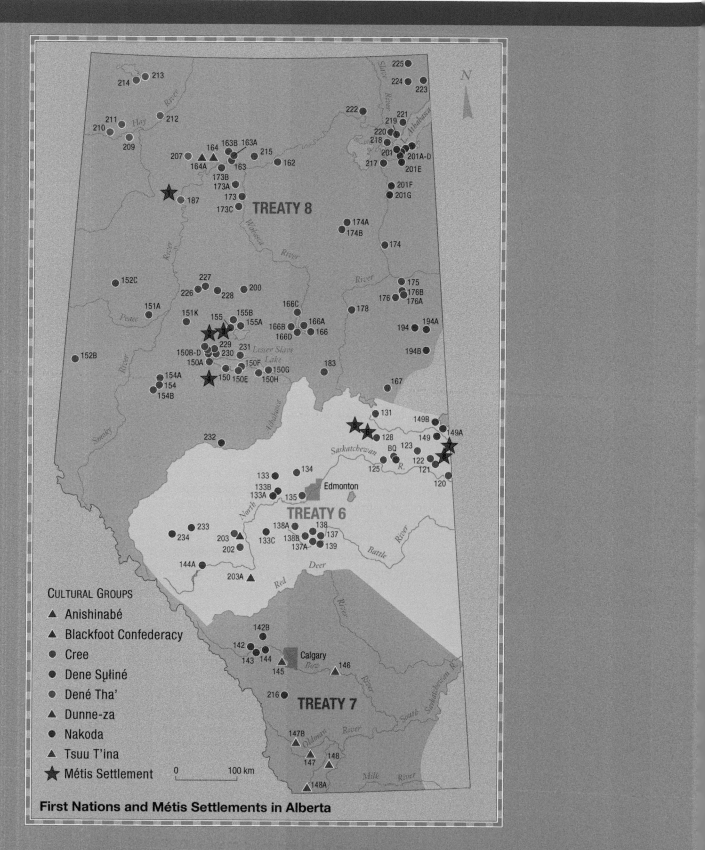

CULTURAL GROUPS

▲ Anishinabé
▲ Blackfoot Confederacy
● Cree
● Dene Sųłiné
● Dené Tha'
▲ Dunne-za
● Nakoda
▲ Tsuu T'ina
★ Métis Settlement

0   100 km

First Nations and Métis Settlements in Alberta

A WEB OF CONNECTION

Talking circles are a type of organized discussion for a topic that has no right or wrong answer. The purpose of a talking circle is to share ideas, feelings, and points of view, but not to reach a decision.

To keep the discussion welcoming to everyone participating, it is useful to follow a talking circle protocol. This activity includes protocol ideas, but your class may want to define your own rules. Your teacher may be able to help you find out the protocol used by local communities.

Speakers may respond to the topic in any way they choose: sharing a personal experience, telling a story, giving an opinion, or relating the topic to another issue or idea.

Whatever protocol you use, remember that the goal is to make everyone feel that they are a valued and respected part of the circle.

It is a good idea to use an experienced facilitator. The facilitator acknowledges participants for their contributions and may clarify comments with non-judgmental language. If necessary, the facilitator may recall the circle to the topic or to protocol. This is a challenging role that takes practice. Your class may wish to approach an Elder in the community to facilitate a talking circle. Your teacher will help you with the appropriate protocol to make this request.

What does a circular seating arrangement imply about those participating? How does sitting in a classroom arrangement have a different effect on participants?

Sample Protocol

1. Only one person should speak at a time. This can be managed by moving from person to person in a clockwise direction around the circle. This technique ensures that all participants have an equal chance to contribute.
2. Everyone else in the circle should listen without judging or speaking.
3. Each person should feel free to speak or to be silent on their turn. Participants may say "pass" without negative reaction from other participants or the teacher.
4. All questions and comments should address the topic under discussion, not comments another person has made.

Each talking circle in this textbook will include a reading that you may use to begin your talking circle. You may wish to focus on the ideas of your classmates without any added perspectives.

Each quotation respects the original choice of words by the speaker including terms, such as *Whiteman* or *Indian,* that are now considered out of date in most circumstances. The word choice by the speaker may reflect a specific situation or time period in which such words were accepted.

Each talking circle will end with a short exercise, such as the one below, to help you reflect upon what you've learned in the circle.

▮ REFLECTION

What is your connection to land? Is it a strong or weak force in your life? Are you connected to a reserve, settlement, or homeland? In your journal, write your answers to these questions or write a response to the talking circle discussion.

We had everything. Well, you just had to go out on the land to get it. We ate healthy foods — meat and lots of fish. We didn't need any pills. If we were sick, there were lots of herbs. There's a plant for everything. There's even herbs for children. The Creator has provided us with everything we need to live a good life. We picked lots of low bush and high bush cranberries and blueberries. We dried lots of saskatoons because they don't lose their sweetness. We always made lots of jam, too.

— Eva Nanooch, Fox Creek Reserve, adapted from *Those Who Know: Profiles of Alberta's Native Elders*

And you know we, the Dene here, we were put here by the Creator on this earth to live with a certain purpose, with a certain way, we know that; we see that in our ways, our land, wildlife that provides for us...The land is healthy as a result of what the Creator does for it. Rain, snow, winter, summer...the seasons of the year, all keep everything in balance and we as people live in balance with those seasons. We go from one season to the next. That's how we lived before the Whiteman came here, we shared, we worked with each other.

— Victor Echodh, Black Lake Dene Sųłiné First Nation, *Treaty Elders of Saskatchewan*

The people respected the land and lived off it, depending on its resources. However, nature is uncertain and changeable. Sometimes there was plenty, and sometimes starvation was a fearful reality. People respected nature because they survived at its whim.

— Phyllis Cardinal, Saddle Lake First Nation, *The Cree People*

We do not exist in isolation from the other living things. My grandfather told me this. He said, "We do not exist by ourselves without the help of other things. This tree here helps us to keep warm because we burn its branches and use them to make stakes for our tipis to hold them down. The rocks we use to hold things down and to heat our sweat lodges." The Indian medicines we used we had to dig up. We were taught about them and we dug for them. The old man's medicines were different from the old woman's. My grandfather would say that he was given these plants to use. It was in the fall when we dug for the roots. They grew in particular places, not just from anywhere. One type of root, which grew in a rocky location, particularly where we hauled water from, was called *aiksikkooki*. It had a bitter taste. Another root was called *sooyiaihts*. It was good for burns. We would also spend much time collecting *ka'kitsimoi*. *Ka'ksimiistsi* was another plant we harvested. We used it to make a tea in the wintertime, especially to help with colds.

— Issokoyioomaahka (Bill Heavy Runner), Kainai First Nation, *Kipaitapiiwahsinnooni: Alcohol and Drug Abuse Education Program*

LOOKING BACK

With your teacher's assistance, use correct protocol to invite an Elder or other community member from a local First Nation or Métis community to your class. Ask your guest to talk about traditional ways of life for his or her community.

WHAT IS YOUR CONNECTION TO LAND?

Chapter One Review

Check Your Understanding

1. According to the Canadian constitution, what does the term *Aboriginal peoples* mean?

2. What are the three most common Aboriginal language families today?

3. Which three provinces have the highest First Nations populations?

4. Name six geographic areas in Canada and list, in point form, major characteristics of each region. In sentences, give at least one example of how conditions in each region influenced the culture of the First Nations or Inuit peoples living there.

5. Name three ways Inuit peoples used Inuksuit.

6. Explain how and why the horse impacted Plains First Nations ways of life.

7. Name nine major cultural groups considered indigenous to Alberta and describe something about the history of each in this province.

8. What is a circular seasonal time frame and why did it prompt the seasonal migrations of First Nations? How did such migrations affect First Nations kinship relationships? How did they affect relationships between different First Nations?

9. What kinds of alliances did First Nations traditionally form? How were they maintained?

10. Why was sign language a part of Plains First Nations cultures?

Reading and Writing

11. Write a paragraph explaining how geography in Alberta affected the culture of the Dene Sųłiné, Plains Cree, and Blackfoot peoples. Offer your opinion of whether these groups were very similar or very different from one another. Use an example from another region in Canada to support your opinion.

12. Read the story told by Glecia Bear on page 35. What lessons might people learn from her story that could be applied to some of the contemporary world's challenges? Write a paragraph with your answer.

Viewing and Representing

13. Different First Nations had animals that were particularly significant to them: the caribou or seal for the Inuit in the Arctic, the salmon for First Nations in the Pacific Northwest, the buffalo for First Nations on the Plains, and the moose for most First Nations in the Subarctic. For example, the Dunne-za used almost every part of the moose for some purpose. They even burned its fat to make offerings to Nahata, the Creator. Dominique and Madalin Habitant, from the Eleske First Nation, explain simply that the moose is meant for the people: *Hayta mayatesee,* which means "moose is used for everything."

   Create a painting, drawing, or other work of art that represents the significance of one of these animals for a First Nation or Inuit group.

What geographic region do you think the people in this photograph are from? What clues help give you your answer?

Glecia Bear was born around 1912 in Northern Saskatchewan. In 1988, she was interviewed by Freda Ahenakew for the book Kôhkominawak Otâcimowiniwâwa (Our Grandmothers' Lives as Told in their Own Words). *In the following selection, Bear describes her own interview with a woman much older than herself. From the background she provides, it is likely that the woman whose story she tells was an adolescent at the close of the eighteenth century.*

Grandmother! I said to her, "How did your family live in the old days?"

"[What] did you sew with, Grandmother?" I said to her. "We took it from the moose," she said, "back there from their back," she said, "and we dried that, 'loin-sinew' it is called," she said, "it was that with which we used to sew," this old woman said.

"But what about needles, what did you use since there were no needles?" I said to her. "Well, some small deer bone," she said, "my husband used to make needles from that," she said. "He used to grind it to a point with a stone," that old woman said....

But then, I said to her, "what did you eat from?" I said to her, "from what did you eat since there were no dishes?" I said to her.

"waskway, kahkiyaw kikway waskway ohc," îtwêw, "wiyâkan[a] ê-kî-osîhtiâhk," itwêw; "êkwa nipiy mîna," itwêw, "êkotowihk

ê-kî-âwatâhk," itwêw, "ê-osîhâ-~ ê-osîhihcik askihkwak," itwêw, "êkota ohci anima nipiy ê-kî-âwatâhk," itwêw.

("Birchbark, everything was made of birchbark." She said, "they made dishes," she said; "and for water as well," she said, "in that kind [birchbark vessels] one hauled water," she said, "pails were made of it," she said, "and the water was hauled in those," she said.)

14. Examine the photograph on page 34. Based on what you have learned about geography, environment, and culture, what can you infer about the ways of life of the people shown in the photograph? Look for clues about their environment, methods of transportation, clothing, building style, and so on.

Going Further

15. Research a map showing the distribution of Aboriginal languages around 1600 (just after Europeans first began travelling to North America). Compare it to the map of Aboriginal language families on page 6. How do you explain the differences?

16. Research a political or trade alliance between two or more nations. Several are mentioned on pages 18–19 if you need suggestions. Why was the alliance established? How was it maintained? Compare it to a contemporary alliance of First Nations, Métis, or Inuit peoples. Present your information in a poster format.

LOOKING BACK

Reread "How the People Hunted the Moose" from pages 2–3 and consider how your ideas about the story may have changed. Discuss your ideas with a partner.

The Oral Tradition

In Chapter One, you learned about the great diversity of cultures among the First Nations and Inuit peoples of North America. Their cultures today reflect a history on this continent that is as old as the land itself.

In Chapter Two, you will begin to learn about the foundations of First Nations and Inuit cultures — the stories that have preserved cultures, histories, and ways of life for generations.

The story on pages 36–37 is one part of a Blackfoot creation story. Although some First Nations people do not approve of sharing important cultural teachings outside traditional situations, this story was approved for publication in this textbook by a round table of Kainai Elders. In this chapter you will learn more about why stories, such as this one, are considered so important to First Nations and Inuit peoples.

As you read this chapter, consider these questions:

▲ What is an oral tradition?

▲ How are creation stories important to First Nations and Inuit cultures?

▲ What role does the oral tradition play in the cultures of First Nations and Inuit peoples?

▲ How do the oral traditions from different First Nations and Inuit communities compare?

The Origin of Death

A Blackfoot story as told by George Bird Grinnell in *Blackfoot Lodge Tales* (1892)

Old Man, also known as Naapi, often appears in Blackfoot oral tradition.

OLD MAN CAME FROM THE SOUTH, TRAVELLING NORTH, MAKING ANIMALS AND BIRDS AS HE PASSED ALONG. HE MADE THE MOUNTAINS, PRAIRIES, TIMBER, AND BRUSH FIRST. SO HE WENT ALONG, travelling northward, making things as he went, putting rivers here and there, and falls on them, putting red paint here and there in the ground — fixing up the world as we see it today.

He made the Milk River (the Teton), crossed it and, being tired, went up on a little hill and lay down to rest. As he lay on his back, he stretched out on the ground with arms extended and marked himself out with stones — the shape of his body, head, legs, arms, and everything. There you can see those rocks today.

After he rested, he went on northward, and stumbled over a knoll and fell down on his knees. Then he said "You are a bad thing to be stumbling against;" so he raised up two large buttes there, and named them the Knees, and they are called so to this day. He went on further north, and with some of the rocks he carried with him, he built the Sweet Grass Hills.

One day Old Man decided that he would make a woman and a child; so he formed them both — the woman and the child, her son — of clay. After he had molded the clay in human shapes, he said to the clay "You must be people," and then he covered them up and went away. The next morning he went to the place, took the covering off, and saw that the clay shapes had changed a little. The second morning there was still more change, and the third still more. The fourth morning he went to the place, took the covering off, looked at the images, and told them to rise and walk; and they did so. They walked down to the river with their Maker, and then he told them that his name was Naapi, Old Man.

As they were standing by the river, the woman said to him, "How is it? Will we always live? Will there be no end to it?" He said "I have never thought of that. We will have to decide it. I will take this buffalo chip and throw it in the river. If it floats, when people die, in four days they will become alive again; they will die only for four days. But if it sinks, there will be an end to them." He threw the chip into the river and it floated.

The woman turned and picked up a stone and said "No, I will throw this stone in the river; if it floats, we will always live; if it sinks, people must die, that they may always be sorry for each other." (That is, their friends who survive may always remember them.) The woman threw the stone into the water and it sank. "There," said Old Man "you have chosen. There will be an end to them."

It was not many nights after that the woman's child died, and she cried a great deal for it. She said to Old Man "Let us change this.

Some First Nations share similar origin stories, but others are very different. Onondaga artist Arnold Jacobs painted Birth of Earth to tell the Haudenosaunee creation story. Based on what you see in this painting, what do you think this story is about? How is it different from the Blackfoot story on pages 36–37? Now research the story and compare it to the painting and your own interpretation.

The law that you first made, let that be a law." He said "Not so. What is made law must be law. We will undo nothing that we have done. The child is dead, but it cannot be changed. People will have to die."

That is how we came to be people. It is he who made us.

❚ REFLECTION

1. Naapi made the first people of clay. How might this be significant to the Blackfoot people's relationship with the land?

2. Think about the ending of the Blackfoot creation story. What lesson can be learned by Naapi refusing to bring the child back to life? Share your ideas with a partner.

3. Sometimes we make decisions without thinking them through. Write a paragraph about a decision you made or an event that you wish you could have reversed or stopped from happening. How did you feel when you realized your error? What did you learn from the experience?

The Oral Tradition

AS YOU READ

Pages 38–43 introduce you to the foundation of First Nations and Inuit cultures: the oral tradition. Within this tradition, storytelling is the primary means of passing on culture from generation to generation. As you read this section, create a list or concept map in your notes that conveys the significance of the oral tradition.

For traditional First Nations and Inuit peoples, the oral tradition was like a library of knowledge. It contained everything people needed to know to live a good life. Today the oral tradition continues to teach new generations. Here teacher Rhoda Ungalaq (centre) teaches her students about the qulluliq, a traditional lamp used by Inuit people for cooking and warmth.

THE CULTURES OF FIRST NATIONS AND INUIT PEOPLES ARE ROOTED IN THEIR ORAL TRADITION. AN **ORAL TRADITION** IS A CULTURE'S COLLECTION OF SPOKEN WORDS THAT HAVE BEEN HANDED DOWN FOR GENERATIONS. THE words of the oral tradition are the inheritance of an entire cultural group. This tradition may include epic poems, prayers, speeches, spiritual teachings, songs, stories, and histories.

Repetition is a central part of the oral tradition. The words are heard many times throughout a person's life. Stories are told and retold. Eventually they become an integral part of an individual's sense of identity and everyday life. The words are then passed on to younger generations in the same fashion. Traditionally, the oral tradition was the primary means of cultural transmission for First Nations and Inuit peoples. **Cultural transmission** is when a society's culture is passed on to individuals who adopt the values and perspectives of the culture as their own.

Today the oral tradition continues in the lives of many First Nations, Métis, and Inuit peoples. Traditional stories and songs are a vibrant part of many communities and many people's understanding of themselves, their culture, and the world.

It can be difficult to describe the significance of a specific First Nation's oral tradition outside its original language. The English word *story* does not adequately convey the significance of the stories that are part of a culture's oral tradition.

For example, the Plains Cree describe stories as either *âcimostakewin* or *âtayohkewin*. An *âcimostakewin* is a regular story or tale that captures everyday events, news accounts, or personal experiences.

Âtayohkewina are sacred stories, sometimes called legends, passed down orally through generations. *Âtayohkewina* provide spiritual messages and sacred teachings.

Within the *âtayohkewina*, *mamâhtaw âcimôna* are stories that relate a miracle or extraordinary experience. These stories often relate to a time long ago when the world was different from the world as it is known today. In these stories, animals can talk, characters can sometimes change their shape at will, die and come back to life, and be many things at once.

Opwanîw âcimona are a second type of *âtayohkewin*. *Opwanîw âcimona* refer to sacred stories that emerge through a spiritual quest. This type of story is seen as direct communication with the Creator or spirit world. As such, it is highly sacred and is normally only shared under special circumstances.

First Nations of the Blackfoot Confederacy call their oral tradition *ákaitapiitsinikssiistsi*, which literally means "stories from the people who lived before us" or "ancestral stories." A Blackfoot storyteller normally indicates what type of *ákaitapiitsinikssiistsi* is going to be told before beginning the story. This lets the audience know what to expect. Some stories might explain how sacred bundles were given to the people, others about armed conflict and bravery, while many are spirit stories, or about Naapi. The latter kind of story often means that something humorous is going to be told.

Among the Dené Tha', all stories are called *wodih*, which means "stories, lectures, or news." This includes recent events, personal stories, prophecies, and ancient stories. A class of stories that might be compared to the

THE TEACHER-CREATOR

He goes by many names in North America and has many shapes: Coyote, Whiskey Jack, Blue Jay, Raven, Mink, and Spider. The Anishinabé call him Nanabozho or Nanabush, the Great Hare; the Blackfoot call him Naapi, or Old Man; to the Nakoda he is Iktomi, the Trickster; and to the Cree, he is Wîsahkecâhk. Half spirit and half human, the Teacher-Creator is often a central character in First Nations oral traditions. Although the specifics of this character vary from culture to culture, he tends to play a similar role.

The Teacher-Creator has extraordinary powers, the ability to create and change things, and many contradictory ways. Sometimes he helps; sometimes he hinders. He transforms himself from shape to shape, male to female, world to world, and even life to death and back to life. Sometimes wise, sometimes foolish, sometimes heroic, and sometimes dishonest and sneaky, the Teacher-Creator is a complicated cultural figure.

Yet trickster tendencies are only one side of this complex character. For example, although many Cree stories show Wîsahkecâhk in his trickster role, he also has a far more serious side. Wîsahkecâhk is an important part of sacred Cree spiritual practices.

This collage, called The Trickster, *was created by Leah Fontaine, an art instructor working with schools throughout Canada teaching Aboriginal culture through art and theatre. How is her choice of collage an appropriate one for the Trickster?*

◨ REFLECTION

Choose a Teacher-Creator figure from a specific culture and create a collage or other artwork that represents his nature.

PERSONAL STORIES

Many stories relate experiences that are more personal than communal. The Plains Cree call these kinds of stories *âcimostakewina*. Such stories may still teach listeners and they may still be passed to new generations, but they are not surrounded by as many protective cultural restrictions about who can tell them and when they can be told. The text that follows, about a Cree Elder in northern Alberta, is an example of this kind of story.

Katy [Sanderson] is a very capable hunter and trapper. At the age of seventy-nine (1991) she remains interested in trapping but prefers a friend or relative to go with her on any treks away from the immediate area of her main trap line home. Her hunting capabilities are well known. For example, in 1975, at the age of sixty-three, she hunted and shot a moose on the shore of the Athabasca River near Fort McMurray. It was a big moose, weighing approximately 500 kilograms. It floundered and fell into shallow water about 1 metre deep. Katy waded into the water and managed to pull the floating animal to where it grounded in 0.7 metres of water. It was late September, and the water was cool. Katy, as quickly as she could, removed its internal organs. If a moose has foraged just before the hunt, its loaded stomach alone can be too heavy for one person to carry. Then she removed the head, cut each leg at the knee joint, and severed each hind and each front quarter from the rib cage. She dragged each piece to the shore. After that she walked back to her home base, approximately 6 kilometres, where she asked other members of her family to return with her to complete the job of skinning-out the carcass and carrying it home.

— Terry Garvin, *Bush Land People*

Katy Sanderson is seen here picking high bush cranberries, a common fruit in the north.

Cree *mamâhtaw âcimôna* are called *tonht' onh wodihé*, which translates as "stories of long ago."

Some stories in the oral tradition, such as those about creation or the reasons for spiritual ceremonies, are passed on with scrupulous exactness. These old stories contain essential cultural teachings. Some stories are a method of prayer. Certain sacred stories are traditionally never told to a person from outside one's own group. Someone might, for example, relate some part of a First Nation's history to an outsider but refuse to share a story about a sacred ceremony.

Traditionally, these special stories were told in the winter. Words were considered so powerful that even speaking of a spirit at the wrong time was believed to cause hardship for an individual or a community. Some First Nations people believed that spirits were asleep in the winter, so it was safe to speak of them at that time of year.

This custom of restricting storytelling to the winter was also practical. Spring, summer, and fall were busy times for most First Nations as they hunted, harvested, and prepared for the winter. In most regions across Canada, winter meant individuals spent long periods of time in shelters with their families. Winter was an important time for reinforcing community bonds and values.

Of course, not all stories were told in the winter. Some stories were told only during other seasons of the year or were restricted to certain types of ceremonies and gatherings.

ELDERS AND THE ORAL TRADITION

Those responsible for passing on the stories and keeping the oral tradition alive are the Elders. In Blackfoot, they are *Omahkitapii*, in Cree *Kihteyaya*, in Dené Tha' *Detⱬye*, and in Nakoda *Ishaween*. In all Aboriginal cultures, Elders are those who are sought after for their spiritual and cultural leadership. They have learned the traditional ways and have been asked by the community to teach this knowledge. An Elder does not have to be old or elderly. Sometimes relatively young people are recognized as cultural advisors because of their special knowledge, gifts, or experience.

The Anishinabé say someone is speaking the truth with the term *w'daebawae*. This means they are telling the truth as far as their words and experience can take them. Elders' experiences make them people who know the truth in this sense of the word. It does not mean they know the one truth and that all others are incorrect.

COMMUNAL STORIES

All First Nations have some stories that are, as the Blackfoot say, *ákaitapiitsinikssiistsi* — stories from the ancestors. This oral tradition is part of a First Nation's **collective** inheritance, like the land. The *Report of the Royal Commission on Aboriginal Peoples* describes these kinds of stories as "truths too deep to be contained in a literal account." As a class discuss what this phrase means. How does it help explain that stories, such as the Tsuu T'ina story of separation below, are held to be true?

A Tsuu T'ina story tells of the time when the tribe split from the Athapaskan-speaking tribes.

The people were crossing a large body of water that was frozen. There was a large horn sticking up from the ice, and an old lady's grandson cried to have this antler. As most Tsuu T'ina grandmothers do, she gave in to her grandson's tantrum. So the Elder proceeded to chop at the antler, for it was frozen in the ice.

In doing so, the old lady disturbed a large serpent from whose head the horn was growing. The large serpent roared, and the people scattered in panic. Unfortunately, the ice crumbled and broke all the way down the lake. The people who were nearest the serpent, in the middle of the lake, perished in the ice-cold water. The people who were nearest the north shore turned back and reached their destination safely, and the people nearest the south shore ran just as quickly to reach safety.

The tribe could not regroup because of the large lake that divided them. So the southern group continued to travel south. They (Tsuu T'ina) adopted the Plains Native way.

— Tsuu T'ina Nation

The Tsuu T'ina oral tradition lives on in new generations. Here a Tsuu T'ina mother wears traditional clothing as she holds her child at an event in Alberta in 2002. (Names of those pictured are not available.)

TSIINAAKI (MRS. ROSIE RED CROW)
Kainai First Nation

Tsiinaaki (Rosie Red Crow)

At eighty-seven years, Rosie Red Crow is one of the busiest Elders of the Kainai First Nation in southern Alberta.

On this day she is off to an all-night ceremony, having recently returned from a Montana conference. She is a member of the Red Crow College Elders Advisory Council, which meets every month, and she is called upon constantly for her knowledge of Kainai culture.

"As long as people will have me, I'll go and share what I can," Red Crow insists. "As an Elder, it's my duty to talk to the young people. Some of them listen to me, some don't. But I keep talking to them so they will be proud of who they are."

Red Crow takes delight in sharing stories her Elders handed down to her when she was young. In them, she finds the very spirit of what it means to be Kainai. "The Blackfoot language is also important, because it embodies the way we believe and express ourselves," she adds.

According to Marie Marule, who heads up Red Crow College "Rosie is just a treasure. She is our matriarch; she's bright, delightful, and very astute. And active! She bakes bread, pies, and picks berries. Most of all, she's a cultural expert."

Red Crow knows the oral history of the Kainai nation and has been a member of the Horn, Brave Dog, and Buffalo women's societies. She has been a bundle keeper and is a grandparent to those who enter these spiritual societies.

Like other Elders of her generation, Red Crow is heartbroken by the fast lives many young people lead.

"Every weekend there's an accident or suicide. We really have a lot of respect for each other, especially us Elders, so we feel the loss when something happens."

My grandfather Askaota'siwa (Owns Many Horses) was one of our chiefs.

People would approach him saying, "Aakaota's, I am on foot. Would you lend me a team of horses?" He would say to the person, "There are two over there who look alike. Why don't you break them?" When the person came back later to report that the horses were broken in, Aakaota's would give the horses to that person. This was sharing and helping each other.

— Tsiinaaki (Rosie Red Crow),
Kipaitapiiwahsimooni:
Alcohol and Drug Abuse Education Program

▌ REFLECTION

Rosie Red Crow describes sharing knowledge as part of her role as an Elder. How might her story about her grandfather relate to this role? In your journal, write your understanding of the term *Elder*. As a class, discuss how a person becomes recognized by their peers as an Elder.

What are your roles in your family, school, and community? Consider how a person's roles change as they grow older. In your journal, describe your roles now and how you see those evolving in the future.

The story below was adapted from *Those Who Know: Profiles of Alberta's Elders*, by Dianne Meili. What does Ella Paul's story about Mary Mae Strawberry tell you about Elders and their teachings? What did Paul learn from her experience?

Ella Paul, from the Alexander Reserve, describes an experience of spending time with Elder Mary Mae Strawberry on the O'Chiese Reserve. Ella explains that she felt anxious about spending the night in the bush with Mary Mae after seeing a bear track in the dirt. Mary Mae said calmly "Don't worry. We're in the hands of the Creator. Whatever happens will happen. The Creator balances all things in his Hands and watches over them." Ella tried to stay calm, but spent a rough night hearing the sound of wolves howling around her. In the morning, as the two women left the bush to return to Mary Mae's home, they saw a fresh bear carcass.

Says Ella, "I realized then about the balance Mary Mae talked about. That bear had come into our little circle to distract the wolves so they wouldn't bother us. Even though I was scared of the bear, he was really our helper because the wolves eventually fed on him. He balanced off the circle. If I'd been scared, maybe I would have upset the balance. I needed to act naturally and have the faith that Mary Mae has. She told me, 'We're just like animals so we blend in. Don't be worried.' She was right all along."

Elders are the living memory of their community. Past generations depend upon Elders to pass along their stories, and future generations depend on the young to learn and remember the Elders' knowledge. Each generation is like a link in a chain that connects past to future.

Elders are called upon to conduct and oversee important rituals, such as healing ceremonies, spiritual quests, Sweat Lodges, and Sundances. They are the people who know, remember, and live the teachings that were handed down to them from previous generations.

They also mediate or resolve differences between individuals, communities, and organizations using their knowledge of traditional customs. This means they help restore balance and harmony within communities. Elders are able to counsel people and help them see their place in the community. They reinforce the importance of keeping harmony in one's own life, with the community, and with the environment. Yet their teachings are often indirect and metaphoric, rather than direct forms of advice. Listeners have a personal responsibility to think about the stories and form their own decisions and plans of action.

LOOKING BACK

Before starting the next section, be sure you can answer the following questions: What is an oral tradition? What are different kinds of stories within an oral tradition? Why might a specific story have a restriction upon who and when it can be told? How are Elders a part of the oral tradition?

Connections between older generations and younger generations are fundamental to the oral tradition. Here Dan Cardinal, an Elder from the Sucker Creek First Nation, is shown with a child in 1998.

Creation Stories as Spiritual Foundation

AS YOU READ

From the beginning of time, people from all cultures have wondered about their place in the world: Who am I and why am I here? What is my purpose in life? How did my people come to be? Where do people go when they die? Why are things the way they are?

Creation stories answer these types of questions and provide people with an understanding of themselves and the relationship between all things in the universe, both seen and unseen. As you read pages 44–49, think about your own answers to these questions. What experiences, stories, or other information influence your ideas about your place in the world?

MORE THAN ONE THOUSAND NATIONS LIVED IN NORTH AMERICA WHEN THE FIRST EUROPEANS ARRIVED. EACH HAD ITS OWN CULTURE WITH PARTICULAR RITUALS, CEREMONIES, AND BELIEFS THAT TIED THEM TO THE LAND the people called home. Creation stories explain how the world and all of its parts began. This explanation for the **origin** of the world can help people understand and accept things that cannot be seen or touched, including their own identity, purpose, and place in the world. An individual's understanding of their place and purpose in the world is part of their **spirituality**. The traditional spirituality of First Nations and Inuit peoples is a way of life infused with the belief that existence includes both a physical world and a spiritual world. The physical world can be seen and touched. It is the humans, plants, water, and earth itself.

The spiritual world is normally unseen, but is nevertheless present everywhere and in everything. All humans, animals, plants, water, and the earth itself have spiritual aspects along with physical presence.

The two worlds are inseparable. Every part of the physical world is connected to the spiritual realm. In turn, the spiritual realm is affected by events, decisions, and actions in the physical world. This sense of connection between the physical and spiritual has a central role in the oral tradition and especially in creation stories.

Creation stories are normally considered sacred stories. People who want to hear one should issue their request using proper protocol for the community involved.

Creation stories affirm that creation is not a matter of the past — it is an ongoing process that is constantly in a state of renewal through the continuation of life.

The crow was the most beautiful of birds; they say he had a lovely voice and sang better than all the rest. But he was proud and was always strutting about while he sang, despising the other birds. One day, they say, a big bird, tired of the sight and sound of him, contrived to seize him by the neck. Then, they say, he rolled him in charcoal and squeezed him so tight that the crow, half strangled, could only cry "Caw! Caw!" That is why he is now black all over and can't sing any more.

— Dene Sųłiné oral history from *Inkonze: The Stones of Traditional Knowledge*

Creation stories describe the origin of and the reason for the rituals, ceremonies, and spiritual beliefs that celebrate the renewal of creation. In Chapter Three, you will learn about some of these ceremonies and beliefs.

PURPOSE AND ORDER

Because the world is a complicated place, creation stories are sometimes long and have many parts — how the world was formed; when people arrived; the origin of important cultural objects, such as the ceremonial pipe; how there came to be light, fire, the moon, and wind; why the animals and plants look and act as they do. For example, various stories explain how the chipmunk got its black stripes, why owls have big eyes, and why the bobcat has a flat nose and long tail.

Common in these stories is the idea that nothing is by chance. The Creator has a purpose for each part of the natural world. Creation stories reveal that the Creator's touch is everywhere.

Creation stories set forth the relationship between all things of the world — animals, birds, plants, insects, rocks, trees, rivers, mountains, oceans, and humans — and the role each of them has in maintaining balance and the cycle of creation. Nothing is too small or insignificant to play a part. A message common in many creation stories is that everything and everyone has a gift to give that should be accepted with gratitude and respect.

Creation stories reveal the important position animals hold in First Nations and Inuit cultures. In many First Nations origin stories, the world was shaped and formed by the thoughts and wishes of an animal. The Secwepemc (Shuswap), for example, tell how Coyote saves the world from darkness and long winters by creating day and night and the four seasons.

Humans are not separate from the land, but part of it. In many creation stories, humans are the last to be created. "When the world was new," as the Sahtú Dene say in many stories, animals were different from the way they are now. They were animal-people with special powers, and all spoke the same language. In traditional Sahtú Dene stories, humans are the only creatures that no other animal or plant depends on for survival. Because of this, people are meant to be respectful and humble in their relationship to nature and the land. The attributes of the land are gifts meant to be used and enjoyed with gratitude.

Many stories look to the natural world and its laws as guides to human behaviour. A Blackfoot story tells how wolves showed the first people how to cooperate with one another to hunt buffalo. The wolves then disappeared but can be seen in the sky as makóyoohsokoyi (the Wolf Trail or Milky Way). The stars are a reminder of how people should live together.

FLOODS, EARTH, AND THE SKY WORLD

Creation stories are among the world's oldest stories — they exist in all cultures. There are often similarities in the stories of different cultures. For example, many tell of a great flood — of a long-ago time when the entire world was covered by water.

In one version of the Cree creation story, the Creator made all the animals and the first people; then he told Wîsahkecâhk to teach them how to live. But Wîsahkecâhk did not obey, and the people quarrelled. The Creator was displeased and sent a great flood. Everything was drowned except Wîsahkecâhk, Otter, Beaver, and Muskrat. They needed somewhere to live, so Wîsahkecâhk asked the others to dive down and bring up a bit of earth so he could make an island. Each one tried, but only Muskrat succeeded. Using the powers given to him by the Creator, Wîsahkecâhk expanded the bit of earth into an island by blowing on it.

The story of the earth diver is told not only by many First Nations, but also by indigenous peoples in Australia, Africa, and parts of Asia.

Other creation stories are quite different. First peoples living in the southern United States, such as the Apache, Navajo, and Hopi, were said to have climbed out of Earth, passing through different worlds before reaching the surface where they live today.

Some stories involve a Sky World of spirits. In a creation story told by the Dene people near Great Slave Lake, the world becomes dark and snow falls and blankets Earth. The animals send a delegation up through a trap door to the Sky World to find out why. There the animals work together to retrieve the sun, moon, and stars from Black Bear who was not yet an animal of this world. The animals throw the sun through the trap door and it melts the snow, causing a great flood. After the waters recede, as the story goes, people come and there is never peace on Earth again.

LAND AND IDENTITY

Creation stories of different First Nations reflect their specific environment and give the people a sense of belonging with their surroundings. In the Blackfoot creation story, Naapi marks off a piece of land with a stick and provides the people with many animals and plants. He then tells them to defend their land and its resources from others.

Many stories describe the creation of specific landforms or features of the physical environment. Dene people say the waters of the Great Slave Lake were left behind after the great snowfall melted. In the Haida creation story, the beaches and rocks of Haida Gwaii (the Queen Charlotte Islands) are formed after the waters that covered Earth receded. In some stories

Lloyd Pinay, a Cree artist from northwest of Saskatoon, made this sculpture, called Re-creating Turtle Island, *to welcome visitors to the First Nations gallery at the Royal Saskatchewan Museum. His sculpture combines elements of Cree, Anishinabé, Nakoda, and Dene oral traditions. In some creation stories, Earth is formed on the back of a turtle, which is why some First Nations call North America Turtle Island.*

from the Pacific Northwest, Raven makes the first people from seashells, and in others he leads them from a clamshell. Some Inuit and First Nations tell stories about the origin of the aurora borealis, the northern lights. A stone along the southern shores of Lake Superior is sacred to the Chippewa. This is where Nanabozho stopped to rest and smoke his pipe while he created the world. Everywhere in the Rocky Mountains, sacred places where Naapi walked or slept or hunted can be found.

The stories show that these places, the traditional lands, were home to each group from the beginning, provided to them by the Creator. These lands are where each nation is intended to live. The intimate sense of connection traditional First Nations people felt with their surroundings was a part of their identity as humans. Many First Nations people continue to feel this connection today.

In addition, creation stories teach that human actions in their surroundings have to be respectful. It is here that their ancestors were taught how to hunt, which plants to use for food or medicine, and the importance of balance and harmony with nature. Here, the lessons were learned on how to live as a person, a family, a community, and a nation. The land is both birthplace and birthright.

There is a hill coming up from the north side of Lake Athabasca called Beaver Lodge. There were once two giant beavers living there. A giant came and chopped their beaver lodge. If you see the beaver lodge, you will see it is split in half. One of these two beavers that lived there hid, and the other one swam south across Lake Athabasca. The giant chased this one across Lake Athabasca and killed him. That beaver kicked the trees south of Lake Athabasca and created the Sand Dunes.

— Trace Deranger, *Inkonze: The Stones of Traditional Knowledge*

Cantara Dune Field, Athabasca Sand Dunes Provincial Wilderness Park, south shore of Lake Athabasca, Saskatchewan

Naapi and the Rock

Noomi Napiiwa ihtapawawahkawa. Ikskaisistsikowa; Itsitohkitsikopi ami ohkotoki. Itohkotsiiwai omaayi. Itotstoyi. Matsitsiskotoyi ami maayi. Ama ohkotoka itsitokiitaki kitomapoksisaiskoyi Napiiyi. Iitanistsiyikh oomiksiiya pist'toiks kiyahkitapakspommakihpowaw. Ki itai'statsiyaihkia'wa ommi ohkotoki ki ai'aitsin'nanitohpat'tsistoyiyihkiaw. Mii Ohkotokskoi itotaisksi nahk ohkotokahk.

(One day Naapi was out walking. He was very tired so he rested on a big rock. Then he gave his robe to the rock as a gift. It got cold, so he took his robe back. The rock got angry and chased Naapi all over the place. Naapi asked some nightingales for help and they dive-bombed the rock with their droppings until it broke apart. You can see that rock by Okotoks.)

— The Siksika Nation, *Aakaitapitsinniksiists (Siksika Old Stories)*

Okotoks, the name of a town just south of Calgary, Alberta, is an anglicized version of the Blackfoot word Ohkotokiksi, which is the Blackfoot name for this rock outside the town.

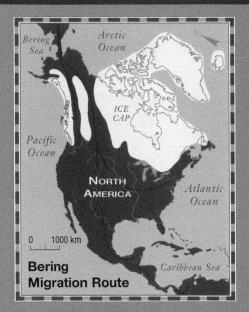

Bering Migration Route

This map shows the route scientists believe First Nations took as they migrated from Asia to North America between 30 000 and 11 000 years ago. Research what the environment would have been like at this time in North America and other parts of the world. Use your research to write a short story about a group of people making this journey.

Many First Nations and Inuit peoples believe that their ancestors originated in North America and that the Creator made the land and its inhabitants, including humans, to exist in a delicate state of balance. These beliefs are based on sacred oral teachings that have been passed down for generations.

Scientists propose various **theories** about the origins of North America's first peoples. Theories are explanations that are not proven, but are scientifically reasonable. Scientific theories are based on the study of artifacts found at archaeological sites across North America. Most theories maintain that the first peoples to live in North America originated elsewhere. These theories propose that the earliest humans on the planet evolved in Africa and then gradually spread to other parts of the world.

Scientists disagree, however, on the exact date and circumstances of humanity's appearance in North and South America. The most widely accepted explanation is known as the Beringia theory, which suggests that First Nations migrated to North America from Asia between 30 000 and 11 000 years ago.

Today Alaska and Siberia are separated by the Bering Strait, a narrow strip of water approximately 88 kilometres wide. During the Ice Age, however, ocean levels were much lower. Vast quantities of moisture were locked in the ice sheets covering North America. Lower ocean levels left a continuous land mass between Asia and North America exposed for several thousand years. Scientists have named this area Beringia. At some point in history, Beringia may have stretched across 1600 kilometres.

Scientists theorize that ancient hunters from Asia travelled across Beringia in pursuit of large game, such as mammoths, giant bison, antelopes, and mastodons. From there, scientists believe the hunters migrated south, either along the Pacific coastline or as shown on the map on this page, through a narrow, ice-free corridor stretching down through what is now Alberta.

The Beringia theory dominated North American archaeology for six decades. Today other theories compete for acceptance. Some scientists, for example, now believe that the first Americans arrived by boat. Following Asia's coastline, they sailed past Beringia and migrated down the west coast as far as South America. Others believe ancient Europeans may have travelled across the North Atlantic. Still others argue that Polynesian islanders and Australian indigenous peoples arrived by raft or boat from across the Pacific Ocean.

No theory yet explains all evidence. Because these theories are founded on discoveries of physical artifacts, new discoveries can support or change scientific theories rapidly. Debate in the scientific community about this topic continues.

> ## ▣ REFLECTION
>
> As a class, discuss the differences between beliefs and scientific theories. What are the strengths and limitations of each form of explanation?

COMPARING CREATION STORIES

Indigenous cultures around the world use creation stories to understand how the world and human life came to be. Animals and nature, and their relationship to human beings, are common themes. Each group's creation story is unique, however, because it reflects the specific environment in which the group lives.

What roles do animals and nature play in creation stories?

WHAT TO DO

1. Select two groups of indigenous peoples that come from different geographic locations. You might select one group from Alberta and another group from a place that you have visited or would like to visit. If you prefer, you might choose two groups from places far apart in the world, such as Canada and Australia.

2. Using literature anthologies, the Internet, or community Elders if possible, find creation stories from the two groups you want to compare. If you approach Elders from your community, be sure to consult with your teacher first about using the proper protocol in your request.

3. Using an atlas, geography textbook, magazines, or the Internet, make point-form notes about the geography of the stories' locations. Consider, for example, what the land looks like, whether there is water nearby, what types of animals live there, and the climate.

4. Make a table to organize the similarities and differences between the stories and the geographic locations. Read the stories carefully and complete your table as thoroughly as you can.

5. Use the information you've found for a creative project. Some ideas include:
   - an educational poster that communicates the information from your table
   - a painting or sculpture that illustrates one of the stories
   - an audio guide for a tour bus that is driving through the landscape involved in the story.

   Once you have an idea, clear your project with your teacher before beginning.

Thinking About Your Project

As a class, discuss how geography influences creation stories. Why might indigenous peoples living in different parts of the world sometimes have similar creation stories?

LOOKING BACK

Discuss the following questions with a small group and make your own notes from the discussion. What are creation stories? What kind of questions do they answer? How are creation stories a part of First Nations and Inuit cultures?

Teaching Stories

BEFORE YOU READ

In the last section, you learned how creation stories provide a spiritual foundation for First Nations and Inuit cultures. Many of these stories also pass on values, skills, and knowledge because traditional spirituality was inseparable from the way people lived their day-to-day lives. You will learn more about spirituality in Chapter Three. In this section, you will begin to learn about the many ways the oral tradition functioned in traditional First Nations and Inuit societies. Among many communities, this tradition continues. As you read, make a list of the ways the oral tradition functioned and the kinds of values it passed on.

Through their oral traditions, First Nations and Inuit peoples pass on their history, customs, and values. Oral traditions also teach practical skills, such as house building, hunting, collection and preparation of medicinal plants, healing ceremonies, and knowledge of fishing spots and migratory routes. The sharing in this knowledge traditionally bound individuals and families together with a common understanding of life and how it should be properly lived.

Oral teachings are very much a social experience. Oral communication normally requires at least two people, one to speak and another to listen. In the oral tradition, members of the community, most often the old and young, must spend time together. The oral tradition therefore reinforces **interpersonal relationships**, or social bonds, at many levels. For example, a story might communicate the importance of relationships while the process of sharing a story reinforces the same idea.

The Royal Saskatchewan Museum commissioned this mural, called The Story Teller, from artist Dale Stonechild. What is your interpretation of Stonechild's work? Discuss your ideas with a partner.

I've learned a lot of lessons about life from stories.

When I was a boy, whenever I asked "Why?" my grandmother and the old people would answer by telling stories. These stories related the marvelous exploits of many wondrous creatures and beings. All the stories had a moral lesson. They taught me how to behave, and they taught me about nature and life on Mother Earth. As I became older, the stories got more serious, for they contained spiritual teachings. I had to listen closely or I would lose the whole meaning of the story.

After my old people died, I forgot these stories. Now, I am returning to them. My art is one way that I am reconnecting with the teachings of these stories.

— Dale Stonechild, Plains Cree-Dakota

THE ART OF STORYTELLING

Do you remember people telling you stories when you were a young child? Most children love hearing stories, especially when the storyteller mimics the characters through voice and body language. Storytelling is an art that First Nations and Inuit peoples have used for centuries as a way to entertain, convey information, resolve conflicts, and teach important values.

Good storytellers structured their story for their specific audience and get them involved. Some have the audience sing a particular song at appropriate points or respond with a "Ho!" to the storyteller's "Hey!" at regular intervals. In old times, such techniques would both keep listeners awake as they sat by the fire and ensure that they stayed involved in the story.

Oral cultures depend entirely upon memory. Storytellers, therefore, have the responsibility to make their stories memorable and listeners have the responsibility to pay attention.

In First Nations and Inuit oral traditions, both speaker and listener are active participants in the exchange of knowledge. Being a listener does not mean being a passive receiver of words. It means responding to the speaker with mind, body, and spirit.

Storyteller Mida Donnessey is one of many Yukon Elders who have performed at the annual Yukon International Storytelling Festival. The festival encourages storytellers to use their first language, with a summary provided in English. Storytellers from across Canada and around the world attend.

Your Project

1. Using appropriate protocol under your teacher's guidance, invite a storyteller to come to your class. With your teacher's help, locate someone who is recognized by a local First Nations or Métis community as a talented storyteller. Let this person know that your class would like to learn about the art of storytelling.

2. During the visit, observe the storyteller and make note of voice, body language, eye contact, and gestures that are used. Also pay attention to pauses and silences. Sometimes these carry as much meaning as the words themselves.

3. After the visit, make notes about any techniques you noticed the storyteller using to make the story interesting.

4. Select a First Nations or Inuit story that you think would appeal to young children. With your teacher, make arrangements to present your story to a class or group of younger children. If that is not possible, present your story to your classmates.

5. Practise your story so that you can present it without the use of a book or notes.

6. Keep the following points in mind:

   - You do not have to present the story word for word, but you need to capture the sentiment.
   - Make use of your voice, body language, and eye contact to bring your story to life.
   - Prepare a dramatic opening to grab your listeners' attention.

Thinking About Your Project

Today electronic media, such as television, radio, and the Internet, can relate oral stories without the presence of a storyteller. Can First Nations and Inuit communities use electronic technology to maintain their oral traditions? What issues or problems do you see with the use of this kind of media? As an extension project, use a Web site design program to create a Web site that makes use of your class's best ideas.

Traditionally, some Inuit peoples resolved differences by carrying out musical duels. Singers would face off against each other, inventing lyrics designed to poke fun at the other and persuade the audience that he or she should be proclaimed the victor in the dispute. Here Anda Kuitsi and Robert Umeerinneq from East Greenland perform a duel song in 1998.

Much oral communication traditionally took place during land-based activities or rituals. Sometimes specific oral communication required a particular activity in order to convey its full meaning. For example, the sights, sounds, smells, and physical experience of digging up a particular root at a specific time of year, in combination with observation of spiritual prayers or rituals surrounding the activity, teach much more than a description of what to do. Much of the wisdom from the oral tradition involves this kind of sensory, experiential knowledge.

THEMES AND VALUES

Most stories from oral traditions are entertaining. Many use humour — in one Wakanabi legend, a man chooses the ability to make a marvelous sound that rings through the hills whenever he belches or passes wind — but it is a story's underlying message that is most important. Stories often teach about the natural world or they illustrate central values, such as truth, love, and respect. A value is a principle, standard, or quality that is considered worthwhile or desirable. The values of a story are rarely stated outright; listeners have to think about and consider the consequences of the characters' behaviour.

Stories are traditionally told over and over. A child's understanding of a specific story might differ from that of a young adult or adult. Children might appreciate the entertainment. Adults might appreciate the spiritual teachings. The same story might offer something to listeners of all ages. Listeners are expected to learn from their experiences and to use stories to guide their decisions throughout life. The Dené Tha', for example, call oral storytelling *emot'li*, which means "words to live by."

The Haudenosaunee tell a story about Opossum, who is conceited about his lovely, bushy tail and is tricked into shaving it. This story and many others explain the origin of particular animal characteristics,

In some communities, land-based activities, such as skinning an animal, still offer opportunities for traditional communication styles in the oral tradition.

but also show the perils of allowing vanity to control behaviour. Trickster characters often appear in such cautionary stories.

Many stories warn of the consequences of unkind or disrespectful behaviour. Creatures who refuse to get along often meet an unhappy ending. As in *The Legend of the Saskatoons*, as told by Eleanor Brass on this page, greed and other forms of selfishness are seldom unpunished.

Teaching by negative example is often tied to humour. Characters in stories are made to look foolish as a way of warning listeners not to bring the same consequences on themselves.

Teaching stories often use negative behaviour as examples, but not always. Inuit oral tradition tells of a hunter who is rewarded by Nunam-shua, the Woman Who

The following story was published in the *Regina Leader Post* in 1956. It was written by Eleanor Brass, who was born on the Peepeekisis Reserve in Saskatchewan. It is one example of hundreds of teaching stories told by First Nations. Describe an experience you've had that is similar to the one Brass describes, or write a story about someone who experiences the truth of a traditional story in contemporary society.

The Legend of the Saskatoons

The Saulteaux tribe who dwelt mostly among the waterways have many legends of a water serpent.

During saskatoon season, a young woman with a baby laced in a mossbag attached to a board, called a cradle, went out picking. She leaned the cradle against a tree in plain view of the berry patch. In peering deeper into the bushes she saw larger berries and went after them and repeated this performance until in her greed she got out of view of the baby. When all her containers were brimming full, she emerged from the bluff remembering her baby, who was not where she had left [the cradle]. In looking around the tree where she stood the cradle, she heard [the baby's] cry down by the lakeshore. On arriving on the lakeshore the cry seemed to be coming over the water from the middle of the lake, and then she knew it was the water serpent that took her baby into the lake and she would never see it again. This was now her punishment for thinking more of saskatoons than the safety of her baby. For generations the cry of this infant was heard on the lake by the Saulteaux Indians to remind them that they must not indulge in greed.

Saskatoon berries were once a staple in the diet of many Plains First Nations, such as the Nakoda, who called the low-growing bush wabasoka, *which means literally "tree spreads out."*

I was picking saskatoons in the Qu'Appelle valley along Ketepwa, where there were a lot of good berries on the bushes. In penetrating deeper into the bluff, finding better and better ones, I was thinking of the Saulteaux woman's legend and was greedily plucking berries for my already overfilled pail, when I was attacked by large ants whose bites were like fire. I hastily retreated, wondering if the old legend had a message still.

— Eleanor Brass, *I Walk in Two Worlds*

Dwells in the Earth, for his respectful ways — taking only what he needs, avoiding females with calves, being thankful, and remembering that the grass is sacred when the caribou migrate.

Some stories demonstrate that even small creatures have power and deserve respect. Many stories explain natural phenomena, such as why deciduous trees lose their leaves in the fall. Stories about food sources vary from region to region — the coming of corn, the gift of buffalo, how salmon originated, and why berries ripen at certain times of the year. The stories explain why something happens as it does, but they also teach listeners valuable knowledge about the environment and its resources.

Other common topics include the changing seasons, the four elements of nature (earth, water, fire, and air), and celebrations of bravery and good deeds.

Whatever a story's subject, it often carries a message about values, such as cooperation, compromise, sharing, and pride in the success of the community. Connections between the personal and the planetary illustrate the interdependence between all things and the importance of establishing nurturing, respectful relationships with oneself, other people, and everything in the world.

Some stories centre on dreams or visions; others predict the future. Most show that the visible world is only the surface. Sometimes a story's message is obvious. Other times listeners might have to think about it over time. Most often the natural world provides answers.

First Nations oral traditions have always related how living and non-living parts of Earth are one. Today mainstream science recognizes this truth. The science of ecology — the study of relationships between living things and their environment — circles back to truths First Nations have known and taught for generations.

The Teaching of Tsęli (Tselly)

The teaching of Tselly... I guess a long time ago in the prehistoric times, the people they got careless, they say, and they got sloppy, filthy. ...They didn't take care of Mother Earth. So the frogs started coming out of the water. And it didn't matter how many they killed; it seemed like there were more and more frogs coming, and they didn't know why. So the leader asked the Medicine Man "Try to find out what is happening. Why are all these frogs invading our camps?" So the Medicine Man somehow communicated with these frogs and the frogs told him "Your people are filthy... and all the garbage you create is going into that water and... we have to live in that water. As long as you don't clean up... us frogs are going to be here. No matter what you do, there is going to be more and more frogs living amongst your people. But if you clean it up, all the frogs will go back into the water again. From this day forward, every evening before the sun goes down we are going to talk to you again, to let you know to keep this earth clean, to remind you to keep yourselves clean."

— Harvey Scanie, *Inkonze: The Stones of Traditional Knowledge*

FINDING INSPIRATION THROUGH THE ORAL TRADITION

Many stories from the oral tradition contain an inspirational message about rising above challenges. Common themes for these kinds of stories include:

- recognizing talents and strengths in ourselves or in others
- overcoming obstacles
- enduring difficult situations
- reaching goals
- virtuous characteristics (e.g., patience)
- positive values (e.g., equality).

What important values or lessons do stories from the oral tradition offer?

WHAT TO DO

1. With your teacher's help, outline the steps of the proper protocol to use when approaching Elders with a request. The protocol varies among First Nations and Inuit communities, but it always ensures the Elder and his or her knowledge is shown respect. In the Cree and Blackfoot cultures, an offering of tobacco and/or a gift is a common form of invitation.

2. Using correct protocol, invite an Elder to your class to share a story from his or her culture. Request a teaching story from the Elder's culture.

3. Following the Elder's visit, discuss as a class what you think the message of the story is (for example, to help understand the importance of patience, to inspire others who face difficult situations, etc.).

4. Song lyrics, like stories, often express ideas about values or messages about accomplishing important goals. Find a song that you think expresses an inspirational message. As you listen to the song, make notes about lines that help support the main idea of the lyrics.

5. Prepare a presentation for your class that includes the following:

   - a brief explanation of the song and Its message

   - a summary of how you feel the song lyrics can be inspirational

   - parts or all of the song used at the beginning, end, or throughout your presentation.

6. As a class, compare how the Elder's story conveyed its message with the techniques used in the song.

LOOKING BACK

Before moving on to the next section, be sure you can answer the following questions: How does an oral tradition teach values to new generations? What kinds of values are common among First Nations and Inuit peoples? Write a short story, poem, or paragraph that uses your answers to these questions and the ideas you have learned on pages 50–55.

Oral and Written Literatures

AS YOU READ

Today words from the past continue to be passed on to younger generations. Many are shared in the traditional way, from old to young through the spoken word. Until recently, people from non-Aboriginal cultures made little effort to understand oral traditions. They tended to evaluate First Nations and Inuit stories according to their own culture's belief systems, which place greater value on the written over the spoken word. In recent years, however, this kind of thinking has declined — even the Supreme Court of Canada has used oral histories in its rulings. As you read, think about the similarities and differences between oral and written literatures. With which form of expression are you most comfortable? Why?

This petroglyph is at Writing-on-Stone Provincial Park in southern Alberta. The name comes from the Blackfoot word Áísínai'pi, which means "writing on stone." Many First Nations visited this site; it was on a common migration route. Research the kinds of information that were recorded there. Compare its symbols to those of petroglyphs or pictographs from elsewhere in Canada and note the similarities and differences.

ALTHOUGH ALL CULTURES HAVE STORIES, ONLY ORAL CULTURES CONSISTENTLY USE THEM AS THEIR PRIMARY TOOL FOR EDUCATION AND **SOCIALIZATION**, WHICH IS A LIFELONG PROCESS BY WHICH INDIVIDUALS absorb the culture of their society. European legends and folk tales once served similar functions of education and socialization, but today are viewed as entertainment for children, rather than integral parts of living cultures.

THE WINTER COUNT

Although the basis of all First Nations and Inuit cultures is the oral tradition, some nations also recorded information in caves or on the sides of mountains. Rather than orthography — a system of written letters — these groups used symbols and figures of animals and people. These symbols are today called pictographs or petroglyphs. Petroglyphs are carvings on stone, while pictographs are made with paint or ochre on stone. The following account describes a Blackfoot system of written history. It is from *Kipaitapiiwahsinnooni: Alcohol and Drug Abuse Education Program* by Makai'stoo (Leo Fox).

The Kainai, Siksika, and Piikani used what has been called the *winter count* to record each year. The winter count depicted the most outstanding event in a particular year and served as a chronological measure of time.

Because there was more than one person who made these recordings, the events could be different from record to record. For example, if one year a solar eclipse took place and this was considered by one recorder as the outstanding event of the year, then they would record this. In the same year, another historian might have recorded something different, such as many deaths caused by a terrible winter storm. When reference was made to either of these events, the people would realize that they were talking about the same year.

Cultures that primarily transmit information through the written word tend to emphasize authors as creators of original works. Written works are seen as a form of self-expression and are greatly respected. Authors legally own the works they create and have certain rights with respect to how their works are used.

Oral cultures have different ideas about literary creation. Stories of a particular culture are seen as the inheritance of a community, not a specific individual. An individual storyteller might be admired for his or her skill in telling a story, but the stories themselves are a part of the community. The ultimate goal of sharing a story is to bring people together in a sense of belonging.

THE MÉTIS ORIGIN STORY

Many First Nations and Inuit peoples believe that their ancestors originated in North America and the Creator made the land and its inhabitants, including humans, to exist in a delicate state of balance. These beliefs are based on sacred oral teachings that have been passed down for generations.

The Métis Nation, like First Nations and Inuit peoples, also originated in this land, although their story of origin is different from those of other Aboriginal peoples. One difference is that Métis people may trace their history through written records. In contrast, First Nations and Inuit peoples trace their history primarily through oral

Every culture has an oral tradition. Those cultures that now have written histories can trace their stories back to an oral tradition. For example, the stories in the most widely published book in the world, the Bible, are based on oral stories.

Both written and oral stories use rules and conventions that are commonly held and understood by the storyteller's audience. These rules or conventions help audiences understand the storyteller's intentions and can make parts of stories quicker to understand.

In general, both written and oral stories need an authentic source or an acknowledgement of the story's origins. First Nations storytellers usually begin with an acknowledgement of who told them the story. This gives the story authenticity. Their stories can be traced back through time and generations.

Both kinds of stories sometimes need to provide explanations of concepts, background, or sources of more information. Oral storytellers often pause and refer to another story or incident in a technique that could be described as oral footnoting.

Many other conventions are used in both written and oral literatures. Some of these include plot, a central character or protagonist, some kind of conflict or problem, theme, suspense, and so on. Furthermore, both types of literature include numerous genres, such as history, philosophy, humour, or mystery. Moreover, education of some kind is often the main purpose for writing or telling a story.

Often, when mainstream society thinks of the oral tradition, its scholars and the general public misinterpret the stories and even dismiss them as mere fables. In this way of thinking, the works of Shakespeare or Plato would be seen as fables.

— Billy Joe Laboucan, Little Buffalo, Alberta

Billy Joe Laboucan is a Cree-language specialist, educator, and storyteller of Cree-Métis origin. His interest in storytelling began with the stories he heard as a child from his parents and Elders. As an adult, he has spent time with many Elders to hear their stories.

records, with relatively recent written documentation (over the last four hundred years). Although some Métis people identify with parts of the oral history of their First Nations ancestors, the origin of their own culture took place after European contact.

PUBLISHING ORAL STORIES

Today many stories from First Nations and Inuit oral traditions can be read online or in books. Even stories about spiritual matters exist in written form. Some people believe sacred stories should not be written or shared outside traditional circles.

Indigenous Knowledge

Sacred teachings form the very basis of traditional First Nations, Métis, and Inuit beliefs. Their closest equivalent would be that of the Bible to Christians. Many teachings lose their original meaning when translated into the English language because there are often no words in English to explain them. When a sacred story is taken out of context, shortened, adapted, translated, and written down, the result is often distorted and misunderstood. These beliefs are best taught by people who speak their own language and in the context of their own culture.

— Bernie L'Hirondelle, Barrhead, Alberta

What do you think about writing down stories that were once considered too sacred to share with outsiders? Is this an important transition for First Nations cultures in the contemporary world? Or should First Nations stories only be shared through the oral tradition? Discuss these questions with a small group and then share your ideas in a class discussion.

One of the problems is that not all published versions are authentic. Some stories have been used by people of other cultures in ways that do not respect the stories' origins and purposes. Many First Nations and Inuit peoples object to this use of their stories as much as they would object to someone taking a sacred object and using it inappropriately.

Other people believe that publishing stories from oral traditions widens the circle of people who can learn from the teachings they contain. Many believe that sharing traditional wisdom helps non-Aboriginal people appreciate and understand First Nations and Inuit cultures.

In addition, many Aboriginal people now live in urban centres or other areas where they might not have opportunities to hear stories told in traditional ways. Some people fear that oral traditions will be lost if they are not written down. These people believe that preserving them in any format should be the priority.

Though much has changed in the world, the stories' lessons on peace, harmony, balance, environmental responsibility, acceptance of differences, cooperation, respect for nature, and the importance of living an honourable life remain relevant to many contemporary problems.

ORIGIN OF THE MÉTIS NATION

As you read the section that follows, consider how the Métis Nation's history is both similar to and different from that of First Nations and Inuit peoples. What might be the significance of these similarities and differences today?

When the first Europeans arrived in what is now Canada, they were amazed at the land's thick forests and strong rivers. They wished to own the land and all its riches, especially the luxurious pelts of the fur-bearing animals.

Initially, First Nations welcomed the Europeans. They were willing to help the newcomers, who did not know the ways of the seasons and suffered many hardships during their first winters. The First Nations expected the Europeans who stayed to join them in living a harmonious life as their ancestors and those of other first peoples had done for all time.

For many years, the Europeans and First Nations existed in reasonable harmony, and a mutually beneficial relationship based on trade developed. This was the early era of the fur trade. As the years passed, two groups of Europeans — the French and the British — competed to gather furs, each group striving to obtain as many as possible, and to claim the land as their own. The successful ones among them sought the wisdom and assistance of First Nations people.

Some European traders married First Nations women and they had children. The French government at first actively encouraged these marriages, believing they would eventually help France establish its hold on the continent. The British government discouraged the unions, but could do little to stop them.

By the early eighteenth century, the French began to understand the independence of the Métis peoples and the unique nature of their culture. Even the French then began to discourage the unions, but Métis communities, especially in the West, were by then firmly established.

These unions — called *mariage à la façon du pays* in French, *country marriages* in English — often combined First Nations and European traditions. The families usually worked in the fur trade. The children learned the ways of both cultures and spoke two languages. As these children grew up, married, and had children of their own, they often carried on the blended culture that they had learned as children. The family units that began as social and economic bonds during the fur trade developed into a distinctive culture.

The culture eventually became stronger than the trade that gave rise to it and today is a source of identity and shared bond for many people.

Many Métis people in Alberta continue to learn Métis cultural traditions. Here members of the Caslan School Dancers, from the Buffalo Lake Métis Settlement, perform at the 2003 Aboriginal Day celebration in Edmonton. (Names of those pictures are not available.)

A UNIQUE CULTURE

- Though people of mixed ancestry exist worldwide, few form a distinctive culture of blended cultural traits. The Métis Nation is an exception.
- Some historians say the first children of First Nations–European parents were born soon after the first group of European traders set foot on North America's eastern shores in the sixteenth century. The Métis Nation developed a sense of distinct culture during the eighteenth and nineteenth centuries.
- Some Métis people are descended from French fur traders who worked for the North West Company. Others have Scottish or English ancestors who worked for the Hudson's Bay Company. Each group had distinctive cultural traits that remain to this day.
- Métis people were officially recognized as one of Canada's Aboriginal peoples in the Canadian constitution of 1982.

CREATION STORIES IN THE MODERN WORLD

For some First Nations and Inuit peoples, creation stories are as important today as when they were first told. The values the stories carry forward are timeless.

For First Nations asserting claim to a part of their ancestors' traditional territory, creation stories have additional political and economic significance. The Supreme Court has recognized that oral testimony should be given the same consideration in the courts that written evidence is given. Read the statements about creation stories that follow and in your talking circle, consider how creation stories might be significant in a First Nation's claim to a specific territory or land.

How does a circular seating arrangement emphasize ideas of renewal and continuity?

As you share your ideas, consider sharing any experiences you have had with an Elder's teachings.

Mushkegowuk of James Bay ancestry dating back 10 000 years hold a belief that the Creator put them on this land, this garden, to oversee and take care of it for those that are not yet born. The law of maintenance or just maintaining that garden means taking care of the physical environment. It also means maintaining a harmonious relationship with other people and the animals depended on for survival.

— Chief Edmund Metatawabin,
Fort Albany First Nation,
Report of the Royal Commission on Aboriginal Peoples

WHAT DO CREATION STORIES MEAN TODAY?

In Aboriginal historical traditions, the particular creation story of each people, although it finds its origins in the past, also, and more importantly, speaks to the present. It invites listeners to participate in the cycle of creation through their understanding that, as parts of a world that is born, dies and is reborn in the observable cycle of days and seasons, they too are part of a natural order, members of a distinct people who share in that order.

— *Report of the Royal Commission on Aboriginal Peoples*

Creation is a continuity, and if creation is to continue, then it must be renewed. Renewal ceremonies, songs, and stories are the human's part in the maintenance of the renewal of creation. Hence the Sundance, the societal ceremonies and the unbundling of medicine bundles at certain phases of the year are all interrelated aspects of happenings that take place on and within Mother Earth.

— Leroy Little Bear, Kainai First Nation, *Report of the Royal Commission on Aboriginal Peoples*

The creation of the Raven is an important part of the Creation story. The Raven was created the leader among leaders. It was the most powerful and clever of persons and its knowledge and experience were sought by one and all. But it was also vain and selfish. When the birds were being painted, it insisted that it should be painted better than all the other birds. Its reward was of course to be painted black. The Raven's weakness was that it did not see itself in relationship with others around it. It saw itself as complete and finished. From the Raven story we derive the Dene perspective that we must continually push ourselves to grow rather than remain complacent and smug in what we are or have become.

— *Dene Kede Curriculum Document*

My people, the Dene, believe that we have always lived in this place, in the North. We don't accept the scientific stories about aboriginal people coming across the Bering Strait land bridge from Siberia. We believe the Creator put us here when the world was new; he put us in this place that Canadians now call the Northwest Territories and the Yukon. It is our place.

I remember well the stories my grandmother, Besiswo, told me. She said the Creator first put animals on the earth and then we humans gradually evolved from them. The stories she told me are thousands of years old and I believe them. These are the stories of my people, even if science says they are legends.

Who are my Dene people? We are people of the land; we see ourselves as no different than the trees, the caribou, and the raven, except we are more complicated. The Creator gave us intelligence to live with and look after the animals and plants on this Mother Earth, and he also gave us free will to do whatever we feel like doing.

— George Blondin, Sahtú Dene, *Yamoria the Lawmaker: Stories of the Dene*

LOOKING BACK

The stories a people tell reveal much about their values. Look back over this chapter and your notes and projects to prepare a list of significant First Nations and Inuit beliefs and values. Use your list as inspiration for a collage, painting, sculpture, or illustration that represents your ideas. In the next chapter, you will learn much more about the values and spirituality of the First Nations, Métis, and Inuit peoples.

■ REFLECTION

1. Following your talking circle discussion, write or draw your own response to the creation stories you have studied.
2. Find a story that you believe asserts a particular First Nation's claim to a specific territory. How does the story provide evidence for the case?

Chapter Two Review

Check Your Understanding

1. What is an oral tradition?

2. During which season were stories most often told? Why?

3. What is an Elder? Does an Elder have to be the oldest person in the community? Explain.

4. How do many stories from the oral tradition portray the relationship between the physical and spiritual worlds? How is this related to First Nations spirituality?

5. How did traditional societies use the oral tradition to resolve disputes between people?

6. Explain two reasons why writing down oral stories may alter their meanings.

7. How do creation stories tie a First Nation's identity to its traditional territory?

8. What lesson or message do you think First Nations and Inuit peoples are trying to relay in some creation stories by attributing to animals as much or more power than humans?

9. What is the relationship between humans and animals today? How does this compare to the way First Nations and Inuit peoples thought about it in creation stories?

10. According to the Beringia theory, where did the first people in North America come from?

11. What is the origin story of the Métis Nation? How is this story different from First Nations and Inuit origin stories?

12. How have first peoples' stories and teachings influenced today's environmental movement?

13. List at least three ways the oral tradition functioned in traditional First Nations societies.

14. Although mainstream society has sometimes misinterpreted the authenticity of stories originating from the oral tradition, oral literature is increasingly recognized in the same light as Shakespeare or other writers. In what ways do you think oral literature is as important as classical written literature?

15. Outline a protocol you have learned for requesting knowledge from an Elder.

Reading and Writing

16. Write a paragraph that describes your answer to the following question: What is the significance of creation stories for First Nations and Inuit peoples today?

17. Many collections of Elders stories have been published in the last few decades. Some are listed on page 241 of this textbook. Read one of these collections and write a book review.

18. Read Emma Minde's story on page 63. Using an appropriate Cree word you learned in this chapter, how would you classify the story? Write a paragraph describing what people can learn from her story.

Viewing and Representing

19. Review the profile of Rosie Red Crow on page 42. Using this and other resources, create a pamphlet about her or another Aboriginal person from Alberta. This pamphlet could resemble one that you might find in a museum or library. Include biographical information, significance, quotations, pictures, and other informative details.

20. Create a poster that depicts the main idea behind one of the stories you studied while working through this chapter. Try to depict the First Nations and Inuit concepts of interconnectedness between the physical and spiritual worlds.

21. Create a work of art to illustrate one of the stories you read or studied in this chapter.

Speaking and Listening

22. Most of the stories in this book are from published sources. Using correct protocol, find an Elder from your own community or a nearby community who is willing to share a creation story with you. If the Elder permits, use a tape recorder or video camera to record your interview of the Elder telling the story. Share the story with your class by playing the tape.

Going Further

23. In this chapter, you read different opinions about trying to preserve oral traditions by writing down stories for permanent record, as well as about the potential for misinterpreting stories and culture. Do you think it is better to have an imperfect record of valuable stories, or is the potential for harm too great? What other ways, besides writing the stories down, might people preserve oral traditions?

LOOKING BACK

Re-read the Focus Questions on page 36 and write answers to each one.

Ê-pê-kiskisiyân aya, aspin ohc âya kâ-awâsisîwiyân, ê-kî-wâpamakik aya, ninîkihikwak êkwa kotakak ayisiyiniwak, kotakak onîkihikomâwak, iyikohk ê-kî-atoskêcik, ê-wî-pimâcihocik. (From the time I was a child, I still remember, I saw my parents and other people, other parents, work so hard at making a living.)

These are the things they used to do: they used to hunt so they had meat, and they also used to trap, at the time they mostly used to trap for muskrat, not so much for beaver. And they also used to fish. All the time they used to prepare for the next winter, storing up food for themselves; they would move their camps out and go to live out there [on the trapline], killing game, mostly moose and deer, and also muskrats; but not as many in the fall, for they used to trap for them in the spring. And then they used to go to live out there, in the spring they used to go to set traps and they used to trap muskrats. That is how the people made a living long ago.

And in the fall, when they found berries, when they found berries out there on the trapline, they also used to pick berries. There were blueberries and cranberries, as these berries were called, they grew over there, and also wild blackcurrants. The women also had various ways of trying to make a living, trying to make a living for their children, and they also used to help their husbands in making a living....

And today these skills are greatly missed; people have largely lost how well they used to shift for themselves, now there is none of that taking place. You just go to the store now, you just go and try to buy something. This is why it is that I am asked to tell about it, so that the young people would know how the old people back then used to run their lives...

— Emma Minde, Saddle Lake First Nation, *kwayask ê-kî-pê-kiskinowâpahtihicik (Their Example Showed Me the Way; A Cree Woman's Life Shaped by Two Cultures)*

Worldview

In the last chapter, you learned that the oral tradition is fundamental to First Nations and Inuit cultures. Transmission of information in an oral culture is a social process that reinforces relationships — those between young and old, those between ancestors and the living, and those between the living and future generations.

The importance of relationships is the focus of this next chapter, which is about traditional First Nations and Inuit worldviews. These worldviews, although expressed in different ways from culture to culture, have elements in common. Generally, the common thread is the emphasis placed on balanced and harmonious relationships.

Métis peoples have a worldview that is shaped by their unique heritage and history as a nation. Although this chapter focuses on traditional First Nations and Inuit beliefs, keep in mind that some Métis people share this way of looking at the world. How Métis people's worldviews differ will be discussed in more detail in Chapter Five.

In "The Story of Eagle Child," you will see examples of many characteristics of the oral tradition from the last chapter. Make note of these characteristics as you read and watch for ideas about relationships. What messages are being expressed?

As you read this chapter, consider these questions:

▲ What is a worldview?

▲ What kinds of relationships are important to traditional First Nations and Inuit worldviews?

▲ What are the roles of sharing, generosity, harmony, and unity in traditional First Nations and Inuit cultures?

▲ What is the cycle of life and how is it related to First Nations and Inuit worldviews and cultures?

▲ How do expressions of First Nations and Inuit worldviews vary from culture to culture?

The Story of Eagle Child

Adapted from a story told by Bernie Makokis of the Saddle Lake First Nation

A BABY WAS BORN IN A VILLAGE. THE ELDERS SENSED THAT HE WOULD BE A GREAT TEACHER AND GAVE HIM THE NAME EAGLE CHILD, SINCE HE WOULD have visions for his people.

One day the village was attacked and everyone died except Eagle Child. Before his mother died, she had hidden him behind a big rock. He lay hidden for a long time.

When Eagle Child began to get hungry, he started to cry. A pack of wolves walking around the village heard this crying. The leader of the wolf pack went to the rock to see what the noise was all about. As he came to the rock, he saw the child crying and felt sorry for him. He called the other wolves to come over. In his wolf talk, he told them that their role as wolves was to protect the elderly and the young. He said that this child must be protected and nurtured, so the wolves stayed with Eagle Child, taking turns feeding him.

As Eagle Child grew, he was astonished by the size of the rock. In his child's mind, he wanted to climb the rock, so one day he decided to do it. Each time he tried to climb, however, he fell down and hurt himself. Finally, one day he succeeded. The wolves celebrated his feat.

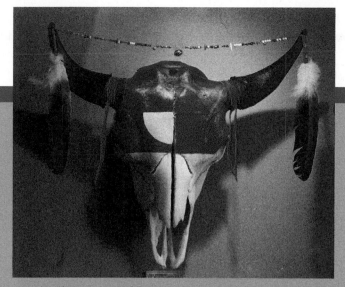

As Eagle Child grew, he became curious about his purpose in life. One of the old wolves advised him to leave on a quest to visit the spirits of the heavens. Eagle Child went on a journey to the Eagle Spirit in the east, the Spirit of the Thunderbird in the south, Grandfather Bear of the west, and the Wind Spirit of the northern heavens. He eventually travelled back to Earth and found a human camp, which celebrated his arrival for four days.

After the celebration, the Elders took Eagle Child to the mountains to show him the teachings that he was seeking.

An old man brought out the pipe and explained to him that the stem was straight and that this represented honesty. The bowl of the pipe was made of rock and that it represented the value of determination. Eagle Child was ecstatic because the spirits had told him this.

An old lady told Eagle Child that in their camp, everyone shared. She explained that the Great Spirit, Kise Manito, had created a natural law that when everyone shares, it is easier to do things.

Another old woman showed Eagle Child some sweet grass. "This represents the kindness of Mother Earth," said the old woman. "She feeds us and she nurtures us. Even animals don't eat this because they respect it."

At last, an old man got up and said "*Nôsim, kiwâpahten Ahcâhkwaskiy. Kise manitô kitôkihtawihik. Mâka mâmayisk ta nistotâsoyan ekwa ta kiskîmisoyan, pôko pita ta tâpwehtaman.* (My grandson, you have experienced the Spirit World. You are a Spirit. The Creator gave you all these gifts.) In order for you to understand yourself and who you are, you must first believe. The Spirit of belief is very powerful. You must also know all of the teachings of the Spirits. They are not difficult to understand. You were given these values. The most difficult task is to live these values. That is your answer, just as every person has their own answer."

Eagle Child grew up to be a wise old man, for he followed these values.

Tsuu T'ina artist Rocky Barstad went through a special ceremony to be allowed to paint on buffalo skulls. This work is called Good Medicine. Barstad gets his skulls from a buffalo farm. Makokis's story makes reference to four spirits who live in the north, south, east, and west. What aspect of Barstad's work reflects this same sense of four directions?

▌ REFLECTION

"The Story of Eagle Child" helps readers appreciate hardships and challenges in life as opportunities for growth and accomplishment. Write your own story about a time in your life when you faced a difficulty on your own. What did you learn from the experience?

Worldview

In the statement on this page, Chief Seattle uses the metaphor of a spider's web to explain First Nations beliefs in the interconnectedness of all parts of the world. Create your own metaphor that reflects this worldview.

AS YOU READ

How do you know what is right or wrong, or how to behave or react in a particular situation? All of your thoughts and behaviour arise from your worldview, even if you cannot state or explain what your worldview is. Your worldview is shaped by your culture and experiences, and it affects every aspect of your life. Your worldview, or perspective, is so ingrained in your way of thinking that it can be hard to understand any other way of thinking. In many ways, another culture's worldview cannot be fully understood or appreciated unless it is experienced.

Pages 66–70 will help you understand what a worldview is and some of the general principles common among many First Nations, Métis, and Inuit worldviews. Keep in mind that these general principles are generic rather than specific. Individual cultures and people have unique ways of describing, celebrating, and expressing their worldview. As you read, think about which aspects of the worldviews under discussion strike a chord of truth with you — they are likely part of your own worldview. In your journal, begin a list of ideas that might help you articulate it.

IN THE LANGUAGE OF THE WAPISIANA PEOPLE OF GUYANA, SOUTH AMERICA, THERE IS NO WORD FOR SORRY. FOR EXAMPLE, IF A PERSON LEAVES A BOOK LYING ON THE FLOOR AND ANOTHER PERSON STEPS ON IT AND DAMAGES IT, that individual might say something like "What a silly place to leave a book." Neither person would see the need for apology because in their culture, the concept does not exist.

People from different cultures have different ways of seeing, explaining, and living within the world. They have different ideas about what things are most important, which behaviours are desirable or unacceptable, and how all parts of the world relate to each other. Together these opinions and beliefs form a **worldview**, the perspective from which people perceive, understand, and respond to the world around them.

People from the same culture tend to have similar worldviews. A culture's worldview evolves from its history, which is the collective experiences of the people within that culture over all the years of its existence. It also includes their beliefs about origin and spirituality.

The traditional worldviews of First Nations and Inuit peoples in Canada differ from the worldviews of people with a non-Aboriginal ancestry. You might compare a First Nations or Inuit worldview to a Euro-Canadian worldview, for example, by drawing a circle and a

> All things are connected like the blood that unites us. We did not weave the web of life. We are merely a strand in it. Whatever we do to the web, we do to ourselves.
>
> — Chief Seattle, Suquamish Nation, 1854

line. The circular First Nations worldview focuses on connections between all things, including the visible physical world and the invisible spiritual world. It sees time as always in a cycle of renewal that links past and present and future. In contrast, a linear Euro-Canadian worldview lays out separations between elements of existence (spiritual and material, life and death, animal and human, living and non-living) and sees time as a progression from point to point.

There is no single worldview common to all First Nations, Métis, and Inuit individuals any more than there is a single worldview common to all European or African individuals. Differences in viewpoints exist between individuals within a single culture or community. In learning about traditional First Nations and Inuit worldviews, however, it is possible to identify several similarities between many first peoples' cultures.

SPIRITUALITY

For traditional First Nations and Inuit cultures, worldview is rooted in spiritual beliefs. Spirituality incorporates a culture's highest ideals, values, morals, and ethics. It defines the behaviour that makes a society survive and thrive. It involves honouring and respecting things that are unseen — the Creator, souls, spirits, the wind, the air — as well as those that are visible. It is an individual's understanding of their place and purpose in the world and

Móókoanssin (Belly Buttes) on the Kainai Reserve, is a sacred site with spiritual significance for the nations of the Blackfoot Confederacy.

their relationship to the seen and unseen forces.

According to western European thinking, the world is clearly divided into **animate** things — human beings, animals, plants — and **inanimate** things — rocks, hills, mountains, land, sky, rivers, water, the wind, and the sun. In contrast, according to traditional First Nations and Inuit spirituality, everything in the universe has spirit and is animate. The entire universe is alive with a constant dialogue or energy between all things that exist. For humans to live in balance with the universe, they must be aware of this dialogue and be careful not to insult or disrupt the spirits of animals, plants, wind, or earth.

In a universe in which everything is alive and has a spirit, certain sites, land formations, and types of matter have great spiritual power. Particular rocks, hills, mountaintops, and sites in a forest are honoured in key rituals and rites of passage. At these sacred places, initiation ceremonies take place, people fast and pray, and visions are revealed. These sacred places strengthen the link that binds humans to the natural world and the Creator.

Within traditional spirituality, creation is an ongoing process. The

Even a task such as picking berries has a spiritual component. Berry-pickers traditionally pray and scatter a few berries in thanks to the earth. (Names of those pictures are not available.)

cycle of life is unending, as can be seen in the migration of birds, the rising sun, and the changing seasons. People walk in the footsteps of their ancestors, as will the generations yet unborn. The presence of the Creator is everywhere.

For traditional First Nations and Inuit peoples, spirituality is part of being alive, and part of everyday life. For example, to honour the corn or squash that they raised, traditional Pueblo people eat gently, reflecting on the plant that is becoming a part of their bodies and minds. Traditionally, respectful Inuit hunters speak to a caribou's *shua* — its "living essence" — before letting their arrows fly. Afterward, they thank the animal for giving its life and place something in its mouth to aid it on its journey.

Most cultures have some version of this ritual of thanking prey and their spirits. Prey are viewed as willing participants in a relationship with hunters. Hunters do not take; prey give themselves. In return for the animal's gift, hunters thank and honour its spirit and continue the cycle of giving by sharing the animal with their extended family.

Spiritual advisors are people who have powerful visions and are thought to have special insight into the spirit world. However, all individuals can receive communication from and can communicate with spirits and the Creator.

RELIGION

Spirituality is not religion. **Religions** are systems of attitudes, beliefs, and practices that focus on groups, while spirituality centres on an individual's understanding of his or her place in the world. However, both spirituality and religion can coexist in an individual's life.

One of the main goals for the first Europeans travelling to North America was **evangelism**, which is the act of converting others to their own religious beliefs. The French, in particular, saw the conversion of First Nations people to Roman Catholicism as an important part of their work in North America. In their worldview, evangelism was one of the best ways one could serve God. You will learn more about this history in Chapter Five.

Roman Catholicism is just one denomination of the Christian religion. Christianity incorporates many different denominations —

I was raised in the Methodist Church, but I don't let my Indian religion go. ... Whatever a person does, that's their way. The sweat lodge — that's some people's way. Church — it's another way. All people have their own way of believing. No way is better or worse.

— Abbie Burnstick, Paul Band Reserve,
Those Who Know: Profiles of Alberta's Native Elders

Roman Catholic, Lutheran, Anglican, and others. Basic Christian beliefs are the same, although their practices and interpretations differ, much in the way that First Nations spiritual practices differ from culture to culture.

Since the seventeenth century, when efforts to convert them began, First Nations and Inuit peoples responded in various ways. Some completely rejected European religions; others completely rejected traditional spirituality. Still others adopted aspects of both.

Many First Nations and Inuit peoples were curious about Christianity and understood it by fitting its teachings within the world-view provided by their traditional belief systems. For example, the idea of the Christian God, the creator of all things, was not new to First Nations, who already believed in a Creator or Great Spirit. The Christian creation story, Genesis, as told in the Holy Bible, could be seen as a new version of the creation stories they knew from their oral tradition.

The use of symbols to demonstrate faith was also familiar to First Nations, who had always used symbols to reinforce their spiritual beliefs. A **symbol** is one thing that stands for another. A cultural symbol is often a simple cue that, when used, causes members of the culture to think about a much more complex meaning. The most widely recognized symbol of Christianity is the cross.

The use of celebrations to affirm faith and give thanks was also a part of traditional spiritual practices. The Christian celebrations of Christmas and Easter are holy festivals centred around the birth and death of Jesus. One of the most important Christian beliefs is that Jesus was the son of God and that he spent time on Earth, sharing God's wisdom with the people before returning to heaven.

Pilgrimages are another kind of religious activity. Worldwide, people travel long distances to sacred places and shrines, hoping to receive a blessing from God. The concept of sacred sites with special significance was long a part of traditional First Nations spirituality.

Despite these similarities, it is incorrect to classify spirituality as a religion. Spirituality is an individual's lifelong journey — it is a way to live within the world that each person must explore and learn for himself or herself. Religion presents a way to live within the world — the challenge there is to learn and live the religion's teachings.

In general, Métis people tend to have a close relationship with Christian religions. Métis people descended from French-speaking Métis families are frequently Roman Catholic. However, some Métis

Today many First Nations, Métis, and Inuit peoples practise some form of the Christian religion. The Roman Catholic faith is important to many Métis and First Nations people and the Anglican religion is common among Inuit peoples. This church at Enoch, Alberta, modifies traditional Christian symbolism to incorporate Aboriginal symbolism. This church includes curved walls, a tipi spire, and a stained glass window with First Nations figures.

Every year, thousands of Roman Catholic First Nations and Métis people from across North America flock to the shores of Lac Ste Anne, Alberta. The lake is believed to be a holy site with healing powers. Another significant site for Roman Catholics is the grave of Kateri Tekakwitha at Caughnawaga, Ontario. In 1980, 300 years after her death, the Lily of the Mohawks became the only First Nations person to be beatified by the Roman Catholic church. This is often a first step toward sainthood.

Many processions and ceremonies are held during the annual pilgrimage. At night, a candlelight procession is held. Thousands of pilgrims walk from the shrine to the lakeshore and back carrying lighted candles. (Names of those pictured are not available.)

people also maintain the spiritual beliefs of their First Nations ancestors.

Lac Ste Anne, Alberta

Lac Ste Anne was known by local First Nations as *manito sâkâhikan*, Cree for "Lake of the Spirit," long before it became an important site for Roman Catholics. *Manito sâkâhikan* was a traditional First Nations gathering place for the summer buffalo hunt.

Oblate priest Jean-Baptiste Thibault started a mission in 1844 at the lake because of the large numbers of Métis and French-speaking Roman Catholic settlers in the area. He renamed the lake Lac Ste Anne, after Ste Anne de Beaupré, the mother of Mary. The Lac Ste Anne mission was taken over by Father Albert Lacombe in 1852. He and the other priests at the site gained a reputation for their special holiness. They cared for the sick and worked to prevent armed conflict among the cultural groups in the region. Many First Nations and Métis people in the area converted to Christianity.

The first pilgrimage to Lac Ste Anne was held in 1889. Several hundred people attended, and it soon became an annual event. Today, the pilgrimage to Lac Ste Anne has become the largest annual gathering of First Nations and Métis people in Canada.

Catholic priests at the Lac Ste Anne shrine offer many services during the annual pilgrimage. Mass is held three times a day, in Cree, Dene Sųłiné, Blackfoot, Dené Tha', and English. Christian beliefs also include baptism as a symbol of spiritual cleansing and rebirth. In a special ceremony, a bishop blesses the water of the lake, asking God to make it a source of renewal and healing for all people. Hundreds of people then wade into the water to receive this blessing.

LOOKING BACK

Before moving on to the next section, be sure you can answer the following questions: How is religion different from spirituality? How do traditional spiritual beliefs held by First Nations and Inuit peoples demonstrate a part of their worldview? Based on what you know of Métis history, how might some Métis worldviews differ from First Nations and Inuit worldviews?

All My Relations

RELATIONSHIPS AND THE PROPER BALANCE BETWEEN THEM ARE THE FOCUS OF TRADITIONAL FIRST NATIONS AND INUIT WORLDVIEWS. The Laws of Relationships on page 72 offer a concise summary of ideas that are shared by all First Nations and Inuit cultures. Because the chart incorporates the ideas of many diverse communities, it is a generic list of principles. In other words, these ideas are not representative of any single First Nations, Métis, or Inuit culture, but they are representative of all to some degree. It is important to remember that each culture has its own ways of expressing these ideas through specific ceremonies, protocols, practices, and languages.

These principles are described as laws to emphasize that they are fundamental ways of thinking. They are not laws in the sense of contemporary Canadian laws — external requirements that individuals must obey. Instead, they are principles that are internalized by individuals and that bind each person to the rest of the world. Acting against these principles would be almost inconceivable. They are principles of a common worldview. This worldview is grounded in the ideas that all parts of creation are interconnected and all have a spirit; that humans must live in respectful, balanced relationships with all in creation; and that the spiritual forces of the world are intended to help survival, not threaten it.

"All my relations" is the English equivalent of a phrase familiar to most Native peoples of North America. It may begin or end a prayer or speech or a story, and, while each tribe has its own way of expressing this sentiment in its own language, the meaning is the same.

"All my relations" is at first a reminder of who we are and of our relationship with both our family and our relatives. It also reminds us of the extended relationship we share with all human beings. But the relationships that Native people see go further, the web of kinship to animals, to the birds, to the fish, to the plants, to all the animate and inanimate forms that can be seen or imagined. More than that, "all my relations" is an encouragement for us to accept the responsibilities we have within the universal family by living our lives in a harmonious and moral manner (a common admonishment is to say of someone that they act as if they had no relations).

— Thomas King, *All My Relations*

LAWS OF NATURE

A Haudenosaunee worldview maintains that while nature can be kind and generous, one of the strengths of its laws is that they are absolute. Nature's laws are evident and clear, and allow no room for compromise. A person who stays outside on a cold winter night without proper clothing will freeze to death. Any creature — a dog, a deer, a person, a flea — that does not eat or drink will die. Natural law prevails beyond the rulings of any human law. It is simple, basic, and eternal, like the circle of life itself. Humans who live within natural law will live well because nature provides all that is needed for life.

Centuries of closely observing the natural world taught the ancestors of First Nations and Inuit peoples how to live in harmony with their surroundings. These ancestors learned that the physical world exists in a natural state of balance within itself and the spirit world. These first peoples believed the laws of the natural world should be closely observed as guidelines for human behaviour. After all, most creation stories describe the human position in the world as a humble one. Humans are not intended to

LAWS OF RELATIONSHIPS

This chart was developed by educators and Elders from the Northwest Territories and the western provinces. It is intended as an educational tool, not as a guide to any particular First Nations or Inuit belief system.

The Laws of Relationships are a model of the relationships between individuals, their community, and the natural world. Balance is more assured when all relationships are strong. What stories from the oral tradition have you read or heard in this course that reinforce these ideas?

Laws of Sacred Life

- Each person is born sacred and complete.

- Each person is given the gift of body with the choice to care for it and use it with respect.

- Each person is given the capacity and the choice to learn to live in respectful relationships.

- Each person is given strengths or talents to be discovered, nurtured, and shared for the benefit of all.

Laws of Mutual Support

- People in groups of mutual support are strong. Alone, a person will not survive.

- Identity comes from belonging in respectful relationships with others.

- Agreement on rules enables cooperation and group strength.

Laws of Nature

- The natural world provides the gifts of life and place.

- A people's sense of place and identity is tied to the land or water body that has given the people life.

- The natural world provides people with the necessities of life.

- People must live in harmony with the laws of nature in order to be sustained by it.

conquer and control the natural world, but to live in harmony within it.

For example, animals in nature never take more than they need. Most First Nations and Inuit cultures reflect this law by discouraging waste. Inuit people of northern Alaska have a story that explains the rules governing their annual bowhead whale hunt. Their story tells how the Great Spirit created the land, animals, and people, and finally the bowhead whale last as his most perfect creation. However, the Great Spirit realized that the people needed the whale to survive, so he made it possible for the people to hunt it. At one point in the spring, the bowhead swim near the water surface as the ice breaks up. In this way, the whales offer themselves to the people. As the Great Spirit designed, this gift would last providing the people took only what they needed and used all that they took.

LAWS OF SACRED LIFE

In First Nations and Inuit cultures, children are gifts from the Creator. They are evidence that the gift of creation that is recounted in creation stories continues in a never-ending cycle of birth, life, and death. According to the ancient teachings of many First Nations, the essence of life's existence is to raise and nurture the young and therefore continue life. In this way, individuals have their own role to play in the whole of creation.

Traditionally, children are at the center of communities, stories, and decisions. The family shown here is from Fort McMurray, Alberta. Left to right (back): Pat Clark, Kathy Cheecham. Left to right (front): Sean Cheecham, Melanie Cheecham, Tiffany Cheecham.

This way of thinking led to cultures in which individuals have great freedom. They are given opportunities to learn and understand, along with **personal autonomy**, or the power to make their own decisions. Seeking control over another would be like challenging the Creator's purpose for that person. Individuals learn to be accountable for both their actions and the consequences of those actions.

This belief in personal autonomy and responsibility served a practical as well as spiritual purpose for cultures living on the land. In a wilderness environment, knowing what decision to make was sometimes critical to life.

Communities traditionally had a sense of personal involvement in individuals' actions, however they did not try to control them. Anyone who demonstrated inappropriate choices received direction and guidance from the community to help them make better choices. Those who would not accept guidance and could not abide by the ways of the community were free to leave. Individuals always had the right to disagree, although the unity of the whole group was considered most important. This sometimes meant that a dissenting person would leave a group rather than disturb the sense of togetherness and common purpose.

LAWS OF MUTUAL SUPPORT

For traditional First Nations and Inuit peoples living on the land, the demands of daily life required that people work together with the natural world, not against it or against each other. They lived within a web of mutual support. **Mutual support** is a concept that is central to First Nations and Inuit worldviews. The Blackfoot term

aisspommootsiiyio'pa, which means "helping one another," captures this fundamental way of life. In mutual support, people are **interdependent**, which means they rely upon one another for some purpose. Interdependence is a **reciprocal** relationship of giving and taking.

Among traditional societies, the structure of this web of support began with the family and extended family system. Individuals turned first to their families for help and support, widening the circle of family around them in accordance with available resources. For example, larger families lived together in times of more abundance or areas with more abundant resources. Kinship bound groups together, beginning with the circle of the extended family, widening with bonds of clan, nation, and sometimes confederacy or alliance.

Identity in traditional First Nations and Inuit cultures stressed the community more than the individual. Many celebrations and ceremonies involved sharing and strengthening these bonds.

Many First Nations held give-aways, a way of honouring an individual or group. Today the give-away is still significant for many communities. These ceremonies include dancing, speeches, songs, and gift-giving. It is an honour to give as well as to receive.

Indigenous Knowledge

With a partner, discuss how the story that follows acts as a metaphor for mutual support.

As geese fly south during their fall migration, they fly in a V formation. During flight they honk loudly to encourage their leader at the point of the V. When the leader gets tired, it falls to the back and the goose next in line takes over. This is done in sequence throughout their long journey.

— as told by Bernie Makokis, Saddle Lake First Nation

Sharing and Generosity

The Anishinabé language traditionally had no word for *savings*. Putting items aside for future use or personal gain was against the value of sharing. Families and communities depended upon each person contributing his or her best efforts, with all sharing in the products of those efforts.

The ethic of sharing also extended to non-human elements of the world. Rituals of returning gifts to the land in exchange for its provision of food and other materials were part of all traditional First Nations and Inuit cultures. For example, when cutting down the centre pole for a Sundance lodge, many prayers of thanks would be given to the tree for allowing its use in the ceremony.

In a similar way, when a Cree hunter was successful, the entire community gathered for a feast. Haudenosaunee villagers shared in the tasks necessary to plant, tend, and harvest the crops that would feed them through the winter. In all First Nations and Inuit cultures, people's status increased not by what they had, but by their generosity — what they gave away.

Harmony and Unity

Traditionally, living on the land required that people work together to perform the tasks needed for day-to-day life. Everyone contributed to the work that provided food, clothing, shelter, and tools. People shared a common purpose in which each individual had a role to play. Roles were clearly defined and all contributions were respected. Principles of respect and sharing meant that conflict-generating emotions, such as envy and greed, were reduced. Most communities lived in harmony most of the time.

The give-away is a tradition that is still strong in many First Nations communities. Carl Quinn, former chief of Saddle Lake First Nation, is seen here presenting a gift to an Elder at Poundmaker's powwow in the 1990s. How is the give-away an example of mutual support?

> A single twig breaks, but the bundle of twigs is strong.
>
> — Tecumseh, Shawnee chief (1768–1813)

> A group of men would go out and hunt and split the animal amongst themselves. They would split the meat with their families... The white society cannot understand that; they say, killing two moose is too much. They don't realize that if I kill two moose I might have one chunk [of meat] by the next day. I would split it with my sons or uncles or relatives and the rest of the people that we hunt with. We still have the distribution that we used to do in the old days... We still share; that is what we do in this community; we still share.
>
> — William Coutoreille, *Inkonze: The Stones of Traditional Knowledge*

The Plains Cree saw honesty in the straight growth of tree trunks. Other cultures would see their values reflected in the growth of corn, behaviour of sea mammals, or the wind. How was a connection to a particular territory partly responsible for the differences in spiritual practices between various First Nations and Inuit cultures?

Values affect thoughts and behaviour — opinions and actions. Values stem directly from a person's worldview and shared values lead to harmony between individuals.

Anishinabé cultures recognize seven core traditional values: bravery, honesty, humility, love, respect, truth, and wisdom.

Dakota traditional values include conformity with the group and harmony within it; taking responsibility for the here-and-now; the development of the ability to make personal decisions; control over emotions; reverence for nature even while using it; and constant awareness of the Creator.

The Plains Cree observe four values in nature that are then incorporated into their culture's symbols and ceremonies:

- Earth's red-hot core teaches that **strength** can be gained by working together. Cree Elders call this centre *atâmaskîw asinîy* — centre rock that holds Mother Earth together.
- Observations of animal and plant life show the value of **sharing**. Animals and plants give life to maintain life. For example, a tree takes nutrients from the soil but gives back to the soil when its leaves fall to the earth and decompose.
- **Honesty** can be observed in the trees, which grow straight to the sky. Individuals committing to the values of strength and sharing will live truthfully, or as they are meant to live — in the balance of the whole of creation. A person who is weak, stealing from another, for example, introduces discord and lack of balance.
- **Kindness** can be observed in the earth itself, which provides the plants necessary for all other life. An individual who shares food, shelter, good feelings, and gratitude also contributes kindness. Such qualities reinforce the strength of the whole community.

▌ REFLECTION

The Plains Cree learned about values, such as strength, sharing, honesty, and kindness, by observing nature. Choose one of your own values and identify something in nature that you feel brings out the meaning. Use a dictionary to define your value. Illustrate your value by designing a poster or by preparing a story to tell your classmates. Briefly explain the association.

Of course not all people got along all the time, and one of the roles of the Elders was to help individuals rid themselves of negative feelings. The goal in resolving or mediating a conflict was to help individuals become whole again and restored to themselves and their community. These principles are still at work today in many communities through restorative justice programs. You will read about how this works in Chapter Six.

Within this worldview, a good life requires harmony with the rest of the physical and spiritual worlds. To the Navajo people, the greatest compliment one could give was to say that someone takes care of his or her relatives. First Nations know that this statement includes not only parents, siblings, and extended family, but also everything in all of creation.

Humour

One of the best ways to reinforce a social bond between people is to share a good laugh. Few experiences as easily forge bonds of unity and common worldview.

Sharon Shorty, a Tlingit and Northern Tuchtone woman from the Northwest Territories, was drawn to storytelling in her youth. She noticed that Elders often used humour in their stories to help make their point. Shorty's character Gramma Susie has strong opinions about everything, and her comments about First Nations people and communities make her audiences laugh. Her style is common among

Good feelings, such as enjoyment and laughter, strengthen social bonds. In this photo, comedians Cash Creek Charlie and Gramma Susie spoof the old-time Elders they grew up with. Gramma Susie waves a bingo dauber for the photo.

First Nations comedians and communities.

First Nations comedy can be described as a kind of satire. Satire is an ancient form of humour found in many cultures. Satirists use humour to poke fun at, make a joke of, and expose hypocrisy, foolishness, and injustice.

One way satire appears in First Nations humour is through jokes about serious topics. Satire highlights injustices, but also tries to spark change through this exposure. In other words, it makes a point while getting a laugh.

For example, some First Nations comedians twist stereotypes into jokes. **Stereotypes** are rigid ideas about a particular ethnic, national, or cultural group. Stereotypes prevent people from seeing members of the group as individuals. Stereotypes characterize all members of a group as being exactly the same.

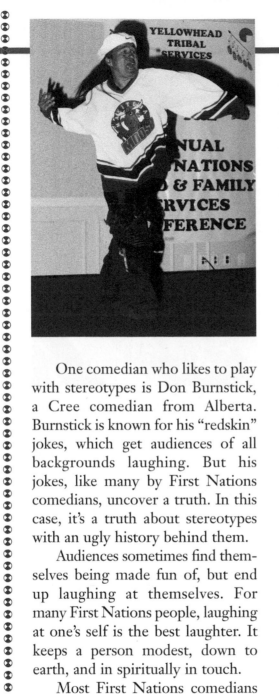

Contemporary comedians, such as Don Burnstick from the Alexander First Nation, continue a tradition of humour that reaches out to audiences from many cultures.

A First Nations sense of humour is evident even on the signs in the parking lot at the Treaty Eight First Nations of Alberta office in Edmonton. Using a play on words, "reserve-d" makes a joke about their claim to a parking space.

One comedian who likes to play with stereotypes is Don Burnstick, a Cree comedian from Alberta. Burnstick is known for his "redskin" jokes, which get audiences of all backgrounds laughing. But his jokes, like many by First Nations comedians, uncover a truth. In this case, it's a truth about stereotypes with an ugly history behind them.

Audiences sometimes find themselves being made fun of, but end up laughing at themselves. For many First Nations people, laughing at one's self is the best laughter. It keeps a person modest, down to earth, and in spiritually in touch.

Most First Nations comedians agree that if you end up laughing at the expense of First Nations peoples, then you've probably missed the point of their joke.

First Nations comedians often use their own life experiences to fuel their humour. Don Burnstick used laughter to get through a difficult childhood and drug and alcohol problems. He says that despite all that Aboriginal peoples have endured, they have never lost their sense of humour.

Charlie Hill, a successful Native American actor, writer, and comedian from the Oneida Nation, would likely agree. He says that by laughing about painful experiences of the past, he "turns poison into medicine."

Mutual Support Today

The values of interdependence that once supported traditional ways of life are still a part of communities across Alberta. At a personal level, intermarriages between groups

Indigenous Knowledge

As a class, watch a video featuring the work of Aboriginal comedians. Analyze the humour when you are done. Who or what is being laughed at? Why is it funny? How does the humour make you feel? Are you laughing at yourself or at other people? Discuss these ideas as a class.

have created a web of kinship ties between communities. For example, most First Nations people have many relatives in Métis Settlements. One Métis woman expressed the closeness this way: "It is no wonder that Métis Settlements are close to reserves. That is where our *kohkoms* live."

An obvious area for mutual support is in the political realm. Political organizations, such as the Assembly of First Nations and the Métis Nation of Alberta, meet regularly and work together to help their member communities or nations.

The Treaty Seven Education Consortium combines the education efforts of five nations in Treaty Seven. This alliance shares information, expertise, and contacts. Most importantly, it speaks with one voice to the provincial government to influence resource and policy decisions.

Some groups have **economic partnerships**. For example, Pimee Well Servicing Ltd. is owned by six First Nations from northern Alberta: Heart Lake, Frog Lake, Saddle Lake, Kehewin, Beaver Lake, and Whitefish Lake. Pimee or *pimiy* is a Cree word meaning "oil." The business cleans oil rigs and was awarded an Alberta Chambers of Commerce Business Award of Distinction in 2001 — the Eagle Feather Business Award of Distinction. Chiefs from each

Pimee Well Servicing Ltd. is an example of mutual economic support. The company is owned by six First Nations. The business benefits the owner communities in many ways, including making generous contributions to local powwows.

owner First Nation are on a board of directors that works together using traditional decision making methods.

The legal world also offers many examples of mutual support in action. Aboriginal groups watch one another's legal battles closely. Because of the system of legal precedent, a victory for one is often heralded as a victory for all. For example, when Métis hunter Steve Powley won hunting rights in a September 2003 Supreme Court decision, many Métis and First Nations groups across the country applauded. Powley's success in Ontario may help other groups working to resolve hunting and fishing rights issues.

Peter O'Chiese

PETER O'CHIESE

Peter O'Chiese was born near Waterton Lakes in southern Alberta. No one is quite sure what year he was born because his clan did not sign a treaty with the federal government. His family believes that he turned 104 in 2003.

O'Chiese is Anishinabé, a First Nation cultural group known for maintaining the traditions of its ancestors. The nation's territory is along the Rocky Mountains from near Rocky Mountain House to Grande Cache.

O'Chiese is well known across Canada for his spiritual teachings of traditional ways of life. His self-sufficiency and generosity inspire people who seek his teachings. One of his favourite sayings is that the Great Spirit gave us eyes to see, ears to hear, a nose to smell, and hands to work with.

O'Chiese was instrumental in First Nations political movements of the 1960s and 1970s, guiding Harold Cardinal, from the Sucker Creek First Nation, to be one of the most respected First Nations leaders in Canada. O'Chiese advised Cardinal on matters of politics and spirituality.

Peter O'Chiese's teachings are based on knowledge of the Elders, animals, and Mother Earth. These values include kindness, honesty, sharing, and determination. He does not believe in violence — his community always maintained peace with European settlers and the federal government.

He has also travelled to other parts of the world and has made connections with other indigenous peoples. He tells the story of a visit he made to Guatemala in Central America, where he was paying his last respects to a wise man who had passed on in one of the villages. In the villagers' culture, when someone dies, the relatives sit the person up for the viewing of the body. As O'Chiese paid his respects, a shovel suddenly appeared in this man's hand. The story spread throughout the country.

A few days later, an earthquake occurred in the same village. The United States government offered assistance, but the villagers refused the American help. However, when O'Chiese offered his services, the people accepted, showing their respect for him.

REFLECTION

What values and principles does Peter O'Chiese embody? How does his life set a spiritual example for all people? Think of another person who embodies these kinds of ideals and write a one-hundred-word profile about them.

LOOKING BACK

Review pages 71–79 and write a definition of each of the following terms or phrases: all my relations, laws of nature, personal autonomy, choice, responsibility, mutual support, interdependence, sharing, generosity, reciprocal relationship, gift-giving, values, unity, harmony. Create a concept map or other visual diagram that helps you remember how these terms and ideas are related.

Language and Worldview

LANGUAGE AND CULTURE ARE INTERTWINED AND CANNOT BE SEPARATED. LEARNING AN ABORIGINAL LANGUAGE MEANS ABSORBING THE very foundation of an Aboriginal identity — the web of relationships that bind the self, community, and natural world. The Royal Commission on Aboriginal Peoples, in consultation with Elders, reported that "thinking and dreaming in a language means that the speaker has internalized the principles for organizing the world that underpins that language." These "principles for organizing the world" are another way of describing worldview. To internalize a worldview is to literally see the world from that view.

A language is rich and varied in its expression of the key cultural experiences of its speakers. For example, there are many words used by the Woodland Cree for *moose*. The prominence of moose in their language is related to the significance of the animal to the traditional Woodland Cree livelihood. Indigenous peoples from Hawaii would likely have few words, if any, for moose in their language. Yet they might have a large vocabulary to describe the behaviour of the tides or particular fish.

Whatever is most important to a culture is described most precisely in its language. For example, Nehiyawewin, the Cree language, has many terms to describe relatives.

AS YOU READ

Language is the window to a culture's worldview. There are gaps between languages because different cultures have different beliefs. Certain concepts may not be shared. While translation from one language to another provides an approximate meaning, subtle distinctions are often lost or need lengthy explanations.

As you read pages 81–85, consider why language education is considered by many First Nations, Métis, and Inuit peoples to be one of the most important goals for their youth.

See the chart on page 82 for examples.

Aboriginal languages reflect a cultural belief in connection and interdependence. Many words eliminate boundaries and emphasize change, transition, and transformation. Nothing is static. Even an object such as a rock can be both physical and spiritual at the same time. Aboriginal languages reflect this dynamic view of the world with many verbs. Verbs are words of motion, action, change, and transition.

CREE WORDS FOR MÔSWA OR MOOSE

George Cardinal, an Elder and hunter from Peerless Lake, Alberta, provided these examples:

onîcaniw	female moose before giving birth
nôses	female moose after giving birth
oskâyis	newborn moose calf
piponâskos	yearling
yikihcawases	one-year-old male moose
waskewceses	two-year-old male moose
okinomwacayeses	three-year-old male moose
oskoweskwamotayew	four-year-old male moose
mistiyâpew	big bull moose

In contrast, the English language reflects a worldview that draws separations between things — black and white; saint and sinner; animate and inanimate. As a language, it tends to emphasize nouns over verbs. Objects are living or not living; stories are fact or fiction.

A shared language unites people with a sense of shared understanding. As one Elder states, "Talking Cree … you have the feeling of your culture, your own feelings, values … you know them better." Language provides a path to understanding that is more difficult to find in another language. One Dene Sųłiné verb, for example, can contain as much information as one English sentence.

ABORIGINAL LANGUAGES TODAY

Today about 26 per cent of the Aboriginal population — about 206 000 people out of 800 000 people — claim an Aboriginal language as their mother tongue which is the first language a person learns to speak, usually at home. The most individuals by far speak Cree,

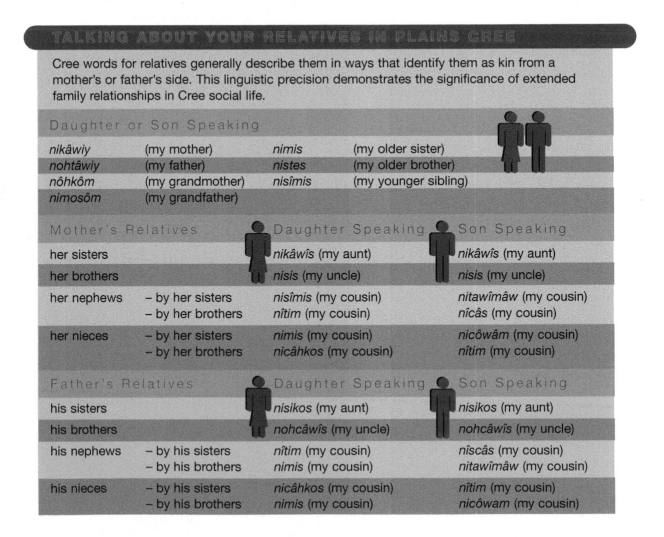

TALKING ABOUT YOUR RELATIVES IN PLAINS CREE

Cree words for relatives generally describe them in ways that identify them as kin from a mother's or father's side. This linguistic precision demonstrates the significance of extended family relationships in Cree social life.

Daughter or Son Speaking

nikâwiy	(my mother)	*nimis*	(my older sister)
nohtâwiy	(my father)	*nistes*	(my older brother)
nôhkôm	(my grandmother)	*nisîmis*	(my younger sibling)
nimosôm	(my grandfather)		

Mother's Relatives

		Daughter Speaking	Son Speaking
her sisters		*nikâwîs* (my aunt)	*nikâwîs* (my aunt)
her brothers		*nisis* (my uncle)	*nisis* (my uncle)
her nephews	– by her sisters	*nisîmis* (my cousin)	*nitawîmâw* (my cousin)
	– by her brothers	*nîtim* (my cousin)	*nîcâs* (my cousin)
her nieces	– by her sisters	*nimis* (my cousin)	*nicôwâm* (my cousin)
	– by her brothers	*nicâhkos* (my cousin)	*nîtim* (my cousin)

Father's Relatives

		Daughter Speaking	Son Speaking
his sisters		*nisikos* (my aunt)	*nisikos* (my aunt)
his brothers		*nohcâwîs* (my uncle)	*nohcâwîs* (my uncle)
his nephews	– by his sisters	*nîtim* (my cousin)	*nîscâs* (my cousin)
	– by his brothers	*nimis* (my cousin)	*nitawîmâw* (my cousin)
his nieces	– by his sisters	*nicâhkos* (my cousin)	*nîtim* (my cousin)
	– by his brothers	*nimis* (my cousin)	*nicôwam* (my cousin)

Inuktitut, and Ojibway. Linguists are confident that these three languages will survive in the future.

However, Statistics Canada considers 95 per cent of Aboriginal languages to be endangered, which means they are spoken by enough people that survival is a possibility, but only if community interest is present and education programs are available. All languages depend on people to speak them and keep them alive. In cultures based on an oral tradition, languages contain the cultures themselves, so loss of language could mean loss of culture. In 1996, 120 people spoke Ktunaxa, one of the most endangered languages in Canada. Fewer than 6 per cent of Métis adults speak Michif; fewer than 5 per cent of Métis children speak any Aboriginal language.

One reason for the different rates of language retention is the number of people in each culture. There are almost 80 000 Cree speakers spread across the country — Cree speakers are the most numerous group of Aboriginal peoples in Canada.

Another factor is geography. In general, the more isolated a region was from European society's impact, the less its people adopted French or English. For example, Inuktitut speakers still tend to live in their traditional territories. The Arctic has historically attracted few settlers and outside influences arrive slowly. This has helped Inuktitut survive as a vibrant language.

In comparison, the Ktunaxa people, a small nation, traditionally

WORLD INDIGENOUS PEOPLES CONFERENCE ON EDUCATION (WIPCE)

The sixth tri-annual World Indigenous Peoples Conference on Education was held in Stoney Park, near Morley, Alberta, in August 2002. WIPCE is an international organization working towards the goal of indigenous peoples' control over their own education. The conference in Morley had the theme *The Answers Are Within Us*, celebrating indigenous peoples' ability to transmit their ancestral heritage from generation to generation.

With a daily sunrise ceremony, evening cultural exchanges and performances, and workshops presented in tipis, the event promoted experiential teaching, which places value on knowledge based on experience. Such experiential knowledge is the knowledge of Elders.

The Answers Are Within Us conference also furthered action on WIPCE goals such as indigenous language education for young people.

The Kainai Grassland Singers are shown here getting ready for a performance during the conference.

◨ REFLECTION

1. Use a dictionary to determine the root word of *experiential*. Why is Elders' experiential knowledge of such value?
2. If you know an Aboriginal language, where did you learn it? How does it affect your worldview or perspective on life? Discuss these questions in small groups.

Many Aboriginal students across Canada learn Aboriginal languages at school, such as this Cree student in northern Quebec. However, unless they also speak the language at home, the students are statistically less likely to pass the language on to their children. How does this fact compare to your own experience? Have you ever learned another language in school?

lived in southeastern British Columbia. Their territory was easily accessible to other nations and was directly in the path of westbound traders and explorers. Communication in other languages had always been an essential part of their culture, even before European contact. The Ktunaxa culture has

The arrival of television in the region in the 1970s presented the greatest danger to culture and language ... Younger people like myself, years ago, would go round and visit with the Elders and sit down and listen to them talk ... [Now,] homes in the area are bombarded with information ... that has little relevance to this land-based culture.

— Billy Day, Inuvialuit Communications Society, Inuvik, Northwest Territories, May 6, 1992

therefore been greatly affected by interactions with other cultures and languages.

There are exceptions to these generalizations. Even some isolated communities are losing their traditional languages, especially today. Global communication technologies mean that few communities are completely removed from the reach of satellite transmissions from mainstream media.

Over the last fifty years, government policies that have resulted in the separation of families, as well as the lack of support for Aboriginal languages, have greatly reduced the number of Aboriginal mother tongue speakers.

First Nations people living in Cold Lake, Alberta, are just one First Nation community in Alberta that is determined to preserve its language. Currently, one in ten residents speaks Dene Sųłiné. Through the Daghida project — a name proclaiming "we are alive" — community members are working with the University of Alberta on programs that will help them retain both their language and thousands of years of traditional knowledge. One program goal for the future is to establish cultural camps. Students who attend these camps will learn traditional skills in Dene Sųłiné, such as trapping, fishing, gardening, and crafts.

HONOURING CANADA'S ABORIGINAL HERITAGE

Toronto, Lake Athabasca, and Canada have names that reflect this country's Aboriginal heritage. Yet many place names in Aboriginal communities are commonly known, but do not appear on maps. For example, a creek known by people living on the Kainai Reserve as Pomiipisskaan was recently labelled Layton Creek by signs on the highway that runs through the reserve.

Some communities are now documenting their heritage by naming or renaming places. For example, Frobisher Bay residents voted to change their name to Iqaluit, the Inuktitut word for "place of fish." A lake in northern Alberta has been named Atihk Sakahikun, which means "Elk Lake" in Cree.

Individuals or organizations can suggest names by contacting the Geographical Names Board of Canada. Your class might wish to nominate a local landmark to be named or renamed in a way that reflects its Aboriginal heritage. You might need to ask community members for information about local places that could be named. If you decide to take on this project, you can download procedures from the Geographical Board of Canada Web site at *www.geonames.NRCan.gc.ca.*

What do place names reveal about the naming culture's worldview?

WHAT TO DO

1. Look at a map of Alberta or Canada.
2. Identify place names that you think have an Aboriginal origin.
3. Using the library or Internet, research the history of the place name you selected to try to identify its origin and meaning.
4. Many times, the spelling of Aboriginal names is anglicized. If you can, locate the original spelling.
5. Research the place to identify why the name was chosen. For example, the name might reflect the geography of the area or an important event.
6. What does the name reveal about the naming culture's worldview and language? Discuss your ideas as a class.

LOOKING BACK

Language education programs, such as the Daghida project, are a positive step towards revitalizing Aboriginal languages. With a partner, brainstorm projects that would help people learn, use, and pass on the languages of their Aboriginal heritage.

Cycles of Life

AS YOU READ

In the western European view of time, events happen and then time marches on in a straight line. In a traditional First Nations or Inuit view, history and the sense of time is cyclical. The observed patterns of creation — seen in the repeating cycles of birth and death, phases of the moon, the days, the seasons — are part of the natural world's order. The cycles of life are perpetual, or never-ending.

First Nations and Inuit stories, symbols, ceremonies, and cultural practices reflect this understanding. Cultural reminders show individuals their place within the natural order and their responsibility to past and future generations. Individuals are not separate from these generations, but are part of the same cycle of renewal. Pages 86–90 describe this important concept and some of the ways it appears in various cultures. Remember that although all First Nations and Inuit cultures recognize the concept of the perpetual cycle of life, they have many ways of expressing it.

A SEED DROPPED INTO THE SOIL GROWS INTO A PLANT, PRODUCES LEAVES, AND FLOWERS. THE FLOWERS BEAR SEEDS, WHICH DROP TO THE GROUND AND BECOME NEW PLANTS, AND SO THE CYCLE CONTINUES. The **cycle of life** is a view of existence in which all things end at the beginning in a never-ending circle of existence. While the plant lives, it thrives on the rain that falls from the sky. It takes in moisture and nutrients from the soil through its roots, and cycles the moisture back to the sky by breathing it out through its leaves, in a process called transpiration.

A deer might wander by and nibble at the plant, grazing on its leaves, which contain some of the soil's nutrients. The deer's body cycles the plant food into energy and passes what it doesn't need back to the earth. Its droppings nourish the soil so that more plants may grow. Later, a wolf could eat the deer. What the wolf doesn't eat will feed smaller animals, birds, and insects. As the wolf moves through the forest, some seeds might stick to its fur, travelling with the wolf for a while before falling to the ground, where new plants will grow. When the wolf dies, its body decomposes, returning to the soil. All things are connected. Birth leads to death and death generates more life.

At the heart of the cycle of human life sits the woman, just as Mother Earth is at the core of all life. Around the woman is the family and extended family, circled in turn by clans or other groups of relations. These wide circles of relations form a nation. A circle of nations makes a cultural group or confederacy. Circles of all humanity are linked with circles of the physical and spiritual worlds that make the planet.

Nature's patterns are circular: flowers, tree rings, and the ripples in water if a stone is dropped in. The round moon revolves around

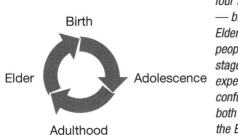

Birth

Elder

Adolescence

Adulthood

The Plains Cree acknowledge four stages in a human life cycle — birth, adolescence, adulthood, Elder. Some First Nations say people move through seven stages in the cycle of life: birth, experience, change, searching, confusion, wisdom, and truth. In both cases, the circle closes with the Elder moving towards the child by sharing the wisdom of experience and the ancestors.

ABORIGINAL PERSPECTIVES

Earth, which rotates as it circles around the spherical sun. All the circular planets orbit the sun. And so the pattern continues beyond the universe into infinity.

In the Cree language, Earth is called *Okâwimaw Askiy* — "Mother Earth." Many First Nations and Inuit cultures make a connection between the planet and women. Both have the power to create life. Mother Earth travels in a path with nine other moons (planets) around the sun; pregnancy lasts nine moons (months). The cleansing night moon (the lunar moon) circles once a month, as does a woman's monthly cycle.

Like Mother Earth, women were highly respected in traditional First Nations societies. Elder women of a community often provided guidance to community leaders. They were seen as the protectors of the community's young and the keepers of the culture.

Because of their gift — the ability to give life — women are considered especially powerful during their monthly cycle. A young woman's onset of this cycle was a cue in many traditional cultures to give thanks through ceremonies for the fertility that continues life.

In most traditional First Nations cultures, certain ceremonies were only for women. Women usually had their own pipe and among people of the Blackfoot Confederacy, only a woman of high moral character could preside over the *Ookáán*, an important ceremony held as part of some Sundances.

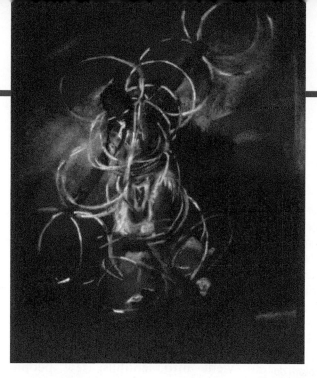

CEREMONIAL CIRCLE

The circle is a universal symbol of connection, unity, harmony, wholeness, and eternity. In a circle, all parts are equal.

In Cree, *miyowicihiwewin* means "having good relations." The circle is a symbol of this cultural value.

When a Cree First Nation's dance is held in a circle, it is a cue that the dance affirms *miyowicihiwewin*. It symbolizes the coming together of the nation, and the unity of the First Nation's social, spiritual, and political institutions with the Creator.

Many ceremonies are performed in a circle, acknowledging the unity and interconnectedness of the participants with each other and the world. The pipe ceremony, for example, follows the sun's path in a circle. Stories are often told to a circle of listeners and various meetings and decision making institutions are conducted with a circle of participants. The talking circle and justice circle are two contemporary examples of how First

Rocky Barstad's Dancer 3 *shows circles of the hoop dance. Find at least one other example of artwork by a First Nations, Métis, or Inuit artist that shows circular symbolism and bring it to class to show other students.*

Edmonton-based
Amiskwaciy
Academy bases its
educational system
on the principles of
natural law. What
symbolism discussed
in this chapter is
used on its logo?
What other
symbolism do
you recognize?

Nations and Inuit peoples continue to acknowledge the significance of the circle in day-to-day life.

If something goes wrong in one part of the circle, everything else is affected. Many contemporary environmental movements reflect traditional First Nations and Inuit beliefs about the necessity of using nature's gifts with respect. Such practices keep the circle in balance. Just decades ago, littering was commonplace and almost all waste went into landfills; few people thought about the legacy of garbage

left for future generations. This kind of thinking reflects a worldview that isolates rather than a worldview that is **holistic** — emphasizing the significance of the whole rather than the parts. Today most municipalities have shifted their thinking with recycling and composting programs. Wisdom and ways of life that were the foundation of traditional First Nations and Inuit cultures for hundreds of years has just recently become commonplace in mainstream society.

In many First Nations cultures, the circle is then divided into four, like a compass. These four directions and the number four have symbolic significance that can be observed in the natural world. Each time that the sun rises in the east to circle across the sky, the day moves through four parts: morning, afternoon, evening, and night. The days join together to bring four seasons.

The concept of four directions is sometimes represented by the idea of four winds that blow from the north, south, east, and west. Many dances incorporate the four directions, which symbolize different things to different nations. In one interpretation, the east represents the sun and fire; the south, the thunderbird and water; the west, plants, animals, and earth; and the north, wind and air. Some First Nations also identify four sacred elements of creation: earth, water, air, and fire.

The Elders stated that the circle symbolized the oneness of First Nations people with the Creator and the spiritual, social, and political institutions of the First Nation. It is at once a statement of allegiance, of loyalty, fidelity, and unity by both the nation and its peoples. This act/statement is rooted in the doctrine of *wahkohtowin* (the laws governing all relations) and *miyowicehtowin* (the laws concerning good relations).

In this particular context, the Elders told us that the circle represents a coming together or a bringing together of a nation. They state that, in coming together in this manner, the nation reaffirms its unity under the laws of the Creator. Under First Nations' traditional teaching, this was one of the sacred ways in which the nation would continue to possess the capability to nurture, protect, care for, and heal its people. It is these annual acts of renewal and spiritual community refurbishment [ceremonies] that enabled the Treaty First Nations to retain their inner strength, cohesion, and spiritual integrity.

— Harold Cardinal and Walter Hildebrandt,
Treaty Elders of Saskatchewan

THE MEDICINE WHEEL

About five thousand years ago, while pyramids were being built in Egypt and Stonehenge was under construction in England, the people of the North American Plains were also laying stones. The form of their low-lying stone creations varied from region to region, but most included a variety of stone circle, cairn, and spoke configurations.

About seventy of these ancient stone structures still exist today, marking hilltops, river valleys, and open prairie in Alberta, Saskatchewan, and some Midwest states. The largest and most elaborate of these, known as the Bighorn medicine wheel, lies atop Medicine Mountain, a sacred site in Wyoming. In the 1880s, someone referred to this structure as a *medicine wheel*, and the term stuck.

To First Nations, the term *medicine* is not restricted to herbal or chemical remedies for illness, although it can, of course, include these things. Medicine traditionally includes spiritual energy and enlightenment. The medicine people of traditional societies were powerful individuals who communicated with the spirit world. They used their knowledge and powers to benefit the community and strengthen spiritual balance.

In many traditional First Nations societies, illness was seen as a sign that a person was not in balance or harmony. Medicine people had the job of restoring a person's balance — physically, emotionally, and spiritually. If the Bighorn medicine wheel and other such stone structures were used for spiritual ceremonies, the name *medicine wheel* may well be appropriate.

However, according to the traditions of the Blackfoot Confederacy, there is no such thing as a medicine wheel. Blackfoot nations built many stone structures, but each had a

First Nations of the Blackfoot Confederacy believe tipi rings are sacred. They believe these rock circles and cairns need to be protected so that future generations can view and learn from them and feel the energy that they radiate. This ring is found on top of a hill in Alberta.

Kathleen McGuire is a counsellor who uses a medicine wheel in her work with people who have suffered substance or sexual abuse. She incorporates humour in her work and sometimes takes on the persona of Smokey Hontus, a wise and witty Elder.

others that the site should be respected as a spiritual location.

Today the term *medicine wheel* can also be used to refer to a concept for learning and healing. This form of medicine wheel has been adopted by many First Nations peoples, regardless of whether it was part of their traditional culture. Generally, the teachings of this kind of medicine wheel help people to attain healthier minds with a greater awareness of how to live peacefully and harmoniously with Earth.

The contemporary medicine wheel is usually presented as a diagram that includes various forms of symbolism and philosophy. For example, a medicine wheel diagram might identify four directions on a wheel and connect each direction with aspects of life, such as spiritual, physical, emotional, and mental health. An individual might examine each aspect to evaluate whether they have balance in their "life circle." There are many interpretations of the medicine wheel charts.

specific identity, purpose, symbolism, and name. For example, some were *mâmma'pis*, which means "tipi rings," while others were *a'kihtákssin*, which means "cairn or memorial." Memorials were built at burial sites to honour prominent leaders, Elders, warriors, or holy women. *A'kihtákssin* were also built to mark the site of sacred lodges or sites where visions were received. The markers indicated to

Indigenous Knowledge

Research an example of a medicine wheel chart and examine the kinds of symbolism and values used. How do these types of medicine wheels connect to what you have learned so far about spirituality and worldview?

LOOKING BACK

With a small group, discuss how the idea of a perpetual cycle is important to traditional First Nations and Inuit worldviews. As a group, prepare a dramatic or dance performance or on your own, create a work of art that demonstrates your understanding of the concept.

Ceremonies

Many traditional First Nations and Inuit practices demonstrate respect and gratitude for the gifts of the physical and spiritual world. Such practices maintain harmony and balance between humankind and the rest of creation.

First Nations and Inuit peoples from across the continent share a tradition of regularly giving thanks, through everyday acts, through rituals, and through ceremonies. A ceremony is a formal act or series of acts performed as prescribed by custom, law, or other authority. Ceremonies can be simple or elaborate, solemn occasions or forms of celebration. First Nations celebrations are often a means of thanking everyone in the community for their contributions.

Ceremonial gatherings remain at the heart of First Nations spiritual and cultural practices today. The significance of these ceremonial practices remains true to sacred teachings that go back to the beginning of time.

Gift-giving is an important part of many First Nations ceremonial gatherings. People traditionally offer their best and most valuable goods to sacrifice or distribute to guests or members of their community. Such gifts are a recognition that resources are meant to be shared. They are also thought to encourage the spiritual world to be as generous.

AS YOU READ

Some traditional First Nations and Inuit ceremonies celebrate and renew kinship. Others praise or thank the Creator, and still others purify thoughts. No matter what the specific purpose of each ceremony is, the overriding reason for ceremonies is the maintenance of harmony and balance within the circle of creation, including human, animal, plant, earth, and spiritual relationships. As you read pages 91–101, consider how ceremonies reinforce First Nations and Inuit worldviews.

Traditionally, giving a gift created a relationship of reciprocity between giver and receiver. If the recipient of a gift could not respond with gifts in kind, the recipient might offer loyalty or service.

Many gifts were given and then re-given. Even today, it is the act of giving that is most significant, not the gift itself. Generous individuals gain status and are thought to receive blessings from the spirits.

In ceremonies from many indigenous cultures from around the world, the four-beat of the sacred drum symbolizes the heartbeat of the nation and Mother Earth's pulse. The sound connects the drum, the drummers, listeners, and Earth.

Plants in general symbolize transformation. Many First Nations use tobacco, sage (pictured here), sweet grass, or cedar for ceremonial, healing, and purification purposes. Each plant symbolizes different things to different nations, but specific prayers and rituals always prescribe collection, preparation, and use of the plant.

Traditionally, the *Mâhtâhitowin* or "Give-Away Dance," was held by the Plains Cree in fall or early winter. It was an important ceremony in which communities would pray for good hunts and long lives. It was no coincidence that the ceremony was held just before winter. The feasts and generous exchange of gifts were thought to ward off starvation or other hardships during the long winter.

The Give-Away Dance is relatively new among the Blackfoot nations. At the end of this dance is a distribution of blankets, money, horses, and anything else that the sponsor wants to give away. The dance strengthens social bonds and is also a way to welcome visitors.

At the heart of every ceremony is gratitude to the Creator for the gift of life. Giving gifts honours this greatest gift of all.

Specific ceremonies address the protocol for use of the land's resources. Some traditional rituals helped communities ensure an on-going food supply, under the belief that the spirits of respectfully treated animals or plants return to replenish the earth. When a First Nations hunter offered part of an animal back to the natural world, this symbolized respect, honour, and thanks for the animal's gift of life to the human community.

Many First Nations and Inuit peoples continue to honour such ceremonial practices today.

Traditional First Nations and Inuit ceremonial gatherings are tied to a seasonal time frame rather than specific dates. In the Pacific Northwest, First Nations held various ceremonies to celebrate the gift of salmon when the first fish of the year was caught. Similarly, eastern First Nations had regular ceremonies to show gratitude for the plants that fed them, with celebrations for green corn, strawberries, and the maple tree, for example.

Many ceremonies use sacred and symbolic objects. For example, to the Dené Tha', the drum is not simply a musical instrument. It is a symbol of identity, a spiritual instrument for singing prayers, communicating with the Creator, and honouring Elders, mothers, children, and nature. Different cultures consider different items, such as the pipe, tobacco, specific kinds of rocks, water, birds, and many animals, to be symbolic of values and beliefs important to the culture.

Sacred objects are seen to have a life, spirit, and power of their own. Symbolic objects are normally considered animate in most First Nations languages. For example, the Cree word *pesowew* or *petâw* means "bring it" — *pesowew* (for animate items) and *petâw* (for inanimate). When Cree people refer to the pipe, they use an animate term — *pesowewospwâkan*. Their language reflects a belief that the pipe is a direct link to the Creator.

A ceremonial pipe used with tobacco represents communication with the Creator — a form of prayer. Ceremonial pipe tobacco is traditionally not for recreational or everyday use. For many First Nations cultures, tobacco represents honesty that is carried in one's heart when words are spoken between people. The smoke represents one's visible thoughts; tobacco travels ahead of the words so that honesty will be received in a kind and respectful way.

First Nations and Inuit spirituality is action oriented, involving the senses of sight, sound, smell, and touch. Dancing is an important part of many ceremonial gatherings. For many people, dancing is a spiritual act, a way of praying that connects mind, body, and emotions to the spiritual world. First Nations have many dances, each with a specific purpose.

Singing performs a similar spiritual purpose, and songs exist for almost every type of ceremony.

CEREMONIAL PROTOCOL

Many First Nations people believe that in order for the balance of all living things to continue, proper protocols must be followed. Protocols ensure that ceremonies will be remembered from generation to generation and that the values of the culture will be upheld through time.

All ceremonies involve protocols. If you ever have the opportunity to attend a ceremony, be sure to find out the preferred protocol for the ceremony and community involved. General protocols for sacred ceremonies usually include not taking a camera or video recorder. Women may be encouraged to wear long dresses and are often discouraged from attending sacred ceremonies during their time of month.

Women are like Mother Earth, who once a year in the spring, washes herself down to the river and then to the ocean. Everything ... all debris is washed away. Same thing with a woman, except it's every month. ... At Sundances, if a woman in her time comes near the lodge, the singers and dancers know. I have to tell the older women to tell the younger ones not to stay around if they are like that. It's not because we don't like them, it's the power they have.

— George Kehewin, Kehewin Reserve,
Those Who Know: Profiles of Alberta's Native Elders

Songs are particularly important to Inuit peoples and are a major component of their oral tradition. Inuit songs can be spiritual or secular, which means they deal with topics from day-to-day life. Among traditional Inuit societies, every Inuk was a poet and singer, but songs from people regarded as prophets and spiritual leaders were especially powerful. From these people, songs were believed to heal or even work miracles.

RITES OF PASSAGE

Some types of ceremonies appear in almost every culture around the world, although the details, of course, vary widely. These common types of ceremonies include ceremonies for births, deaths, marriages, and other rites of passage. An important rite of passage for First Nations youth was traditionally the transition from child to adult. The signs of this passage differed from culture to culture and between boys and girls. Female Elders generally described and guided female rites of passage and male Elders did the same for boys and men.

In some cultures, a boy's transition to manhood was marked by hunting or warfare, or sometimes by a personal event such as going on a spiritual quest. During a spiritual quest an individual sought guidance from a guardian spirit. This rite of passage usually involved a period of a few days in seclusion without food, water, or shelter. The person prayed until a vision was received. The Dené Tha' describe a vision as *mendayeh wodekéh*, which means "something appearing in front of someone." Purification ceremonies were held before and after. In some cultures, Elders would later assemble a sacred bundle of objects related to the vision.

In many First Nations cultures, the onset of a girl's monthly cycle was the event seen to mark her transition to womanhood. Many cultures recognized the event with important ceremonies. Among the Plains Cree, a young woman would spend the first four days of her first monthly cycle in isolation with a grandmother. It was an important time of education and spirituality for the young woman. When the four days were over, her family would celebrate with a community feast and give-away.

Your Project

1. Identify a First Nations or Inuit rite of passage that interests you. If you prefer, you may choose one from an indigenous culture outside North America.

2. Find out about the ceremony, including information such as
   - when it takes place
   - symbolism used
   - protocol or etiquette involved
   - how it expresses the culture's worldview.

You may need to research background information about the culture that practises the ceremony for context.

3. Organize your information in a PowerPoint™ presentation. Include your information in point form only. Supplement the information on your slides with your own thoughts and ideas while you present. If you have personal experiences of this ceremony, you may wish to share parts of them in your presentation.

4. Be sure that all of your information deals with non-sacred aspects of the ceremony. If you are not sure, check with your teacher or a knowledgeable member of your community, such as an Elder.

5. Your PowerPoint™ presentation should have a maximum of six slides.

6. Present to your class.

COMMUNAL CEREMONIES

If rites of passage celebrate an individual's transition from one phase of life to another, then communal ceremonies celebrate and reinforce social and spiritual relationships.

Among the Plains Cree, traditional communal ceremonies included the Sundance, Shaking Tent Ceremony, Masked Dance, Prairie-Chicken Dance, Pipestem Bundle Dance, Round Dance, and Medicine Society Dance.

Major Plains Cree dances were traditionally sponsored by an individual. Such sponsorship was an enormous project for that person and for that person's relatives. Some dances would require many months of preparation by the whole extended family. Families supported one another in these preparations, which drew kin together and reinforced systems of kinship responsibilities.

Contemporary ceremonial gatherings preserve ancient teachings and serve important social and spiritual functions, much in the way they always have. Most specific information about ceremonies is considered sacred. In-depth knowledge is a personal understanding that is gained through an individual's experience of ceremonial gatherings. The following pages touch upon some of the ceremonial gatherings still held in Alberta First Nations communities.

The sacred knowledge is what we cannot discuss. What we see, what is evident, we can talk about. For example, when the Horns dance outside in a circle, or when the Buffalo Women dance inside their lodge. What cannot be shared is the knowledge derived from membership. A person has to be a member to know the information.

— Rosie Red Crow, Kainai First Nation, *Kipaitapiiwahsinnooni: Alcohol and Drug Abuse Education Program*

CEREMONY REVITALIZATION

In 1885, the Canadian government outlawed the ceremonial distribution of property through potlatches and other ceremonies of First Nations in British Columbia. Potlatches are important political, economic, and social ceremonies that involve a distribution of possessions throughout communities. You will learn more about the potlatch in Chapter Four.

A decade later, the federal government banned certain ceremonial gatherings of other First Nations cultures, along with some rituals of the Sundance and give-away. Some communities continued to secretly practise banned ceremonies, though they could have been arrested for doing so, and some people were.

These bans were not lifted until 1951. Many people, however, remained unaware of this change and almost twenty years passed before ceremonial traditions were widely reinstated.

Ceremonies are now being revitalized in the everyday lives of First Nations people across the country. In the interactions that First Nations leaders have with government, representatives honour and respect traditional teachings by participating in pipe ceremonies, prayer, and other ceremonial practices.

❚ REFLECTION

Research the reasons behind government legislation to ban ceremonies. What were the effects on specific communities? Were the effects the ones the legislation intended? Write a short story or prepare a dramatic monologue that presents your ideas and research.

Members of the Dené Tha' Traditional Dancers — Bobbi Tecomba (left) and Trina Netannah — perform at a Tea Dance in Grouard, Alberta, in 1999.

[My father] used to sleep and dream to get his songs. I still have my drum, too, and I've been singing and dreaming since I was sixteen. The songs that we sing today have been passed along to us from old prophets that lived long ago, and some are the songs of animals that we live on for food — we sing their songs.

— Adam Salopree, Meander River Reserve, *Those Who Know: Profiles of Alberta's Native Elders*

PROPHETS, VISIONS, AND SONGS

For traditional Dené Tha' people, spirituality revolves around the teachings of visionaries and prophets. One of the most famous prophets from Alberta is Nogha (No-ah), whose name comes from his animal helper — the wolverine.

Nogha was a famous *ndátin* or "dreamer," as such prophets are known to the Dené Tha'. Visions and dreams are important to Dené Tha' spirituality, as they are to many other First Nations. Most First Nations see visions as forms of messages from the Creator or the spirit world.

Although all Dene Tha' people can receive visions, certain individuals are especially receptive. These people are recognized as prophets by their community. Songs often come with visions and young Dené Tha' are sometimes told "*Shin kaneya*," which means "Go for a song!"

In the late nineteenth and early twentieth century, Nogha travelled from community to community in northern Alberta, sharing his vision of change and prophecies for the future. His prophecies foretold difficult times ahead for the Dené Tha' — a black cloud hanging over his people. Many Dené Tha' today see Nogha as one of their people's most powerful prophets. Nogha inspired many people to hold Tea Dances, avoid drinking alcohol, and maintain their traditional spiritual ways.

Tea Dance

For Dené Tha' people in Alberta, the *dawots'ethe*, which means simply "dance" in Dené Tha', is the most significant ceremonial gathering. The English name for this ceremony — Tea Dance — comes from the tea served at the gathering, although the beverage itself does not have a particular spiritual significance.

Tea Dances are traditionally held to commemorate a death, mark a change in seasons, or celebrate the end of a successful hunt. The purpose of each Tea Dance is revealed to prophets in their dreams. Prophets are spiritual leaders in Dené Tha' communities. A Tea Dance involves prayer, feasting, dancing, socializing, storytelling, and speeches by Elders. *Shin*, which are songs, are the primary means of addressing the spirits.

Round Dance

The Round Dance held by the Woodland Cree is called the *mâskisimowin*. The Plains Cree call it *pîcicîwin*. It was once held only in the winter, although today it is sometimes held at other times of the year. It is similar in function and form to the Tea Dance.

Sweat Lodge

The Sweat Lodge ceremony involves a physical and spiritual purification. The Cree word for the Sweat Lodge is *matotisân*. There are many types of lodges and they can be used for purposes such as purification, healing, and prayer. Different types of lodges are constructed for different purposes and different First Nations and communities follow different protocols for construction of a lodge and its ceremony.

Often, lodges are constructed with a frame of bent willow branches. The number of branches varies depending on considerations such as the type of lodge being built and the number of people attending the ceremony. Different symbolic meanings are attached to each of the willows. Everything from the entrance to the lodge and which direction it faces, to the symbolic meanings of the rocks and water used in the ceremony, have symbolic and spiritual significance.

Today many Aboriginal people use the Sweat Lodge to seek spiritual solutions for themselves and their communities.

Sundance

For Plains First Nations, the Sundance is traditionally a celebration of community well-being, world renewal, and thanksgiving. It was and is the most sacred ceremony.

Among the Plains Cree, sponsoring the *Pâhkwesimôwin* (Sundance) was one of the biggest spiritual, social, and economic commitments a person could make. Women could pledge to sponsor the dance, but it was customary for a male member to do it on her behalf.

Today, as in the past, the *Pâhkwesimôwin* is a sacred place to visit people, to fast, purify, be safe,

Sundance, *by Plains Cree artist Allen Sapp, reflects the significance of the centre pole in a Sundance lodge. Sapp was born on the Red Pheasant Reserve in Saskatchewan.*

and learn. The dance involves sacrifice as a way to be close to the Creator. People offer gifts to the Creator and commit to important cultural values, such as hope, peace, and harmony.

For nations of the Blackfoot Confederacy, the *Akóka'tssin* (Sundance) was traditionally a time to reaffirm their faith in the Creator and the sun as a major force in the gift of life. Sometimes the *Ookáán*, or "Chaste Woman Ceremony," was a central feature of the *Akóka'tssin*. It was only held if a qualified woman came forward to sponsor it.

The Blackfoot *Akóka'tssin* was sponsored by a group, such as the Horn society. The gathering was and continues to be a time for ceremonies to transfer memberships in societies.

Some people do not like to see photographs of the Sundance shared, because they say that a photograph does not capture the sacred meaning of the Sundance. You have to experience it to understand the sacred meaning. You might have a personal vision between the Creator, the centre pole, and you. You cannot explain the Sundance — you have to experience it.

— Bob Cardinal, Enoch First Nation

Powwows, such as the one pictured here at Wetaskiwin, Alberta, are important ceremonial gatherings that reinforce social bonds, spiritual beliefs, and a common cultural heritage. Young and old attend and take part in the event.

The *Akóka'tssin* remains one of the most important social activities of the year. Today First Nations people from all over Alberta attend the *Akóka'tssin* on the Kainai Reserve each summer.

Powwow

The powwow is the most popular and far-reaching form of celebration among First Nations communities today. Although many First Nations host these gatherings, the powwow is a contemporary gathering and not all communities host or participate in them. For those who participate, the event is often a way to reaffirm their cultural heritage.

Indigenous Knowledge

Invite an Elder to your class to discuss a ceremony that is important to his or her cultural group. Remember to follow proper protocol when issuing your invitation.

After the Elder's visit, write a paragraph that relates what you learned to other knowledge you have gained so far in this course.

There are four main types of powwow dances: Traditional, Fancy, Grass, and Jingle-dress. Jingle-dress dancing is derived from the Anishinabé people of northern Ontario, while Traditional, Fancy, and Grass dancing have their roots in Plains culture.

The Cree word for powwow is *pwât'simowin*, which means "Lakota Dancing," since the Lakota were the originators of what is known as the powwow today. The Blackfoot call it *passkaan* and the Nakoda call it *wagicibi*, which simply means "dancing."

Today powwows celebrate First Nations traditions through singing, dancing, and drumming. The powwow takes place in a circle, as do many other ceremonies.

Some powwows are competitive, which means they offer prize money for some dances. For example, the Skydome Powwow in Toronto offers $75 000 in prize money. Some of these powwows are huge gatherings lasting two to three days or longer, with contests in different categories.

During powwow season, from April to October, people of different nations renew old friendships and make new ones.

Powwow protocol includes proper procedures for everything from when photographs are allowed to not touching a dancer's regalia without permission.

THE POWER OF POWWOW

Author Dianne Meili, from Edmonton, Alberta, interviewed powwow dancers from Alberta about what the powwow means to them. The passage that follows is a summary of their conversations. If you have powwow stories of your own, you might choose to share them with your classmates.

Stan Isadore: I'll start off this circle with a few words to make people think. To me, dancing is not a talent. I've come to realize it really is more of a gift from the Creator.

Adrian LaChance: It's a gift, all right. It turned my life around. I was doing drugs — cocaine, heroin, you name it. Skid row kind of stuff. Well, it was in my whole family ... I was raised with it. In '97 I was just out of the Edmonton Max [penitentiary] and I was on parole. I was a singer, so I decided to go to a powwow in Kamloops. So there I am, sitting on the bus with my big drum and some drum sticks. I just went. When I got there, this dancer friend of a girl I used to get high with gave me tobacco and asked me to dance for him. I said "Sure, sure." I was so nervous. Man, I was stiff, I didn't want to ruffle any feathers out there, literally [laughs]. But then, I felt good. It was the best feeling in the world. I was getting looks from the girls. Then I began to cry. I was so emotional. This Elder dancer said to me "What's your name?" and he encouraged me. I began to get my regalia together. Eagle plumes. Eagle talons. Eagle head. Now, I guess you could say it's my path. You have to walk in a good way. I take care of myself. I don't even eat sugar, if I can help it.

WHAT IS THE SIGNIFICANCE OF POWWOW DANCING TODAY?

Shirley Hill: Dancing is my life. I love dancing. It strengthens me ... I'm fit and flexible ... and I've always had a spiritual connection with it. I started when I was five. Then my parents split up and I didn't dance for many years. I knew part of my culture was missing. It was a tough time. Then my mom took me to a powwow at Blackfoot Crossing when I was eighteen and I just knew I would make a dress. Now, I make dance regalia for other people, too. I learned to bead at the Calgary Indian Friendship Centre. Elders like Louise Big Plume, Maggie Black Kettle, and the late Brigette Crow Chief, they taught me how to sew properly. Oh, and Myna Lefthand. What a sweetheart she is! She always encouraged me and kept me going. I teach Fancy Shawl dancing with Wandering Spirit Native Awareness in Calgary. A student of mine from there went to the World Hoop Dance Championships in Arizona and was complimented on her fancy footwork. She came to me and said "I want to thank you, Shirley." That made me so happy and proud! She had the perseverance, effort, and willingness to dance. When you dance, you have to love yourself and stay motivated to keep going. It brings you so much.

Shirley Hill

Warren Bird: I used to abuse alcohol and the powwow trail changed my life. It got me off the reserve and hanging out with other dancers, and more into ceremonies and prayer. I was nervous at first. I didn't know what I was supposed to do. But people gave me a chance. They made me feel comfortable. After a year, I was going to the big powwows in Kamloops, down in the States at Rocky Boy, and in Saddle Lake, and over to Saskatchewan. My baby, Wyatt Bird, is gonna be dancing soon. He'll be a chicken dancer, like Kevin.

WHAT IS THE SIGNIFICANCE OF POWWOW DANCING TODAY?

Kevin Buffalo: I know what you mean, Shirley, about being a little kid and having a spiritual connection to dancing. When I was nine, I was riding my bike and I heard that thumping sound grouse make in the springtime. I stopped and went over to this little plateau, and there they were! The males were doing their mating dance and the female was on the sideline, watching. The males had their eyes closed while they were dancing. You'll notice some chicken dancers shield their eyes; it relates to that. Or they wear sunglasses. When I was ten, I asked my grandfather to get me some dance regalia, but he said "Nôsim, you won't dance until you have bells on your knees." I didn't know what he meant because no dancers were wearing bells like that. Then I saw the chicken dance — the dancers had a band of bells around their knees. The chicken dance was being revived and I knew I could

Warren Bird

Kevin Buffalo

do it. Then it all kind of came together for me. There is a ceremony of healing related to the chicken dance. I once danced for a sick girl in a wheelchair. She had a newborn baby. She gave me tobacco to dance. I did, and then it started to rain. It was a sad time. I was pretty emotional. And then, later, I saw the sister of the woman I danced for, and she said "There's my sister's favourite dancer." Man, that felt good.

Jackie Soppit: I grew up in a non-Native family and struggled with my sense of cultural identity during my younger years. My life changed when I started seeking out my culture and began dancing when I was sixteen. I went from being the most incredibly shy person to today being the director of my own company. I now teach cultural programs to youth and families with similar backgrounds to my own. I've been a jingle dancer for twelve years and believe the jingle dress dance still holds the healing power it once did.

Felix Lewis: I guess I'd just like to add how dancing is such a physical challenge. Especially men's fancy dance. In the championship, it's easy to get on top. The hard thing is staying on top. There's always someone trying to take your place. It keeps you sharp. I like the "iron man" event. I danced twenty-seven songs straight. That's about fifty-six minutes of fast dancing.

Stan Isadore: You guys have reminded me of something that happened when I was a little kid. I must have been four or five. I was watching the men's traditional on the sidelines — sitting with my aunts and uncles. I remember distinctly how the bells on the dancers were so loud and the dancers looked so huge. One dancer came so close to me, my aunt pulled me back. When he came towards me, he dropped down on one knee and our eyes met. I saw his feathers, his face paint ... I never forgot that. My aunt, Roselie Ward, started a dance group when I was ten and took me across Alberta to perform. Now, I'm a fancy dancer and it's taken me all over the world. I received a lot of encouragement and support from people from my reserve and my mother. She helped me recognize the importance of dancing and how meaningful it is to people. Dance has really helped me. The drum does something to you. Long ago it was a way of praying, a way of communication, a way of prayer. It helps us as people. It tells us where we're from and where we're going.

Jackie Soppit

LOOKING BACK

Before ending this chapter, check to see if you can answer the following questions: What are ceremonies and why did traditional First Nations and Inuit cultures perform them? How are ceremonies related to spirituality and worldview? Name three ceremonies that are common today and briefly explain their significance for at least one First Nations culture.

Chapter Three Review

Check Your Understanding

1. New vocabulary in this chapter is indicated by bold type. For each new word, create a word scramble. When you are finished, exchange it with a classmate and complete each other's word puzzles. To create your word scramble, follow this example:

   A person of European and Aboriginal ancestry. (simte)
   Answer: Métis

2. What is a worldview? How is a worldview acquired?

3. What are some of the main principles of traditional First Nations and Inuit worldviews?

4. Write one sentence that summarizes each of the Laws of Nature, Laws of Sacred Life, and Laws of Mutual Support listed in the chart on page 72.

5. Can religion and spirituality co-exist? Explain your answer.

6. What is mutual support? Explain how communities demonstrate mutual support today.

7. This chapter demonstrates how language reflects culture. Identify two specific examples and explain them.

8. What is a perpetual cycle? How is this cycle represented in ceremonies and symbolism?

9. What role do Elders play in teaching a First Nations or Inuit worldview?

10. What is personal autonomy and how does it fit within a worldview that values community highly?

11. Think about the purpose of a talking circle. Why is the circle used as a structure for this kind of discussion? How is a circle both symbolic and functional?

12. Use a specific example to explain the nature of First Nations humour.

13. What is the purpose of ceremonies in First Nations cultures? Describe at least one contemporary ceremony.

Speaking and Listening

14. Learn at least five words or phrases in an Aboriginal language. If you already speak one, learn words in a new Aboriginal language. You may need to consult with someone in your community who can help you correctly pronounce the words.

15. How does Ken Saddleback's story from page 103 incorporate aspects of traditional Cree worldviews? List as many ideas as you can.

Viewing and Representing

16. Use the phrase "All My Relations" to create an art project that expresses what this phrase means to you.

17. Research artwork by Aboriginal artists that uses circular symbolism. Bring at least one example that you like to class to share with other students. Include information about the artist as part of your presentation and, if possible, information about the work of art you show them.

Going Further

18. Identify an aspect of traditional First Nations or Inuit worldviews presented in this chapter, such as the symbolic significance of the circle, the four directions, or animals. Design a tattoo, piece of jewellery, badge, or other personal item that reflects a traditional First Nations or Inuit value that you share. You may focus on one symbol or a combination of symbols. Be prepared to share your creation with your class, as well as to explain the details of your creation, where and how you would wear or use it, and its symbolic meaning.

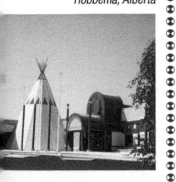

Ermineskin Junior Senior High School, in Hobbema, Alberta

19. In a group of two or three students, imagine that you are an architectural firm that has been asked to design a new high school that incorporates a First Nations worldview. Create a blueprint of the school, including the schoolyard, to show how the building and surroundings reflect First Nations cultural elements.

You may select the symbolism and values of a specific group, such as the Piikani or Dené Tha', or a combination of ideas from many groups. You will likely want to think about who the students for your school will be and make your choices accordingly.

Your blueprint should be poster size so that it can be displayed. For ideas, you might research a few schools from around Alberta that already demonstrate these principles, such as Oski Pasikoniwew Kamik, on the Bigstone Cree reserve in Wabasca, Alberta, Saddle Lake School on the Saddle Lake reserve, or Ermineskin Junior Senior High School in Hobbema, Alberta. Prepare a brief presentation to explain your choices to the class.

LOOKING BACK

Re-read the three chapter opening stories that you have read so far in this book: "How the People Hunted the Moose," "The Origin of Death," and "The Story of Eagle Child." For each, list at least three ways that the story reveals elements of traditional First Nations worldviews. Give specific points to back up your ideas.

The following story tells one person's experience of connecting with his past.

Ken Saddleback grew up on the Samson reserve in Hobbema, Alberta. His upbringing was very traditional and he had a strong connection to his culture. Nevertheless he also had an interest in higher learning and was preparing for a career in public administration when his grandfathers intervened and sent him along the traditional path of his ancestors. They told him that this path was one he would not regret.

The Samson Cree First Nation Cultural Advisor explains "In the summer of 1981, Jonas Cattleman wanted me to be *oskapiyos* (a helper) for him. He transferred his Sundance songs to me, and took me to see Red Bear, an Elder from the Sunchild O'Chiese First Nation. Red Bear told me 'you don't know what you're doing' to be putting up a Sundance." At the time I didn't understand his truthful warning. Sundances are a heavy responsibility for lodge keepers to carry.

Saddleback did not put up the Sundance that summer, but began preparing for it the following January. Part of the preparation involves fasting.

"I was fasting so much. My blood pressure was so high … it felt like I might die. I didn't see anyone supporting me … no Elders were joining me. I was giving up. I thought 'is this worth it?'"

At his lowest point, he envisioned four old men who encouraged him and told him to keep going. They said, Don't ever think you're alone in this work. We are here with you. We are listening to you.

"What they said made me cry. I knew I would finish my first Sundance Lodge," recalls Saddleback. He did, and twenty-three years later he is still serving the people. Employed by his band, he counsels members of his community and provides a wide range of cultural ceremonies. Whether he's called upon to pray with the pipe, sing the ancient songs, or speak at conferences, he is honoured to help in any way he can.

"We can't go back to the old days, but we can bring balance to this world by understanding the universe and the sacredness of it. That's what I help people to do," Saddleback affirms.

Traditional Societies

AS YOU READ

As you learned in Chapter Three, traditional First Nations and Inuit worldviews were infused with spiritual beliefs. People in these traditional societies lived their spiritual beliefs in their political, economic, and social ways of life. As you read Chapter Four, watch for evidence of the values and principles of these traditional worldviews.

Leo Fox is an author and educator working with the Kainai Board of Education. In the reading that opens this chapter, Fox describes the social organization of the traditional Kainai extended family. Other First Nations might have different roles and responsibilities for family members. As you read, think about how the traditional Kainai family organization reflects the principles of worldview that you learned in Chapter Three.

As you read this chapter, consider these questions:

▲ How did traditional First Nations and Inuit political, economic, and social organization systems reflect traditional worldviews?

▲ How were roles and responsibilities assigned and learned in traditional cultures?

▲ How did traditional First Nations and Inuit peoples resolve conflicts and settle disputes?

▲ How did kinship systems and mutual support form the basis of traditional systems of social organization?

▲ How were decisions made in traditional societies?

▲ How did systems of political and economic organization differ between various First Nations and Inuit peoples?

Roles in the Traditional Kainai Family

By *Makai'stoo* (Leo Fox) in *Kipaitapiiwahsinnooni: Alcohol and Drug Abuse Education Program*

THERE WAS ORDER AND ORGANIZATION IN THE TRADITIONAL FAMILY. NATURE HAD AN ORDER AND ORGANIZATION. THIS IS WHAT THE PEOPLE FOLLOWED. EACH MEMBER OF THE TRADITIONAL extended family had a role to play.

The father was the head of the family. What was to be done was indicated by him. He was the *aohko'tsimaawa* or "provider." This meant he was the main food gatherer, hunting and bringing in the meat. If he was also the *ninaawa* or "clan leader," the father was the one who decided when a camp was to be taken down and a new one established at a different location. With his wife, the *ninaakiiwa*, he led the others in this move. As he matured and gained more experience, he became wiser in his leadership skills.

As a leader, he had a lot of respect. He knew that he was only one of many leaders of the tribe. The tribe was made up of different clans. A leader had to earn the respect he got from others. He earned this respect through war, through acquisitions, bravery, kindness, and generosity.

The woman was responsible for looking after the immediate home and surroundings. She was responsible for acquiring herbs for medicines. She was also responsible for picking berries, which she would use then and later on throughout the year.

The *pookaiksi* — "children" — were there to help. They all pulled together. That is how there was order.

The Elders' role was an advisory one. Great emphasis was placed on their wisdom and knowledge gained through experience. From time to time, they counselled and gave nature lessons to the youth.

The people of that time *aiksimstatoomiaw opaitapiiwahsowayi*, that is, they "thought out their lives." From the bison that their fathers and uncles hunted, the boys made little horses from bones taken from around the hooves of the bison. When someone asked "Where's the boy?" he would be told "He is outside, thinking." That is when they "thought out" their future lives.

The same thing happened for girls. When someone asked "Where are the girls?" she would be told "They are playing outside, they are thinking." The reason why this play was referred to as "thinking" was that the children were mimicking real life in their play. The boys played with their "horses" and the girls played with their dolls and their "lodge" (homes), thinking and planning out their future lives.

Life was good for the people then. There was a spirit of belonging and a sense of family. Everyone worked together. Respect was valued. There was reverence for nature and the spirituality that we were given.

Meeting with the Chiefs *was painted in 1994 by Zoey Wood-Salomon, who paints in the style of her Odawa-Anishinabé heritage. It is an artistic interpretation of traditional Anishinabé leadership. What kinds of leadership does Leo Fox mention in his description of Kainai traditions? What role does experience play in the forms of leadership he describes? How do Fox's ideas compare to Wood-Salomon's? Read the artist's explanation of her work on this page. What aspects of traditional First Nations worldviews do you see represented in her painting and statement?*

[In this painting,] the Anishinabé and the chiefs have gathered together to unite their plans for the next seven generations. They look to the Medicine Wheel and its teachings for guidance. The three little circles that are united by power lines represent the good and the bad that is always around us. We have to be able to discern which is which so that we can teach our youth to take the right path.

— Zoey Wood-Salomon, Sault Ste Marie

▊ REFLECTION

Based on what you learned in Chapter Three, what aspects of traditional worldview are represented in the text and image on pages 104–105? Make a list of as many ideas as you can. What roles do family members play? Does referring to children's play as "thinking" affect your ideas about its significance and role in family life?

Traditional Social Organization

AS YOU READ

Since the earliest times in human development, people have organized themselves into social groups in order to meet the needs of the whole community. Individuals or small groups may be able to meet their needs in some situations, but larger groups generally make everyone's life easier and more secure. As groups grow larger, an organization, plan, or rules are essential.

As you read pages 106–115, watch for examples of how kinship ties and other relationships between people formed the foundation of traditional societies.

ALL SOCIETIES HAVE SOME FORM OF POLITICAL, ECONOMIC, AND SOCIAL ORGANIZATION. THE RULES OF THESE SYSTEMS OF ORGANIZATION MAY BE WRITTEN DOWN OR THEY MAY BE JUST UNDERSTOOD BY EVERYONE; THEY MAY BE BASED on tradition and cultural beliefs or they may be based on simple necessity or efficiency. No society, large or small, could survive if there were not rules or some shared understanding about how to work together and get along with each other. Social structures answer questions such as, How should food be acquired and distributed? Who should make decisions? How should conflict be resolved?

Traditional First Nations and Inuit social organizations revealed a high degree of cooperation and mutual support because individuals relied on the people around them for all of their needs. Kinship was the glue that maintained the bonds between people. Communities were held together through trust and the closeness of family relationships. A large extended family was necessary in order to perform all the work necessary for day-to-day life, including taking care of shelter, food, transportation, and defense needs.

Each branch in a kinship system, such as the bond between an aunt and niece, carried with it particular roles and obligations. These involved responsibilities to share resources, to educate, and to offer mutual support in times of hardship. Such responsibilities ensured that everyone was cared for, because everyone had family.

Family ties extended to adopted individuals and their relations. The Blackfoot expression *nitohkoikso'kowaiksi*, which means "my newly acquired relatives," included such adoptions. Adopted individuals became part of their new family with their own set of roles and responsibilities.

Some adoptions did not mean a person would necessarily live with their adopted family. A woman might, for example, adopt a young man who reminded her of a lost son. Other adoptions might occur between important individuals in different First Nations. These kinds of adoptions forged bonds between different groups. Because of these ties and their obligations, kinship bonds helped make political and trading alliances between nations.

The primary living group of most First Nations varied with the season. People living in the area now called Alberta, for example, usually lived in extended family groups during the winter and larger groups at certain points during the summer. Group size was not based on a specific number or family size limit, but instead on the practical requirements of the people. Groups had to be big enough to provide for themselves, but not so big that they had to struggle.

EXTENDED FAMILY AND CLAN

Traditionally, the Plains and Woodland Cree's basic social unit was the extended family. This group included uncles and aunts from both the father's and mother's sides. All children in a group were cousins. Grandfathers and grandmothers could include both the parents of an individual's parents, and the brothers and sisters of the grandparents. Often families would adopt children or older people that did not have a family of their own.

Kinship ties were so fundamental to Plains Cree social relationships that even strangers would establish some kind of kinship bond with each other, even if it were only through a distant ancestor. Strangers might be addressed as *nîstâw* (if spoken by a man) or *nîtim* (if spoken by a woman), which means "brother-in-law." Another form of address is as *niciwâm*, meaning "parallel cousin." Through such ties, newcomers would soon have roles and responsibilities in the family.

Among nations of the Blackfoot Confederacy, the basic social unit was traditionally the clan. The Blackfoot clan was similar in size and function to the Cree extended

The traditional social organization of all First Nations and Inuit groups began with the family, as with this Dene Sųłiné family in the Northwest Territories. Traditional obligations of sharing, education, and mutual support that went along with specific kinship roles in the extended family were fundamental to First Nations social networks. How did such obligations help to take care of people's needs?

family. A clan was generally made up of a chief, his brothers and parents, and others who were not necessarily related. Clan memberships were flexible and individuals were free to join other clans. During hard times, a clan could split up and join with other clans. Among the Piikani, such living groups could include 80 to 240 people, depending on the season.

Beyond the basic social unit of the extended family or clan, First Nations had a variety of social structures. Each family group was generally linked to wider groups sharing common ancestors, language, and other ties. These wider relationships could include societies, nations, alliances, and confederacies.

Clan systems among Eastern Woodlands and Pacific Northwest First Nations were slightly different. For these nations, clans were kinship associations that went beyond the

Kainai

Mamioyiiksi	Fish Eaters
Niiipokskaitapiiksi	Thirty-Trees People
Aakaipokaiksi	Many Children
Pottstakiiksi	Chokers
Mo'toisikskiiksi	All Black Faces
Mo'toisspitaiksi	All Tall People
Mo'toikkakssiiksi	All Short People
Ni'taitsskaiksi	Lone Fighters

Cree

Maskwa	Bear (Plains)
Amisk	Beaver (Woodland)
Wâpôhô	White Owl (Woodland)
Okosâpâhcikaw	Conjurers (Woodland)

Tsuu T'ina

Naa tsis t'a yi	The Clan That Are Reclusive

extended family. Families were often so large and so dispersed over a territory that individuals would not necessarily know all their relatives. Clan memberships simplified kinship connections. Strangers could introduce themselves to a group by identifying their clan and the group could immediately recognize them as a relative, or if not, then most likely as a relative of someone they knew.

All clans had strict rules and traditions, but the specific customs varied from nation to nation. All had marriage rules to ensure that closely related individuals would not marry and have children. Clan members were connected by stories about a common spiritual origin and

important ancestors. Most clans identified themselves with a symbol or totem. The Anishinabé living in the Eastern Woodlands, for example, believed that the Creator had given Earth's people seven clans. Each clan had an animal symbol and each was known for particular kinds of gifts. For example, members of the Bird clan were known as spiritual leaders, while those of the Fish clan were seen as intellectuals or teachers.

Some social groups followed a patrilineal system, which meant a daughter would normally leave her family to live with her husband's family. In **patrilineal** systems, people received their clan identity from their father. Among the Blackfoot, clan lineage was traced primarily through paternal lines, but in some cases was traced through the maternal side if children were descended from a mother from an influential family.

In a **matrilineal** system, sons generally moved away from their families to marry a woman some distance away. Women in these unions retained their family lineage and the men sometimes maintained their own along with their wife's.

SOCIETIES

Nations of the Blackfoot Confederacy had many societies with responsibilities that covered the confederacy's spiritual and administrative functions. Societies included members from all clans so that decisions would have a wide base of consensus. Most of the societies were male oriented and age graded, meaning that as a boy got older, his responsibilities grew more complex. The societies at the top of this order were responsible for the spiritual aspects of traditional Blackfoot life.

The *Kanáttsoomitaiksi* "Brave Dog society" or "Police society" became active at the annual Sundance. They ensured that the orders of the political or war chiefs were enforced. There was also a special women's society, *Máóto'kiiksi* (Buffalo women's society). The rituals of the older societies were known to initiated members only.

The Plains Cree also had a Police or Warrior society, but it was only active during the summer months when hundreds of families gathered for ceremonies and celebrations. The Warrior society ensured that order was kept in the camp and during the communal buffalo hunt. *Okihcihtâwak* (the young men who were part of the Warrior society) had to show exemplary behaviour and uphold the values of the community. Elders who were heads of societies were held in great esteem and, when necessary, would be supported by younger members of the society.

ROLES AND RESPONSIBILITIES

Traditional First Nations communities had greater social equality than European societies at the time, although individual First Nations varied in the degree of equality. In general, people needed each other

to satisfy the requirements of food, clothing, and shelter and to move across large geographic areas. The best way to achieve these objectives was through a culture of sharing and mutual support. Each member of the community contributed something to the other members.

All First Nations and Inuit groups had institutions to ensure that resources were shared fairly. For example, food was distributed equally, regardless of who had killed the game. Trade and gift-giving were common, and everyone was somehow part of a large family group that had obligations to support and help each other.

No person had noticeably more than anyone else. If they did, it was given away. These practices maintained good relationships. Feelings

Les Buckskin Jr.

Nitssaakiaii'nakstssi'si nitsitsitsinssi litskina'yiiksi kii Kanattsoomitaiksi anoo Kainaawa, kii Kiitokiiksi amii Siksikayi. (At a young age I became an active member of the Blood Tribe Horn society, Brave Dog society and Prairie Chicken society of the Siksika Nation.) Through these society memberships I have received knowledge of traditional teachings and doctrines from my spiritual grandparents. I encourage youth to pursue these societies as they assist in your understanding of our unique culture and language. The ability to speak and understand your language makes it a lot easier to comprehend these teachings and society rituals.

— Les Buckskin Jr., Blood Tribe

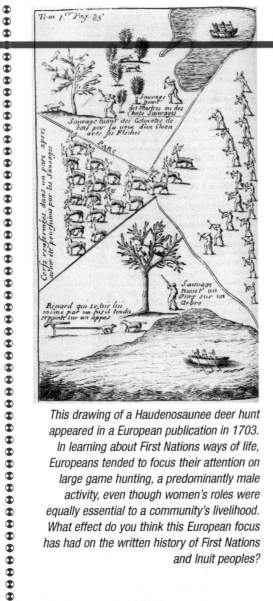

This drawing of a Haudenosaunee deer hunt appeared in a European publication in 1703. In learning about First Nations ways of life, Europeans tended to focus their attention on large game hunting, a predominantly male activity, even though women's roles were equally essential to a community's livelihood. What effect do you think this European focus has had on the written history of First Nations and Inuit peoples?

ONE WITH TWO SPIRITS

First Nations cultures traditionally welcomed individual differences and saw diversity as a gift for the community. For example, in some First Nations communities, the most powerful and respected spiritual people were those with two spirits. Two spirited is a contemporary term that refers to people who are believed to house both male and female spirits in one body. In some cultures, two-spirited individuals were seen as having the ability to see from two perspectives at once. This gift of greater vision was something to be shared. Two-spirited people were sometimes valued leaders, mediators, teachers, artists, and spiritual guides.

of envy and greed were reduced and there was little incentive to acquire more material goods than could be used or given to others. All social incentives encouraged sharing, not possession — the most generous individuals were the most admired.

Each member of a social group had roles and responsibilities. People chose roles that complemented and supported each other. Responsibilities were voluntarily accepted and tasks were shared. Every member of the community had a purpose, including Elders and children.

Men were generally hunters, scouts, and defenders. Boys learned skills related to these future roles.

Women organized the camps, cared for the children, and prepared the game that had been killed in the hunt. Girls generally assisted with tasks such as picking berries.

In some nations, women were also considered the primary teachers and moral keepers of the culture. In Métis history, it was primarily the First Nations women who combined First Nations and European dance, music, clothing, and languages. Through their instruction, the Métis Nation was born and raised.

Roles were flexible and sometimes men and women could and would do one another's jobs, especially in small groups.

Although all members of a group would contribute to the success and security of the whole, individual skill was also admired. People were encouraged to specialize — in spiritual activities, hunting, storytelling, art, or other roles — if they showed special ability. Competition existed, but the reward for excellence was recognition and respect rather than material goods. Mastery of a skill was considered more important than competition with other people. Superior skill enabled an individual to better contribute to the community, which was an honour.

EDUCATION AND SOCIALIZATION

The education system used by traditional First Nations and Inuit communities both taught their culture's worldview and reflected it through example. Often one relative took a child under his or her wing, sharing knowledge about the culture through storytelling.

In traditional education, knowledge was given a practical purpose. Education involved passing on skills, information, and perspectives necessary for spiritual and social balance in the community. The classroom was everyday life, and students understood the relevance of what they learned. Lessons combined learning with laughter, exercise, family, spirituality, and active contribution to the community.

The content of the lessons had been passed on from generation to generation. People would hear the same stories many times throughout their lives. Education was considered an ongoing process, and people were expected to continue learning throughout their lives.

Children often spent time with their aunts, uncles, grandmothers, and grandfathers. During tasks such as picking berries or curing fish, older generations shared stories with younger generations. The stories contained lessons about the natural world and the importance of respect for the land. Stories from the oral tradition taught by offering examples of behaviour — sometimes positive and sometimes negative — but would not dictate what to do. Individuals were guided, but had to make their own decisions.

Children learned a variety of practical skills by observing those around them. For example, in their day-to-day work with others in their community, children learned many ways of sharing and giving to the community and Earth. These practices helped provide for future generations.

Traditional First Nations had a worldview that saw an inherent goodness in all around them. They believed that the Creator made people and everything else in the world with a purpose. They viewed the natural world as generous and giving, as long as humans lived

Many schools today invite Elders and other cultural advisors into the classroom to teach traditional values and skills. Patricia Rain is shown here with a class of elementary students demonstrating how to crush chokecherries for making pemmican. How might this demonstration benefit students?

Learning traditionally took place through storytelling and activity as family members worked alongside one another. What effect would this form of education have on social bonds? How did this system naturally help to enforce a community's laws and customs?

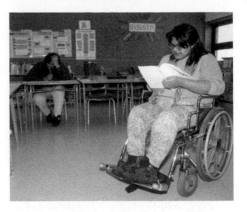

Formal education is a structured system of learning that involves standard curricula, schools, and tests. How do today's methods of formal education in classrooms differ from traditional methods? What are some of the reasons for these differences?

within the natural laws that surrounded them.

Belief in the generosity and good in the world encouraged parents to allow their children the freedom to learn by experience. Each child was seen as having his or her own path to follow — a path given directly by the Creator. It was not up to others, even parents, to change this path.

Every child advanced through his or her own curiosity and need to learn. Children made decisions (and mistakes). Rarely were they physically punished; instead, they experienced the consequences of their actions. The freedom of this personal autonomy allowed individuals to discover their unique gifts.

Elders played a role in guiding young people towards discovery of their gifts and in identifying their skills to other members of the community. As children grew older, they were recognized for their accomplishments in public ceremonies and with songs or give-aways in their honour.

Yet even while the education system encouraged personal autonomy, it also stressed responsibility to others. Children learned to think for themselves and yet act for the good of all.

Traditional teachings embrace the pursuit of living in harmony with oneself, one's family, and one's community, including the community of the natural world. Individuals were expected to regenerate these cultural teachings through their actions, thoughts, and words. In this respect, education was considered everyone's responsibility.

Indigenous Knowledge

If your school regularly invites Elders to be part of the classroom, consider how their presence affects you. Is your educational experience different from that of your parents or grandparents? Write a paragraph comparing your educational experiences with those of a family member from an older generation.

RESOLVING CONFLICT

In traditional First Nations and Inuit communities, appropriate behaviour was considered a personal responsibility. Traditional teachings encouraged people to take this responsibility.

A person who did not respect the customs and laws of his or her community was viewed as lacking self-discipline. Within a traditional worldview, a person who behaved in a disrespectful way to other people, the natural world, or the spiritual realm, was a person who did not recognize the importance of the Creator. Few incentives to break the law existed because individuals saw themselves holistically, as members of a community. They saw rules that were good for the community as being good for themselves.

Conflicts did occur, however, as is typical in all human societies. First Nations and Inuit communities had many ways of handling problems that were in keeping with their worldview. All methods had the restoration of harmony as their ultimate goal.

In traditional First Nations and Inuit communities, laws were viewed as standards of conduct that determined what a person could and could not do in a situation. Customs and laws were not written down, but were passed through the oral tradition.

All teachings reinforced the idea that people needed to respect customs and traditions. Compliance was seen as the natural result of a spiritual understanding of one's place in the world. Family, clan, and community worked together to ensure that every person understood the meaning and importance of proper behaviour. When individuals disobeyed customs and laws, they were reminded of the error of their actions, usually by close relatives. They were given the opportunity to correct their behaviour and make amends for the discord or hurt their actions caused.

If the disruptive behaviour continued, additional reminders were given, sometimes by other relatives and sometimes by other members of the community. In many First Nations, public shaming and embarrassment were tools to encourage conformity. Sometimes unflattering names would be given to people — preventing them from hiding their inappropriate behaviour from others.

Communities might soften the shame by joking or using humour, but their point was clear. If an individual earned a name that pointed to his or her greedy behaviour, the individual and that person's family would be disgraced. Community disapproval was usually enough to curb any further actions that did not respect community laws.

Indigenous Knowledge

Think for a moment about what you know of the Canadian legal system. What is often the goal of its justice? Describe this in your own words. How does it differ from traditional First Nations or Inuit worldviews?

Traditional methods for resolving conflicts reflected respect for all people involved. Each person was given an opportunity to speak to an issue, usually in a talking circle. Every participant in the circle was required to be respectful. This mutual support helped the community reach a resolution while retaining or restoring the dignity of those involved.

If a problem arose in an Inuit village, for example, the entire community would assemble, including the individuals involved in the dispute. An Elder would ask everyone to think about what should happen in a certain situation. He or she might describe the immediate problem, but speak rhetorically, as though it were something that might happen in the future. Everyone, including the disputants, was expected to contribute ideas about how to avoid or correct such a situation.

Most First Nations used similar methods to settle disputes. The priority was on making peace and restoring harmony in the group and between the individuals involved. Problems were resolved without witnesses blaming or speaking against another person, and without anyone being labelled with a criminal record or as a bad person.

Issues for Investigation

COMPARING FORMS OF SOCIAL ORGANIZATION

First Nations had diverse systems of social organization, but they all reflected values such as respect, sharing, generosity, harmony, and unity.

How do different forms of social organization compare?

WHAT TO DO

1. Your job is to compare two systems of social organization with a partner. Compare social organizations from different First Nations or past and present systems from the same First Nation.

2. Consult the library, Internet, or community Elders to find out how the First Nations organized themselves. If possible, invite a guest speaker from the community following protocol set out by your teacher.

3. Make point-form notes in a comparison–contrast chart for the two social organizations you are studying. Consider questions such as, What was the role of women? What role did children play? What kinds of rules structured the society and how were they learned and enforced?

4. Draw two organization diagrams showing the different roles and responsibilities.

5. At the bottom of each, explain the values upheld by the First Nation's social organization. For example, nations that value equality would likely reflect this with systems that share decision making and resources.

6. Prepare a Powerpoint™ presentation of your comparison for your class.

Thinking About Your Project

As a class, discuss common elements of social organizations, as well as variations.

Instead of a fine or jail term, the consequence was a greater understanding of how to live together by everyone in the community.

Where problems occurred during large gatherings, such as during a Blackfoot or Plains Cree Sundance or communal buffalo hunt, they were handled by the Warrior society. If, for example, a hunter ignored the rules of the annual Plains Cree buffalo hunt, the Warrior society might destroy his tent and take his belongings. If the individual showed that he was sorry, however, society members would return his things and perhaps give some of their own to take away bad feelings and restore harmony once again.

For serious infractions, punishments could include banishment from the group and for rare crimes such as murder, in some communities a victim's family might be allowed to retaliate by taking the murderer's life. Once this was done, the matter was considered over. Harbouring a grudge or bad feelings was not acceptable.

The Blood Police were originally considered a continuation of the Brave Dog society or "scouts," which is the traditional policing and protecting service of the Blood people. The half circles with the squiggly lines in the lower half of the circle represent the people in this society. They are arranged as they appear on the badge because, when the people were on the move, the scouts would go up ahead and watch out for danger. If they saw a problem, they would go back and warn the group — always returning in a zigzag pattern so they couldn't be followed.

The Kainai First Nation operates its own police force. The Kainai's traditional Kanáttsoomitaiksi — "Brave Dog society" — today incorporates contemporary law-enforcement techniques with cultural understanding.

The peace pipe is there, first, because the police exist to preserve the peace. Second, it is a symbol of the signing of Treaty Seven. When it was signed, the different parties smoked a peace pipe. Above the pipe is a sun, green grass, running water, and a mountain: when the treaty was signed, it was to be in force "as long as the sun shines, the rivers flow, and the grass grows." The mountain is Chief Mountain, which is visible from the reserve and is part of the Blood people's traditional lands, although it is now in the US and outside the reserve. It is a holy site to the Blackfoot people, and they go there to worship.

— Constable Joe Many Fingers, Blood Tribe Police Service

LOOKING BACK

Before moving on to the next section, be sure you can describe the following institutions for traditional First Nations: extended family, clan, society, education, conflict resolution.

Economic Organization

AS YOU READ

In general, traditional First Nations and Inuit worldviews led to economic systems that stressed self-reliance, thoughtful use of resources, and sharing through family networks. Everyone contributed and was in turn taken care of in a system of mutual support. As you read pages 116–119, compare how European economic models differ from traditional First Nations and Inuit models.

I N ORDER FOR ANY SOCIETY TO MAINTAIN THE WELL-BEING OF ITS PEOPLE, IT MUST HAVE SOME SORT OF ECONOMIC SYSTEM IN PLACE — AN AGREED-UPON SET OF RULES OR CONVENTIONS THAT ALLOWS FOR THE SATISFACTION OF BASIC human needs. All economic systems address the same fundamental questions. What is to be produced (food, material goods, clothing, shelter)? How are goods to be produced (human labour, machines, animal power)? Who gets what has been produced (those who can afford it, those who need it most, shared among all)?

All over the contemporary world, the European model of supply and demand — also known as capitalism, the market system, or private enterprise — is increasingly becoming the dominant economic system.

What goods or services are produced (supply) is determined by what people want (demand). Who gets those goods and services (distribution) is based on who can afford them. Price is established by the available supply of the product. The greater the demand and lower the supply, the higher the price. For example, only some people can afford to buy gold or diamonds or a private jet because these things are expensive and not many are available. However, T-shirts are cheap and plentiful. Many people therefore own one or more.

In capitalist systems, people generally work in one part of the economy and purchase everything else they need. Complete **self-sufficiency** or independence from goods and services provided by other people is rare.

Many people in today's industrialized nations work hard to accumulate wealth. With this wealth, they consume more goods. This kind of consumption has more to do with status and desire than need.

Many people are concerned that the natural world cannot replenish itself in the face of such exploitation. In this sense, **exploitation** is the unethical use of the planet's natural resources to satisfy short-term desires at the expense of future generations. Keep in mind, however, that there are more people in the world today than in centuries past. Some people argue that the world is running out of certain resources because more people need more food, homes, and material comforts. Others maintain that more moderate use and consumption habits would ensure enough for future generations.

In communism, another economic model that is used by a few countries in the world, the society also exploits the planet's resources to achieve comfort and security for the human population, but the

The capitalist system can mean a great standard of living, as shown in the photograph on the left of a kitchen from an affluent home. However, it can also mean enormous differences in lifestyle between the wealthy and poor. Compare the photograph of the kitchen to the photograph on the right of the homeless shelter in Edmonton, Alberta. How did traditional institutions such as the give-away help deal with such economic differences between people?

distribution of these resources is more equitable. Everyone shares what is produced according to need rather than ability to pay. In reality, however, many inequalities persist, even in societies with communist ideals.

Traditional First Nations and Inuit peoples' economic systems are distinctly different from capitalist and communist systems because their worldviews see a fundamentally different relationship between humans and the planet.

Through the oral tradition, First Nations and Inuit peoples learn that the Creator and the natural world supply everything needed for life. This provision is not, however, without restriction. All things in nature — plants, animals, mountains, and streams — are equal to humans and must be respected as such. Demand for Earth's resources must therefore be modest and according to need.

Traditional First Nations and Inuit ways of consuming resources also differed markedly from those of capitalist systems. People took from the land only as much as they needed. In part, this practice reflected practicality. It did not make sense to possess an abundance of goods that had to be moved from

place to place each season. More importantly, collecting more than was needed would be wasteful and show a lack of respect for Mother Earth's gifts.

To be sure, a hunt might be very successful and the community might enjoy an abundance of food, hides, or fur, but no one would have hunted extra animals just for fun. Strict rules governing the use of resources meant that plants and animals could replenish themselves regularly.

Traditional First Nations and Inuit economic systems were based on harmony with nature, but also on equality and sharing within the community. As you learned on page 75, the method of food distribution after a large game hunt illustrates principles of sharing and equality. If group of ten hunters went out in search of deer, even if only three actually participated in the kill, all the families of the ten hunters received equal portions of meat. This arrangement meant that the whole group ate, regardless of luck or circumstance.

Theoretically, a single hunter might get lazy or choose not to work hard, knowing that he would benefit from the hunt anyway. This tended not to happen because pride and status were important incentives.

TRADE

As you learned on pages 16–22, First Nations and Inuit peoples were adept at using all their territory's resources, moving seasonally to take advantage of them. In most regions, people could supply all of their basic needs within their own territories.

However, seasonal migrations often brought different nations into contact with one another. At certain times of the year, territories might overlap. For example, Nakoda peoples once spent summers on the prairie and winters in the parkland, the region between the woodland forests of the Subarctic and the grasslands of the Plains. There they often encountered Plains Cree who followed a similar pattern of movement. The two nations coexisted peacefully, exchanging ideas and knowledge that benefited them both.

Groups that encountered one another would trade stories and news of other regions, often passing along useful technologies or ideas. Sometimes groups could immediately use a new technology and other times the group would adapt it to meet the specific needs and resources of their environment.

Because groups migrated in regular patterns, many such cultural encounters led to trading relationships that were sometimes centuries old. The map on page 119 shows some of the established routes and goods that were common trade items during the centuries before European contact.

Obsidian, a volcanic glass, was an important trade good. It was highly valued for its ability to cut other materials. Groups also likely traded food and other perishable products, but there is no archaeological evidence of this.

Sometimes groups travelled very far for specific trade items. For example, northern Plains First Nations sometimes made long trips to trade items made from their staple — the buffalo — for things such as shells, paint, and salt from groups living near the Great Salt Lake.

Most of the time, however, objects travelled farther than the people who made them. Nations traded with neighbouring nations as part of their seasonal migrations and as part of established alliances. Archaeological evidence indicates that Ena K'ering Ká Tuwe (Cree Burn Lake), along the Athabasca

Indigenous Knowledge

Read the perspective below about how the Haudenosaunee Confederacy agreed to organize itself economically. Describe the arrangements in your own words.

The Great Law of Peace used a metaphor to describe how the nations of the confederacy would share the land's resources:

We shall only have one dish (or bowl) in which will be placed one beaver's tail, and we shall all have coequal right to it, and there shall be no knife in it, for if there be a knife in it, there would be danger that it might cut someone and blood would thereby be shed.

— translation of the Great Law of Peace from a committee of chiefs including Skaniadariio (John A. Gibson), Kanongweya (Jacob Johnson), and Deyonhegwen (John William Elliott), Grand River Territory (1907)

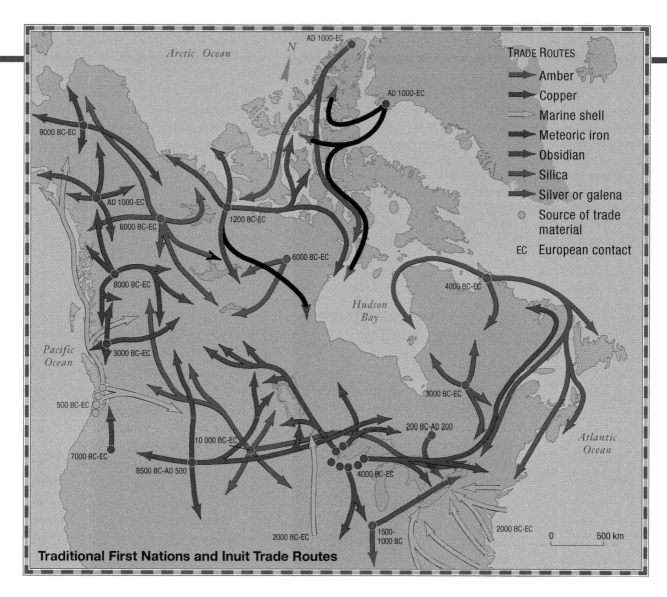

TRADE ROUTES

→ Amber
→ Copper
→ Marine shell
→ Meteoric iron
→ Obsidian
→ Silica
→ Silver or galena
○ Source of trade material
EC European contact

Arctic Ocean

AD 1000-EC

AD 1000-EC

9000 BC-EC

AD 1000-EC
6000 BC-EC

1200 BC-EC

6000 BC-EC

8000 BC-EC

Hudson Bay

4000 BC-EC

3000 BC-EC

Pacific Ocean

500 BC-EC

3000 BC-EC

3000 BC-EC

200 BC-AD 200

Atlantic Ocean

7000 BC-EC

10 000 BC-EC

8500 BC-AD 500

4000 BC-EC

2000 BC-EC

0   500 km

2000 BC-EC

1500-1000 BC

Traditional First Nations and Inuit Trade Routes

River between Lake Athabasca and Fort McMurray, was a major trading centre. Many First Nations visited the site to take advantage of the area's tar sands (used for repairing canoes) and stone (used for making pipes).

Head-Smashed-In near Lethbridge, Alberta, was also a major trading centre. The buffalo was such an important resource that many nations gathered there each summer to make use of it. A group might trade for an item and then later trade the same item with another nation who lived farther away. This process might continue until some goods ended up hundreds or thousands of kilometres from the original people who produced them.

LOOKING BACK

Write a paragraph describing traditional First Nations economic systems by comparing them to contemporary systems such as capitalism and communism.

Traditional First Nations and Inuit peoples had diverse forms of governance. Common to all forms, however, was a worldview that stressed relationships between people, the land, and the spiritual world. Before beginning this section, work with a group to discuss how you would expect traditional First Nations and Inuit worldviews to influence their systems of government and decision making. What values would influence how decisions would be made?

GOVERNANCE IN TRADITIONAL FIRST NATIONS AND Inuit COMMUNITIES WAS HIGHLY DECENTRALIZED AND DEMOCRATIC, ALTHOUGH NOT DEMOCRATIC LIKE CANADA'S CONTEMPORARY ELECTORAL SYSTEM. THESE traditional peoples were democratic in the sense that everyone in the community had the opportunity to voice their opinions and participate in making decisions for the common good.

Individuals held equal power in decision making councils and consensus, rather than voting, was the method used to make decisions. A **consensus** is a collective opinion. As a decision making method, it allows for a resolution that respects many viewpoints and ideas. Leaders had the role of guiding or assisting the group in reaching resolutions. Leaders did not make unilateral decisions or try to impose their own ideas on others. In disputes or disagreements, respect for different opinions was maintained and efforts were made to find a middle ground that would allow all parties to retain respect and status.

The people were the government. Leaders were the servants of the people. People with leadership skills — the ability to speak well, build consensus and agreement, and resolve conflict — also needed to be those who could acquire many material goods (and distribute them). The ability to give generously was an important qualification for leaders in all First Nations.

In most traditional First Nations, leadership was not concentrated in the hands of a chief. Power was dispersed among groups of people and individuals. For example, Elders were highly influential. They often guided and advised other leaders and they helped the community identify people who displayed leadership qualities.

Spiritual leaders — those responsible for the spiritual health of the community — were also highly influential. No decision was made without considering the spiritual consequences.

Various customs and values gave the community effective control over their leaders. Leadership accountability was based on the shared belief that the well-being of the community was more important than individual self-interest.

The regional director general for Indian Affairs, Barrie Robb, greets 106-year-old Rapheal Cree from the Gregoire Lake reserve in July 1999. Cree presented the department with a statement of claim for $1.6 billion in damages suffered by members of the Paul Band. Why do you think the band had an Elder present the statement rather than an elected leader?

DECISION MAKING

As you learned on page 81, traditional worldviews as reflected in Aboriginal languages see the world in a constant state of change. Because of this perspective, traditional communities accepted all viewpoints as important contributions to decision making. No single person could know or understand everything about the world because the world was always changing. Views of children and young people were considered seriously, although Elders, because of their experience, generally had the most influence.

During meetings, differences of opinion would naturally appear. Everyone was expected to listen to those who held dissenting views. When differences were great, Elders were consulted to establish a common position that could be shared by all. This was often accomplished

Non-Aboriginal historians have tended to focus their attention on chiefs, such as Issapoomahksika (Crowfoot) of the Siksika First Nation, as the leaders of First Nations communities. In reality, traditional First Nations leadership was found in many individuals. Leaders such as Issapoomahksika became important during treaty negotiations in the late nineteenth century because the Europeans would usually insist upon negotiating or speaking with only one leader from a community.

Spirituality is the highest form of politics, and our spirituality is directly involved in government. As chiefs we are told that our first and most important duty is to see that the spiritual ceremonies are carried out. Without the ceremonies, one does not have a basis on which to conduct government for the welfare of the people. This is not only for our people but for the good of all living things in general. So we are told first to conduct the ceremonies on time, in the proper manner, and then to sit in council for the welfare of our people and all life.

— Oren Lyons, Onondaga

Indigenous Knowledge

Read the story told by Bernie Makokis below. In your own words, explain what the story is saying about traditional First Nations leadership.

There was a great chief who gathered his people every morning to inform them of his leadership. One man was always pessimistic and questioned the chief on every matter he presented. The people were often annoyed with this negative man. One day the man died and the people rejoiced. They went to the chief and asked him if he would rejoice with them. The wise chief went silent for a while and then said softly "He was the only one who kept me on my feet."

— Bernie Makokis, Saddle Lake First Nation

This photograph shows a meeting in 2004 of all First Nations chiefs in Alberta. The leaders meet four times a year to discuss common concerns. From left to right at the meeting table: Alexander First Nation Chief Victoria Arcand, Ermineskin First Nation Chief George Minde, Saddle Lake First Nation Chief Eddy Makokis, Driftpile First Nation Chief Rose Laboucan, and Beaver First Nation Chief Barb Wendt. Research how this group runs its meetings and makes decisions. Are their systems First Nations, European, or a combination?

through negotiations with the dissenters. If a person could not agree with the emerging consensus, custom required the person to withdraw from the discussion to preserve group harmony.

Consensus was important to group unity and harmony. It was considered more important to take time to develop common agreement than to reach a quick and efficient decision. Groups were small enough that these systems of discussion and consensus were practical, even if they were sometimes slow.

Decisions were adopted if they promoted the common good of the whole community. The common good meant not only the community making the decision, but also the good of future generations and the natural and spiritual world. First Nations took a holistic view of decisions.

Once a consensus appeared, the discussion of the problem came to an end. Custom required that all members of the community accept the group decision or law. Acceptance of a decision was necessary for group harmony.

Issues for Investigation

MAKING GROUP DECISIONS

In a direct democracy, every individual has the right to vote on decisions that affect the community. The majority vote wins.

What are the differences between direct democracy and consensus decision making?

WHAT TO DO

1. As a class, decide upon two issues or problems that affect your school.

2. For the first problem, have at least two students give speeches about how they would like to see the problem solved. As a class, vote with a secret ballot to decide upon a solution.

3. For the second problem, use consensus decision making to arrive at a solution.

Thinking About Your Project

After the exercise, debate the merits of the two systems as a class. Which was faster? Compare how people felt after each decision was made. Were leaders necessary? Did leaders who guided the decisions emerge naturally from the class or was a more formal selection of leaders necessary?

ABORIGINAL PERSPECTIVES

DOROTHY MCDONALD
Fort McKay First Nation

Dorothy McDonald

Dorothy McDonald is a courageous woman who stood up against a corporate giant — an oil sands plant that was finally brought to justice for polluting the water her people had depended on for centuries.

"When you walk the good road, you know what is right. Your spirituality guides you, and anything is possible," she says of her battles with industry. She was never afraid of her powerful opposition and describes her efforts as a necessary obligation as a "keeper of the land."

As chief of the Fort McKay First Nation between 1980 and 1986, McDonald made many improvements in the quality of life for her people, working to develop such services as a sewage system, water treatment plant, upgraded roads, and improved housing. She also initiated the Fort McKay Group of Companies in the mid-1980s, which currently earn more than $2 million a month.

McDonald comes by her leadership abilities and strong convictions naturally. As a young woman, she wrote proposals for her father, Phillip McDonald, who was chief of the Fort McKay First Nation for thirty years. When he passed away, McDonald followed in his footsteps to "finish his work."

Her mother, Victoria, told her stories of growing up near the Athabasca River and how important it was to the Dene Sųłiné people.

"We lived on the river. It was our life," recalls her mother, explaining that the people depended on the Athabasca River for drinking water, fishing, and travel.

Says McDonald "We'd both like to see the environment remain the way it is. We can never go back to the old ways, but we can make the future better by taking the best of the non-native and native worlds and preserving our lands and waters using technology and respect."

McDonald is a passionate advocate for the environment and continues to protect it to the best of her ability. She is hoping young people will take up where her generation leaves off.

"I have always said to young people 'We are the keepers of the land. As keepers of the land we are also the spirit of the land. If we lose that spirit, we lose everything, and we will be like the buffalo. Learn your people's ways and your local history. Know who you are and that you are part of that source.'"

"If you take care of the land, it will take care of you," McDonald concludes.

◼ REFLECTION

Research the story behind Dorothy McDonald's fight against pollution in her community.

How do First Nations, Métis, and Inuit leaders balance concern for the environment with the economic needs of their communities? Study an economic development project in Alberta that impacts a First Nations or Métis community and prepare a one-page summary that shows the benefits and drawbacks of the development.

CASE STUDIES OF TRADITIONAL GOVERNANCE SYSTEMS

Leadership within traditional First Nations required respect, wisdom, and caring. Leaders were expected to show initiative, guidance, and consideration for the will of the people. Although different groups had different methods of choosing leaders, all leaders were expected to manage the affairs and issues of their people fairly and equitably.

On pages 125–129, you will read about traditional governance systems from four different regions in Canada. Each system reflects the needs of the people living in that region. As you learned on pages 8–15, both the Haudenosaunee nations and the nations of the Pacific Northwest had relatively settled lifestyles. Although both incorporated some form of migration into their social and economic systems, they tended to live for extended periods of time in one or two locations.

Large numbers of people lived together most of the year. This lifestyle encouraged complex social and political systems. On page 124, you will read about the Haudenosaunee Confederacy of the Eastern Woodlands region. On page 125, you will then study one of the most important political, economic, and social institutions of the Pacific Northwest — the potlatch.

In contrast, the First Nations of the Plains, Subarctic, and Arctic regions tended to move much more regularly. People usually lived in smaller groups in these areas. Their groups were normally based on the extended family. On page 126–127 you will learn how Inuit peoples looked upon leadership in their communities. Finally, on pages 127–129, you will learn about how First Nations from Alberta traditionally chose their leaders and governed both small and large groups of people.

Haudenosaunee Confederacy

The Haudenosaunee Confederacy of the Six Nations — Cayuga, Mohawk, Oneida, Onondaga, Seneca, and Tuscarora — was a remarkable model of large-scale organization. Beginning in 1451, five (later six) nations of similar (but not the same) language and culture lived peacefully side-by-side south of the St. Lawrence River.

This photograph shows a meeting of the hereditary council of the Six Nations in 1898. Although leadership tended to fall in specific families, individuals had to earn their authority and status by making decisions that benefited the community.

The nations were independent and autonomous in internal matters, but drew together in a larger group to resolve issues among themselves and to defend their territory from outsiders. This confederacy's structure and organization is believed by many to have influenced the design of federal democracies that came later, such as the United States.

A **constitution**, called the Great Law of Peace, provided rules for a democratic system in which each family clan had a female and male leader to speak on its behalf.

The confederacy's government included the Grand Council. This council met annually to discuss common concerns. It included representatives, or chiefs, from each nation, who were all considered equal in power and authority. Elder women consulted with clans on the selection of their chiefs.

Although people regarded most other members of the community as equal in status, some differences in wealth and rank existed. Some people and their descendants became leaders on the basis of their hereditary rank as well as their skill and personality.

Grand Council debates were bound by rules that promoted order and unity. Decisions had to respect the rights and status of all the confederacy's member nations. Decisions needed to be unanimous and were achieved through the process of consensus. This system of shared leadership was important for maintaining unity among the nations of the confederacy.

Indigenous Knowledge

How are economic principles of sharing a part of the government systems of the Haudenosaunee Confederacy and Pacific Northwest First Nations? How do these principles relate to the ideas you learned in Chapter Three about traditional worldviews? List as many examples as you can.

Pacific Northwest

Among the Pacific Northwest First Nations, power and influence was concentrated in hereditary groups with greater status and higher rank. However, as with Haudenosaunee governance, leaders were chosen for their personal qualities as well as for their family rank.

Leaders could request a share of the production of every community member for public functions and ceremonial gatherings. The leaders also had the ability to organize work in the community, regulate the use of land, and make decisions about trade and relationships with other nations.

Leaders held potlatches to enhance their social prestige and demonstrate their ability to promote the well-being of the community. The potlatch was a gathering of people from different villages and coastal communities. It involved fasting, songs, spiritual dances, speeches, and the distribution of gifts. An important potlatch could be many years in the making and last for several days. The goal of the potlatch was to strengthen ties between different communities and to affirm a common sense of identity within a single community.

First Nations all the way up the Pacific coastline and even into inland regions in northern British Columbia held potlatches. Here dancers attend an 1895 potlatch at Chilkat, Alaska.

The distribution of gifts during the potlatch helped maintain harmony in the community so that disparities in wealth did not grow too large and lead to tensions.

The potlatch acknowledged and affirmed the status of the chief. A leader who governed the community wisely and fairly enjoyed greater wealth and prosperity, which was then redistributed among the members of the community. It was a matter of great pride for a chief to be able to give generously to those in need or those of lesser means.

If a chief managed the community poorly, community members might ignore requests for the materials they produced or they might give only a small share. A chief brought disgrace on the community during the potlatch if he could not demonstrate great generosity to the community and to chiefs of other communities. Such disgrace would probably lead to a change in leadership.

Inuit Leadership and Community Organization

In a submission to the Royal Commission on Aboriginal Peoples in 1986, Paulus Maggo, a Labrador Inuk hunter, describes how he became a leader. After many hunting trips with Maggo, an older man who was respected in the community as a hunter and leader started asking Maggo questions about where to go and when to stop. At first Maggo was taken aback, thinking "Me? Instructing the one who once was always my leader?" Gradually, however, Maggo began to make more decisions. In doing so, a transfer of leadership took place.

The example provided by Paulus Maggo demonstrates the gradual, natural process of leadership selection that worked well for traditional Inuit communities.

Most traditional Inuit groups were led by an *isumataq* (or *ihumataq*), which means "one who thinks." This leader was usually an older male with some kind of kinship status in the group — a respected father, uncle, or grandfather. In addition, the *isumataq* would be recognized by the community as a good hunter and wise decision maker, as well as being a role model of Inuit values such as sharing. People followed the *isumataq* of their own free will and could ignore his advice or even leave the group if they lost confidence the *isumataq*'s decision making.

Living groups were generally formed on the basis of kinship, although the composition of kinship groups varied from community to community. Beyond the family group, Inuit peoples lived in camps that varied in size depending on the season. Several camps would have a sense of common identity.

A typical camp had thirty to fifty people. A winter seal-hunting technique called *mauliqtuq* "breathing hole" sealing required at least this many people.

When the ice is frozen over in the winter, seals use breaks in the ice called breathing holes to surface for air. Hunters wait quietly at these holes until a seal appears. Because seals use many breathing holes, hunters spread out over a territory so that they can watch as many as possible. This increases their chances of a successful hunt.

Plains First Nations

Like Inuit peoples, Cree and Blackfoot First Nations tended to have smaller and less formal governance systems compared to the Haudenosaunee or Pacific Northwest First Nations. Within extended families or clans, people usually had the same status and there were no major differences in wealth or rank. Everyone was entitled to the same treatment and had the right to receive food when it was needed.

Members of a group contributed to the selection of their leader, which was often a gradual or natural process. Leaders would emerge through recognition (sometimes

— SKINNING THE SEAL —

unspoken) by other group members who would consistently turn to that person for guidance.

For an outsider, understanding who were leaders in a community might require spending time closely observing people's behaviour. Respect was evident in the influence an individual's opinions held at meetings. Similarly, a more respected member of a community might sit farthest from the door of a council meeting lodge, while a community member with less status might sit near the door or have no buffalo robe to sit upon.

Sometimes leadership was inherited by members of the same family or clan, but only if the leader's abilities warranted the role. Leadership qualities that were

Inuit peoples made economical use of every animal they hunted. The seal provided meat and fat for oil. Its waterproof skin was used for everything from clothing, beds, and boots, to kayaks, umiaks, and tents.

I knew the land well so I didn't mind taking charge of a hunting party and did it to the best of my ability. I was always able to take them back to home base in the dark or through stormy weather as long as it didn't get too stormy, and we were able to keep on moving as long as I could see the stars at night. … Although I was not the most clever hunter, they'd always pick me as leader. I guess it was because I had the most experience travelling in the country.

— Paulus Maggo, Labrador Inuk,
Report of the Royal Commission on Aboriginal Peoples

much admired were also useful qualities for day-to-day life — skills in hunting or war, bravery, generosity, spiritual knowledge, and personal initiative.

Leaders remained leaders only as long as they had the support of their fellow group members and as long as a leader was required for specific circumstances. Leadership might change to suit different needs. One person might have exceptional skill in hunting and might lead that activity, while another individual might be a better leader in dealing with other nations. Someone else might be good at resolving disputes or advising the group about spiritual matters. If a leader lost respect for any reason, followers would begin to turn to someone else for guidance.

Large gatherings of many groups were opportunities for

Issues for Investigation

LOOKING INTO LEADERSHIP

The issues facing Aboriginal peoples today have changed from earlier times. However, the skills required for leadership today are much like those of in the past.

What leadership qualities are admired in First Nations, Métis, and Inuit communities?

WHAT TO DO

1. Choose an Aboriginal leader of the past. You can select one from any geographic area, but make sure you can find enough information about the person. To get an idea of which region you might want to focus upon, read the case studies discussed on pages 124–129.

2. Using history books, the Internet, or information from an oral tradition, examine the leader's upbringing and traditional education. If possible, find out how the leader's personal experiences (as a hunter, spiritual advisor, warrior, etc.) helped him or her assume a position of leadership.

3. Select a contemporary Aboriginal leader (preferably from the same cultural group or region as the leader you chose in number 1). Using books, television reports, newspapers, magazines, the Internet, and possibly interviews, investigate his or her upbringing and education. Include both traditional and formal education.

4. In point form, note the major issues and challenges that each leader, past and present, has had to face.

5. Role play one of your leaders to show how he or she would handle an issue affecting their community. Be sure that your portrayal reflects the research you have done. You might, for example, present a speech, ask for input, and give guidance on how to manage the issue. Effective role playing focuses upon the issue rather than the person. Be sure your role play does not bring to life any stereotypes.

6. Ask for class feedback on how well they think your role play reflected Aboriginal leadership qualities and values.

Thinking About Your Project
In an essay, summarize the similarities and differences between the leadership qualities of the leaders you researched. Are there common characteristics that are reflected in both leaders? Be sure to include an analysis of why you think these similarities and differences (if any) exist.

people to realign themselves with different leaders. The Woodland Cree had their large gatherings in the spring, while the Plains Cree and the Blackfoot Confederacy met in large groups in midsummer, when buffalo herds gathered in large herds for grazing. While sharing the work of a large buffalo hunt, groups would live together for a few weeks, sorting out issues and discussing matters of common concern.

At large gatherings, leaders from each group formed a council to discuss issues and make decisions. A **council** is a formal group that discusses issues and advises upon courses of action. Councils of many nations could not force groups to comply with their decisions. Group leaders and their followers were free to comply with the group consensus, leave, or join other groups.

Leaders rarely gave orders in day-to-day living, and only did so when order was required at large gatherings.

Leaders recognized the right of other members to have a say in decision making. Good leaders set

Many leaders are informal rather than formal, elected officials. Informal leaders are individuals who other community members consistently turn to for guidance. As in the past, community leaders in Aboriginal communities today are often informal, such as these Fort Chipewyan Elders — Red Adams (left) and Joseph Marie Marcel.

an example by respecting the opinions of others in the group.

Leaders were recognized partly because of their ability to recommend solutions to their community. Elders discussed and approved a leader's recommendations. If an issue was a difficult one, it took some time before the Elders could reach a decision because they wanted a consensus. Once the Elders approved a leader's recommendation, everyone in the group accepted it.

When we chose our leaders in the past, we always chose those who lived well-ordered lives. We did not refer to such a person as "chief," we just said that this person "led us" and that we "followed this person."

— Adam Delaney, Kainai First Nation, *Kipaitapiiwahsinnooni: Alcohol and Drug Abuse Education Program*

LOOKING BACK

Using a specific example for each, describe how principles of equality, mutual support, sharing, generosity, and harmony were fundamental to traditional First Nations and Inuit government systems. How was leadership both hereditary and earned in traditional communities? Give a specific example of how this worked.

Chapter Four Review

Check Your Understanding

1. Why do human societies organize themselves into social groups?

2. Why was cooperation important to traditional First Nations systems of social organization?

3. Beyond the extended family, what other kinds of ties united wider groups? Name at least three.

4. What Is the difference between a matrilineal and a patrilineal system? How do they work?

5. Describe how traditional First Nations people educated their children.

Many day-to-day tasks in traditional societies were labour intensive, as shown by this Woodland Cree woman scraping a moosehide in northeastern Alberta. Cooperation between members of a family was important in making sure needs were taken care of. Traditional First Nations political, economic, and social institutions helped ensure that people had this cooperation.

It usually takes more than one person to prepare a hide; five women could do it in one day. They put it on a stretcher and scrape all the moose hair off. The People used to make a moose-scraper out of the calf bone of a moose. After all the fur is scraped off, brains or fat are put on top of the hide to soften it. You keep stretching it, taking it off the stretcher to stretch it manually. Then you smoke the hide.

— adapted from a story told by Alice Boucher in *Inkonze: The Stones of Traditional Knowledge*

6. What was the traditional First Nations philosophy of child rearing? How did children learn responsibility?

7. What values did traditional First Nations economic systems maintain?

8. How did traditional First Nations manage the natural resources of their territory? How does this compare with contemporary use of natural resources?

9. Why did First Nations living in the Arctic, Subarctic, and Plains regions tend not to accumulate many material goods in the past?

10. How was game distributed after a hunt in most traditional First Nations? Why was this system used?

11. What were the functions of the potlatch among Pacific Northwest First Nations?

12. Describe traditional First Nations methods of conflict resolution. What was the primary goal?

13. Building on what you learned in previous chapters, describe the roles of Elders in traditional First Nations.

14. What is consensus decision making?

15. How did leadership change depending on specific circumstances? Give examples.

16. What role did Elders play with respect to important decisions?

17. Why did people in traditional First Nations and Inuit groups usually follow their community's laws and customs?

18. Why was generosity an important leadership quality in traditional First Nations?

19. How was trade an important part of traditional economic and political systems?

Reading and Writing

20. Read the statement by Mary Wells on page 131. How does the story demonstrate traditional First Nations educational methods? Contrast these traditional systems of education with contemporary systems of formal education. What are the benefits of each system? Prepare a chart that presents your ideas.

Viewing and Representing

21. Look at the photograph on page 130 and read the statement about the work involved in preparing a single moose hide. Write a short story about a person living in this traditional society.

22. Watch a documentary about traditional First Nations ways of life (your teacher may be able to order one). Write down your reflections in a journal entry about what you admire about these traditional ways.

23. Research the kinds of objects that were used in traditional trading relationships. Make a model or draw a picture of one or two and display them in the classroom.

24. What leadership qualities were usually admired among traditional First Nations? Make a collage from magazines and newspapers that shows your own ideas about leadership.

Going Further

25. Invite a guest speaker to talk about a contemporary First Nations, Métis, or Inuit government. Ask your speaker to discuss ways the government is similar to or different from traditional forms of governance. Invite the whole school to attend. After the talk, discuss how this contemporary government compares to traditional styles of governance. What are the reasons for these differences?

[My] grandmother went berry-picking and found blueberries. Oh my, I had never tasted blueberries until then, I really liked the taste, especially with sugar on them. And my grandmother went berry-picking again and fed me some and I asked for sugar, but my mom told me: "There is not enough sugar for you to put on your berries." ... But I had seen where my mom had stored the sugar. She had put it in a syrup pail and hung it in a tree. Well, as soon as I thought no one was looking that way, I went up the tree, climbing up for the sugar. Well, climbing up far enough to reach it, I just used my bare hands to dip into the pail for the sugar. But a bee must have gotten inside the pail, too, trying to steal the sugar, too, and wouldn't you know it, it stung me! By gosh the sting really hurt, and I just fell down off the tree; oh, I cried as hard as I could. When my grandmother came running, "What's wrong iskwêw?" (she used to call me iskwêw), I was crying so hard. "A bee stung me while I was trying to take some sugar for myself over there," I told her through my tears. *Wâh-wahwâ, kiwawiyatisin!" k-êsit awa nôhkom, "ahpô êwako kika-kiskinohamokon êkây kîhtwâm tita-kakwê-kimotiyan kîkway."* ("Oh my oh my, serves you right!" my grandmother said to me, "maybe this will teach you not to try and steal things again.") No one felt sorry for me when the bee had stung me so hard.

— Mary Wells, Elizabeth Settlement, Kôhkominawak Otâcimowiniwâwa (Our Grandmother's Lives As Told in their Own Words)

LOOKING BACK

Re-read Leo Fox's story from pages 104–105, thinking about the roles and responsibilities of young people in traditional First Nations communities. How do these roles compare to the responsibilities of young people today?

CHAPTER FIVE
Contact and Cultural Exchange

AS YOU READ

As you've learned in previous chapters, First Nations and Inuit peoples lived well on the land for thousands of years before the arrival of Europeans to North America. Contact with European cultures that began at the end of the fifteenth century did not immediately change this situation. In general, early relationships between First Nations and Europeans were mutually beneficial, with First Nations acquiring useful trade goods and Europeans acquiring skills and technology needed for life in North America. Over time, however, benefits for the Europeans began to far outweigh benefits for the First Nations. This chapter will help you understand how and why this significant shift occurred.

In the reading that follows, Sahtú Dene Elder George Blondin describes traditional life and post-contact life for his people. As you read the rest of this chapter, consider how contact affected the lives of his people and how these effects are similar to and different from the experiences of other First Nations and Inuit communities.

As you read this chapter, consider these questions:

▲ In what ways was early trade between Europeans and First Nations mutually beneficial?

▲ How did the relationship between Europeans and First Nations change over time? Why did this change occur?

▲ How does the history of the Métis Nation provide examples of innovative and adaptive cultural exchange?

▲ What were the roles and contributions of Aboriginal peoples to the historical fur trade?

▲ How did the decline of the fur trade affect Aboriginal peoples?

A Way of Life in Transition

Adapted from *Yamoria the Lawmaker: Stories of the Dene* by Sahtú Dene Elder George Blondin

---

Yamǫǫzhaa ts'edi sì dǫne wegondi ło hǫt'e.

Yamoria was possibly the greatest medicine power person in the world when the world was new.

BEFORE EUROPEAN CONTACT, MUCH LABOUR WAS INVOLVED IN FINDING FOOD AND PREPARING CLOTHES, SHELTERS, AND TOOLS. FORTUNATELY, "WHEN THE WORLD WAS NEW," fish and game were plentiful. My people moved within the seasonal circle of life, hunting moose and caribou, tanning hides, picking berries, and gathering for ceremonies and celebrations. Storytellers say it was a time when people could communicate with animals and fly across the land in spirit form. Medicine powers governed my people's lives as in the story that follows:

When the world was new, animals and humans held a conference to see how they would relate to each other. Yamoria used medicine power to control everyone's mind to arrive at a fair resolution. The meeting lasted a long time and involved humans and every bird, fish, and animal that lived on the earth. All agreed that humans could use animals, birds, and fish for food, providing that humans killed only what they needed to survive and treated their prey with great respect. Humans must use every part of the animal and never waste anything.

It was also made law that humans take the bones of the prey and place them in a tree or scaffold high above the ground. And finally, humans were told to always think well of animals and thank the Creator for putting them on the earth.

When the conference was over, communication was still possible between humans and animals, especially when medicine people needed to talk to animal leaders regarding issues not resolved at the conference. Slowly, communication between the two life forms dwindled, until today it is rare to find someone who can talk to animals.

Before contact, my ancestors travelled constantly, hunting caribou herds for meat or looking to find good year-round fish lakes. They were born on the land and died on the land. They roamed across Denendeh and settled nowhere. But when trading posts were built, people began to stay in one place. The traders did not feed the Dene; my people still had to hunt and fish as before, and now they had to trap fur for the trade goods that made their lives easier. Between 1750 and 1850 many Dene starved as populations of fish and game disappeared quickly around trading posts. One of the Dene laws about living off the land is to never overharvest an area.

Anishinabé artist Ron Noganosh created this shield — titled That's All It Costs — to comment on the Hudson's Bay Company's decision to close the last of its northern trading posts in 1991. For over 300 years, the Hudson's Bay Company had encouraged Aboriginal people to hunt and trap for furs. Once demand for furs from the United States and Europe dropped off, the company abruptly abandoned these northern communities, leaving many in a drastic economic decline.

▌ REFLECTION

1. According to George Blondin, what are some of the major changes that have taken place in his people's history? How does his story about "when the world was new" reinforce what you know about the kinds of stories in First Nations oral traditions?

2. Working with a partner, discuss each element of Ron Noganosh's shield: the head office tower surrounded by silver coins, the Hudson's Bay Point blanket, the dangling figures, the soiled and torn American flag, and the title. Hint: The Hudson's Bay Company once used the jingle "That's all it costs when you shop at the Bay." What comment do you think Noganosh is making with his work?

3. On your own, write a paragraph summarizing your ideas about Noganosh's work, or create a visual representation of Blondin's story.

Exploration and Early Trade

AS YOU READ

Pages 134–139 describe the establishment of the fur trade and European presence in what is now Canada. As you read, think about the following questions: What motivated Europeans to come to North America? How did First Nations respond to the newcomers? The Issues for Investigation activity on page 135 will help you organize your notes as you read the rest of this chapter.

IN THE LATE FIFTEENTH CENTURY, EUROPEAN COUNTRIES SUCH AS SPAIN, BRITAIN, FRANCE, AND THE NETHERLANDS BEGAN TO EXPAND THEIR TRADE WITH FOREIGN COUNTRIES. IN 1492, CHRISTOPHER COLUMBUS SAILED across the Atlantic Ocean and reached the Caribbean islands. His journey is usually considered the beginning of European colonization of North America. **Colonization** is when one country takes political and economic control of another, while also attempting to impose its culture on the indigenous people, often by importing settlers to the colonized country.

After Columbus's now-famous journey, Spanish and Portuguese ships began travelling to South America regularly. On each return trip, their ships were heavy with treasures from South American indigenous peoples.

Other European countries eyed this source of gold and other riches with jealousy. Blocked from South America by the Spanish fleet, these countries decided to search for gold farther north. They also hoped to find a route across the Atlantic that would give them access to Asia's markets.

In 1496, the British financed explorer John Cabot to find this route. The next year he returned, not with gold or a route to Asia, but

THE BEOTHUK

The Beothuk people were the original inhabitants of what is now Newfoundland.

In the sixteenth century, the Beothuk were likely one of the earliest First Nations to make contact with Europeans who arrived to fish the Grand Banks, a rich fishing region off Newfoundland's shore. By the eighteenth century, European settlements had begun to appear on Beothuk summer hunting grounds. As Europeans intruded more often on their land, the Beothuk were compelled to take up arms against the intruders. Clashes occurred and casualties resulted on both sides. For a time, English settlers actively hunted Beothuk inhabitants, even paying other First Nations people to kill them.

In 1769, a royal proclamation forbade any European to attack a Beothuk person. The last known Beothuk was Shawnadithit, who lived in St. John's until her death from tuberculosis in 1829. With her died her people's language, history, and culture.

This illustration shows Europeans trading with a group of Beothuk people. Draw an illustration that represents the Beothuk point of view of either these early visits or the European settlements that began to appear later.

with a story about a "New Found Land" and seas so full of fish they could be scooped up by the basketful.

At this time, inexpensive fish such as cod were in great demand by Europe's large Roman Catholic population. Devout Catholics did not eat meat on Fridays and Saturdays, so fish was an important source of protein. Because of Cabot's journey, early British activities in what is now Canada concentrated on Newfoundland, Labrador, and the north shore of the River Kanata — now known as the St. Lawrence River.

The British showed little interest in settling permanently in the region. They just visited each summer to fish, landing temporarily to dry their catch. Other countries also fished in the region and some hunted whales farther north.

The French financed several exploration trips in the early sixteenth century, including three by explorer Jacques Cartier. However,

French explorer Jacques Cartier is shown here greeting inhabitants of the St. Lawrence region in 1535. The Haudenosaunee he met at Stadacona (now the site of Quebec City) tried to discourage Cartier from travelling past them up the St. Lawrence River. The Haudenosaunee already recognized the benefits of monopolizing trade into the interior of the country.

after Cartier's last trip in 1542, the French temporarily lost interest in further North American exploration. They were distracted by political events in western Europe and were disappointed by the results of Cartier's exploration. He had only found people and worthless iron pyrite, also known as fool's gold — hardly the wealth of the Incas. The French, like the British, were content for the rest of the sixteenth century to use North America as a fishing resource. French activities focused on the area explored by Cartier — the St. Lawrence River.

Issues for Investigation

BUILDING A TIMELINE

In this activity, you will construct a timeline to help you organize and visualize the information in this chapter. You will use this timeline as a study aid and as part of an activity on page 165.

How did First Nations and Europeans interact during the early and later years of the fur trade?

WHAT TO DO

1. Label one piece of paper for each century between the fifteenth and twentieth.
2. As you read through the rest of this chapter, write notes on these pieces of paper each time you encounter an important date or general time period, such as "the seventeenth century."

Your notes should include the date, the event, and enough detail that you will remember why the event is important. These notes will help you draw your timeline together and see the significance of specific events. You may also want to note the page number in case you need to refresh your memory later.

This illustration by a European artist shows how little the Europeans initially understood about the North American environment. How is the beaver and its behaviour portrayed in the drawing? How might a First Nations artist have depicted the same scene? Sketch your ideas.

THE FUR TRADE

Just as First Nations had always adapted their lifestyles to accommodate nature's changes — the seasons, migrating animals, climatic variations — so they adapted their ways to take advantage of the European visits.

A profitable sideline soon arose during the occasional encounters between fishers and First Nations. While on their annual summer fishing trips, visiting Europeans traded with First Nations, taking home furs that met a growing demand in Europe. Hats made of beaver pelts were a status symbol in Europe during the sixteenth and seventeenth centuries.

First Nations had traded with each other since time immemorial, mostly as a way of sharing and building relationships and alliances — producing and obtaining only enough for their needs. European societies had different ideas about wealth and their traders wanted as many furs as possible. During the early sixteenth century, for example, 15 000 to 20 000 furs were traded in one summer.

This early trade was relatively simple and beneficial to both parties. First Nations brought furs and the Europeans brought other trade goods. After a brief period of ceremony and negotiation, they exchanged. Early in the seventeenth century, this simple trade began to change. As the importance of the fur trade grew in Europe and North America, so did the involvement of both First Nations and European partners.

NEW OPPORTUNITIES

This early fur trade existed only with the cooperation, knowledge, and skills of First Nations communities. Only they understood how to find, catch, and properly process the thick winter beaver pelts that were most prized by the Europeans. First Nations had been trapping beaver for centuries for fur and meat. They processed the furs simply by wearing them next to their skin. This wore off the outer hairs, leaving only soft, supple fur.

Some First Nations stories about first trading experiences show their surprise that the foreigners would trade valuable iron goods for what they saw as old clothes. It seemed like an incredible bargain, as it did for the Europeans who returned to Europe to sell the pelts for good profits.

France was the first country to develop a permanent European settlement in Canada. In 1608, Samuel de Champlain established a post at Stadacona. Over the next few years, Champlain built Stadacona into an important trading centre that helped move the fur trade into a new era. Until then, the trade had been concentrated on the eastern coasts. Now France began to draw on the resources of the interior.

Champlain lacked both the knowledge and people needed to travel to this region, so he formed alliances with the local First Nations — members of the Ouendat Confederacy, the Innu (Montagnais-Naskapi), and the Odawa. These nations worked with France as **middlemen** in the fur trade. They ferried trade goods up the St. Lawrence, traded them with the inland nations, and brought furs back to the post. In return, they kept part of the profits.

First Nations that had the geographic advantage of being close to the coast or the St. Lawrence were quick to see the economic opportunities of working with the foreigners. Indeed, as the fur trade expanded, it was the middlemen and the Europeans who made most of the profits, not the trappers who provided the furs.

The First Nations were skilled traders who demanded quality goods. The Ouendat nations quickly adopted the strategy of refusing to trade with the first European ship to arrive each season. They recognized that they would get better prices for their furs if they waited for several ships to arrive. The Ouendat had the upper hand in these early trades. They refused to learn French, forcing the traders to learn their language.

Other nations along the coast and waterways also showed an enterprising approach to their

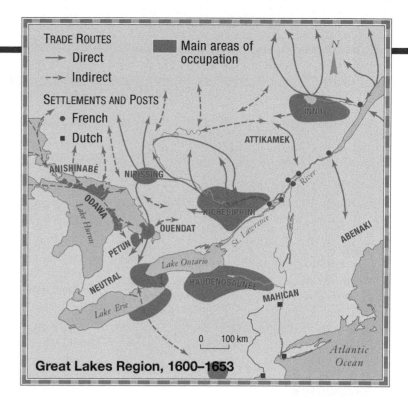

Great Lakes Region, 1600–1653

relationship with the Europeans. For example, the Kichesiprini (Algonquin) First Nation of Allumette Island on the Ottawa River demanded a toll from traders who wished to pass through their territory. As middlemen traders, groups such as the Haudenosaunee and Innu made profitable trades. While they often gave away or shared trade goods with clan members freely, they were not as generous with members of other nations. To maximize their own profits, they would sometimes trade worn or inferior items with inland groups.

This map shows both direct trade routes (used by First Nations who traded directly with Europeans) and indirect trade routes (used by middlemen). Although main areas of occupation are shown for some First Nations, each group also had a much wider territory that was also used. All of the land area shown on this map was occupied or shared by various nations.

Indigenous Knowledge

A traditional rule of trading that many First Nations observed for centuries held that the family or clan that began trade with a foreign people retained the exclusive right to control trade with that people. How was the middleman role consistent with this tradition?

Many missionaries wrote about their lives among First Nations people. Such accounts were extremely popular in Europe and encouraged people to give money to the church to pay for more missionary work. How does the cover of this 1632 account reflect a European worldview of the missionaries' efforts?

In the seventeenth century, France added religion to its list of goals in North America, which already included fish, fur, and exploration. **Missionaries** arrived with the goal of converting First Nations people to Christianity. Among the earliest missionaries were the Récollet and Jesuit who lived with the Ouendat Confederacy between 1615 and 1625.

The First Nations regarded the missionaries with varying degrees of curiosity, puzzlement, and suspicion. The Europeans sometimes brought pets, European-style doors, and clocks, all of which amused and interested First Nations people who saw them.

However, if the missionaries refused to work with First Nations spiritual leaders, many communities were puzzled and somewhat annoyed. They did not, at first, have a cultural reference for a belief system that denied the validity of other beliefs. They were curious about, but somewhat suspicious of a faith that refused to acknowledge their traditional spiritual beliefs.

Many missionaries did a little trading along with their religious work. They quickly realized that without a trading relationship, few of them would have been welcome in First Nations communities.

Although they were willing to trade, most First Nations people showed little interest in the religion the missionaries promoted. A few converted out of curiosity. Others converted when illnesses began to strike their people in record numbers. Still others, like the Ouendat nations, converted in order to receive weapons from their French allies. First Nations people who chose to convert sometimes did so to help their trading relations with the French. Many of these converts ignored Christianity when they were with their own people, while others followed a blend of Christian and traditional practices.

Missionaries were frequently frustrated by such temporary or partial conversions. However, just as variations exist in spiritual practices among First Nations cultures, so do differences separate various Christian approaches to their faith. For example, early Jesuit missionaries among the Ouendat focused their efforts on changing First Nations migratory practices and tolerated other traditional ways of life. They believed that a more settled life would help the missionaries control and convert the First Nations population. Other missionaries tried to completely replace traditional spirituality, values, and ways of life with Christian European ideals.

THE HUDSON'S BAY COMPANY

In 1659, two French brothers-in-law, Médard Chouart Des Grosseilliers and Pierre-Esprit Radisson, made a trading expedition past Lake Superior into what is now Michigan. They returned with sixty canoes full of furs, plus an idea. Why not use the sea route through Hudson Bay to trade directly into the interior? This would eliminate much costly and time-consuming overland travel for the Europeans.

Their idea did not receive a warm welcome from the French government. Angry at the response, Des Grosseilliers took the idea to London. With the help of financial backers, he made a successful trading voyage to Hudson Bay in 1668–1669.

The following year, on May 2, 1670, the Hudson's Bay Company (HBC) was born. The British Crown granted it the exclusive right to trade in the territory where rivers flowed into Hudson Bay — in other words, a huge portion of western Canada. The First Nations who lived in this area were not consulted about this land grant. Within a few years, the HBC had built three forts on the coast of Hudson Bay.

Before then, the First Nations living in this region — Cree and Nakoda — had been on the outer edges of the fur trade. Now they found themselves at the centre, with the French on one side and the HBC on the other.

Unlike the French, British traders did not travel directly into First Nations territory. Instead, they stayed at their posts and waited for First Nations to bring furs to them. This limited the HBC's reach because many inland nations were not able or willing to make long voyages to the bay to trade.

As a result, the Cree and Nakoda became new middlemen, travelling back and forth to the nations of the interior. They became experts at playing the British and French against each other, transporting the furs to whomever they believed would give them the best price.

The Cree and Nakoda flourished in their middleman role, expanding their territory to the west and the south. Today the Cree are Canada's most populous and widespread group of First Nations people, stretching from northern Alberta to northern Quebec and into the United States.

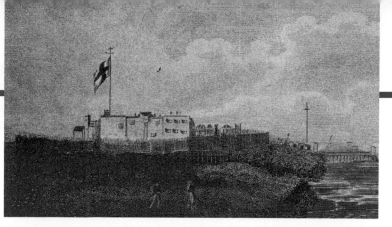

The Hudson's Bay Company established York Factory in 1684. Contrast this coloured engraving of the post from the 1770s with the image of the voyageurs on page 141. Based on what you see, compare British trading approaches to those of the French. Which approach do you think was preferred by First Nations who worked as middlemen? Why might the preference of inland groups differ?

LOOKING BACK

Before moving to the next section, be sure you can answer the following questions: What were the first European motives for visiting North America? How did the fur trade arise from this? How did First Nations initially respond to the Europeans? What economic roles for First Nations developed out of the trade?

Exchange and Adaptation

AS YOU READ

Pages 140–149 discuss the exchange of tools and knowledge that made a trading relationship between First Nations and Europeans of value to each group. Over time, both cultures changed as a result of contact with each other.

ALTHOUGH THE EUROPEANS WERE QUICK TO SEE THE VALUE OF NORTH AMERICA'S NATURAL RESOURCES, THEY WERE NOT AS QUICK TO EMBRACE FIRST NATIONS AND INUIT TECHNOLOGIES. AT FIRST, THEY THOUGHT FIRST Nations had little to offer them beyond furs and fresh meat. In their view, Europe represented the modern, technologically advanced, and superior world of countries, cities, capitalism, and Christianity.

This false sense of superiority prevented them from seeing that much of their knowledge and experience was useless in their new surroundings. Many Europeans failed to live through their first winter overseas, dying of exposure or malnutrition. Those who survived often did so only because First Nations and Inuit peoples shared knowledge, medicine, and food with them.

Gradually, many Europeans came to value First Nations expertise. They found that they needed First Nations and Inuit knowledge and technology in order to work and survive in North America. From the Inuit, Europeans learned techniques such as travelling by dogsled and hunting whales with toggled harpoons. Farther south, they walked in moccasins or snowshoes in the winter and travelled by canoe in the summer.

The First Nations taught the newcomers which vegetables would grow in the northern climate and how to successfully cultivate them. European settlers learned about soil fertilization from First Nations who put fish heads in holes before planting seeds. Before long, Europeans were able to harvest their own corn, beans, pumpkins, and squash. They also learned which wild plants were edible and how to tap maple trees for their sweet sap.

Europeans also depended on First Nations people to help them travel and explore. In 1535, a Mohawk man touched Jacques Cartier's copper whistle and pointed off in the distance. He then drew a detailed map in the dirt — complete with lakes, rivers, and portages — showing a 1450 kilometre route leading to a source for copper.

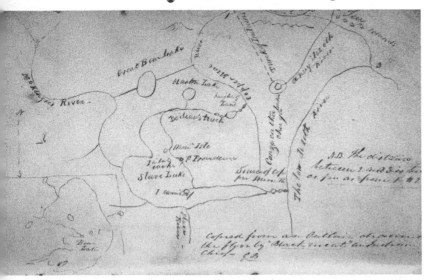

First Nations and Métis peoples were guides and interpreters for explorers and traders and did much of the physical labour required to get from one place to another. This map was drawn in 1820 by Blackmeat, a First Nations leader in the Northwest Territories.

Some Europeans, especially young French men, adapted readily to First Nations ways of life. The freedom and independence of the First Nations suited many of the men. Some had come to New France to escape the rigid social structures of their European homeland. Lured by the promise of fur profits, some of them travelled into First Nations territory to begin trading directly with the inland nations. These men became known as *coureurs des bois* — "runners of the woods" — or voyageurs.

The voyageurs often stayed inland for years at a time, marrying First Nations women and raising families. They and their descendants, the early Métis people, increasingly took over the middleman role in the St. Lawrence fur trade.

The British were generally less adaptive to First Nations ways of life than the French were, but found they had to make some accommodations. For example, to First Nations the act of trading was more than an exchange of goods. It represented a meaningful transaction between friends.

European traders realized that if they were to develop the trust needed to cement an economic bond, they had to respect and follow the customs that stemmed from these beliefs. Before beginning negotiations, First Nations and European traders smoked a ceremonial pipe and exchanged gifts. To the First Nations, the gifts symbolized a mutual

understanding of the sharing and generosity that was the foundation of a friendship and trading partnership between two peoples. In traditional First Nations worldviews, gifts were often more significant and important than goods exchanged in trade. Gift-giving remained an important tradition throughout fur trade history.

The voyageurs adapted to many First Nations ways of life. What evidence of this adaptation do you see in this painting?

Indigenous Knowledge

Bernie Makokis's story below shows the relevance of traditional First Nations knowledge of the natural world as well as the growing appreciation among contemporary scientists for this knowledge. Find a First Nations technology or a story from a First Nations oral tradition that demonstrates scientific knowledge of the environment. Make a poster promoting the value of traditional knowledge using an example from your research. If possible, display your class posters in your school or a public building in your community.

One spring morning, it was quite windy outside. I overheard my grandmother speaking to my grandfather in Cree. She was saying that the trees were mating. I thought that she was a crazy old woman. About thirty years later, I told this story to Dr. David Suzuki and asked him what my grandmother meant. He told me that my grandmother was absolutely right, but in scientific terms, it is called pollination. He said, "Your grandmother knew what she was talking about."

— Bernie Makokis, Saddle Lake First Nation

European trade items changed the lives of First Nations almost overnight. Instead of methods such as cooking in birchbark baskets, they now had metal pots and kettles that could be placed directly over the fire. They acquired metal axes and other tools that were lighter and more durable than stone. They began making some of their clothes with cloth, needles, and thread, rather than hide, bone needles, and sinew. Some decorated their clothes with beadwork as well as the dyed porcupine quills and other natural materials they had used for centuries. They set steel traps to gather furs and carried guns for hunting.

Guns changed the way First Nations hunted, but also made them more dependent on the fur trade. Hunters could not supply their own ammunition, as they could with a bow and arrow. As people became less dependent on their environment for the tools of their livelihood, they became more dependent on trading posts. Europeans began to gain dominance in their relationships with First Nations because European trade goods were increasingly seen as essential. In addition, trading companies paid for furs with credit at the company store rather than cash. People became dependent on the stores for their everyday needs.

Traditional First Nations economic life revolved around the food supply, not around the accumulation of possessions. This outlook frustrated European fur traders who tried to entice First Nations to supply as many pelts as possible. They felt that First Nations, like Europeans, should be eager to accumulate as much individual wealth as possible. However, once a group acquired all of the goods it needed (and could carry), people lost the incentive to keep trapping. The idea of working hard to deliberately accumulate a surplus was at first puzzling to people whose principles were based on values of only taking what they needed.

Magnifying the cultural difference, First Nations people used European trade goods as part of their traditional system of mutual support and gave them away to kin.

Over time, however, European attitudes about economic prosperity began to take hold. People knew they could support themselves, but they wanted a few luxuries.

For example, steel traps became popular among trappers because they made life easier. Trappers worked hard to gather enough furs to trade for the metal instruments.

However, these traps were fundamentally different from traditional snares and handmade traps. Steel traps (and their catch) were owned by an individual, not the community. Some individuals became wealthier than others, leading to tensions and conflict in some communities. In these cases, communal values began to erode.

This photograph shows an Inuit hunter with large bundles of furs for trading. Traditionally, any kind of abundance of food or other materials would have been distributed to family or clan members. How was a surplus increasingly handled among individuals who had contact with Europeans?

◼ REFLECTION

Sharing is still part of many First Nations communities, as seen in give-aways at powwows and the tradition of distributing wild meat or fish to Elders or others in the community. With a partner, discuss why you think these traditions have survived in the face of many other cultural changes.

CHANGING FIRST NATIONS

The fur trade slowly transformed ancient First Nations ways of life. After thousands of years supporting themselves on the land, First Nations found themselves adapting to European-style commerce and politics.

European and First Nations leadership structures contrasted dramatically. No First Nations leader had the kind of formal power wielded by someone like the **factor**, the trader who controlled each Hudson's Bay Company (HBC) post. If the factor's power was incompatible with First Nations beliefs, then the idea of a monarch ruling over a colony from a distant land across the sea must have seemed nonsensical. First Nations leaders were usually those among the group who were seen to have experience and wisdom. How could a monarch with no experience of a land govern it well?

Over time, however, European ideas took hold. For example, European fur traders identified **trading captains** among the First Nations peoples they dealt with and gave them special status. These trading captains were often the most successful hunters or trappers, so they also tended to be individuals who began to accumulate material wealth. Among some groups, this led to a fundamental change in leadership to favour people who possessed material wealth, rather than those who gave it away.

The Homeguard

Unlike their First Nations and Métis partners, most HBC employees lacked the skills needed to support themselves through hunting. To ensure a fresh supply of meat, they encouraged First Nations people to camp near the posts. These people became known as the **homeguard**.

Each year, the homeguard began setting up camp in time for the spring goose hunt. They received brandy or strong beer to celebrate the start of the hunt, along with powder and shot. The homeguard then returned to the post with meat and feathers to trade. Inside the post, HBC employees preserved and stored the birds for the winter.

After the hunt, the homeguard dispersed to their favourite family fishing spots, occasionally returning to the post to trade some of their catch.

At times, the posts relied heavily on the homeguard for their survival. At other times, the homeguard depended on the post. Because they spent much of their

Many First Nations women were curious about Europeans and were eager to facilitate trades by acting as interpreters or marrying and working with European traders. Traditional skills, such as making pemmican, were welcomed by European fur traders as an asset to their work.

time gathering furs and provisions for trade, the homeguard sometimes found themselves short of food. Many of the areas immediately surrounding the posts became over-hunted, providing less and less to those who lived near them. When famine threatened, the homeguard looked to the HBC for support. Sometimes the company gave this support in the form of credit, which put First Nations peoples in debt to the company.

SKIN DRESSING AND MEAT DRYING

Scraping flesh from Moose Hide with Beaming Tool made from leg bone of Deer

Bone-handled Scraper with stone blade

The essential economic role that women played in traditional First Nations communities, as shown in these instructions, carried over to an essential role in the fur trade.

Leather

Method of using Scraper & holding it rigid

Rubbing fat into the skin

Matonabbee, an Anishinabé guide for explorer Samuel Hearne, explained that the lack of First Nations women on Hearne's first two expeditions had caused the expeditions' failures. He said

...when all the men are heavy laden, they can neither hunt nor travel to any considerable distance; and in case they meet with success in hunting, who is to carry the produce of their labour? Women ... also pitch our tents, make and mend our clothing, ... and, in fact, there is no such thing as travelling any considerable distance, or for any length of time, in this country, without their assistance.

WOMEN IN THE WESTERN FUR TRADE

For almost two centuries after the formation of the Hudson's Bay Company in 1670, the fur trade expanded its reach across western Canada. After 1776, the trade expanded rapidly due to competition with the Montreal-based North West Company. The trade was driven by economics, but was also a cultural and social force with the *mariage à la façon du pays* or country marriage as its central institution.

These marriages were essential to the success of the fur traders, particularly in the early years of the western trade. European men who married First Nations women acquired a companion and, in most cases, beneficial kinship bonds, a skilled linguistic and cultural interpreter, and a business partner.

The women performed many tasks that made day-to-day life on the land possible. With his marriage, the European trader gained kinship ties with First Nations people who now had traditional obligations of mutual support towards him and his family. Kinship ties to Europeans were also viewed among many First Nations as valuable commercial contacts.

First Nations women who married European traders had an easier life in some ways. They generally had more material goods and were required to do less physical labour, especially if they lived at one of the trading posts. In

other ways, however, their marriages may have been a hard bargain. The women went from a society in which women's roles were valued, to a society dominated by European thinking, in which the contributions of women to the home and family were not highly regarded.

THE MÉTIS FAMILY

The earliest Europeans to marry into First Nations families were the voyageurs. By the mid-seventeenth century, many voyageurs lived among First Nations in the Great Lakes region. Most of the children from these marriages were either raised as First Nations or Europeans and did not view themselves as being part of a distinct culture.

As the children of these marriages grew up and married other individuals with similar backgrounds, a new and distinct culture began to emerge that was neither European nor First Nations, but a blend of the two. This cultural evolution began in the 1600s and reached its peak by the 1800s.

These people — the Métis — tended to have one of three types of lifestyle, although all were involved in the fur trade. The Great Lakes Métis had a more settled lifestyle living near the trading posts where they were employed as clerks, interpreters, canoeists, and packers. The Plains Métis were semi-settled, living on small farms or settlements in the winter and hunting buffalo in the summer. Other families preferred to follow a life patterned

after their First Nations heritage and were sometimes known as Winter Rovers.

Métis people had an enviable position in the fur-trading world, which encouraged them to have a sense of pride and distinct cultural identity. They learned about European technology and values from their fathers, many of whom insisted their children be educated and raised as Christians. They learned traditional First Nations skills from their mothers, who encouraged their children to be multilingual. Their mothers bridged both cultures and influenced children to adopt beneficial elements of each.

Red River Métis

While some European men eventually left their First Nations families to marry European women in North America or Europe, many Europeans lived the rest of their lives with their Métis families. Significant numbers of these families settled in what is now Manitoba.

These families tended to live more settled lifestyles in comparison to their First Nations relatives. They also adopted European religions and beliefs. Yet they had kinship

Many of the Métis people who moved to Alberta preferred the buffalo-hunting life of their First Nations relatives to the agricultural economy taking over the east. Based on what you see in this photograph of a Métis family from Fort Chipewyan, Alberta, what aspects of their lives differed from traditional First Nations ways of life?

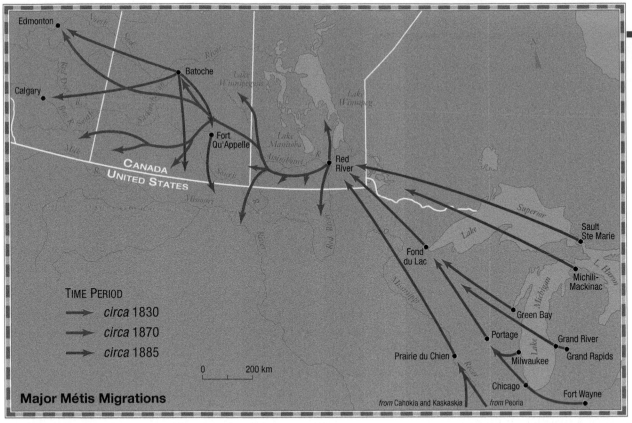

TIME PERIOD

→ *circa* 1830
→ *circa* 1870
→ *circa* 1885

0 ——— 200 km

Major Métis Migrations

bonds with the First Nations and a cultural familiarity that people with only European ancestry lacked.

The Red River settlement was actually two settlements that were founded in 1812. One was at the junction of the Red and Assiniboine Rivers at the site of what is now Winnipeg. A smaller centre (Pembina) was set up to the south in what is now South Dakota. Both were populated mainly by Scottish settlers until 1821. After that time, most of the population growth in the region was due to the Métis people who had been living and working in the area for decades.

Social Structure at Red River

The descendants of French fur traders from the North West Company were referred to as

Métis, while the descendants of English or Scottish fur traders from the Hudson's Bay Company were called half-breeds, mixed-bloods, or Country Born. These terms are today considered offensive and are not used. Métis is the preferred term for people with a dual cultural heritage, whether with a French or British ancestry. At Red River, however, the divisions between the French-speaking and English-speaking Métis populations were strong.

English-speaking Métis at Red River tended to adopt many of the values of the English and Scottish population in the settlement, such as the Protestant faith. These Métis families had a relatively settled life based on business and agriculture. They often did administrative work for the Hudson's Bay Company.

French-speaking Métis shared the Roman Catholic faith and French values and attitudes. These attitudes generally accepted traditional First Nations ways of life. Most French-speaking Métis from Red River hunted buffalo from June to September, and harvested their crops later in the fall. In the winter, many French-speaking Métis worked as freighters or cargo transporters for the North West Company, the HBC's competitor.

There were two class structures at Red River. One was established by the European settlers, who assigned social status to the Métis population on the basis of occupation. In European eyes, Métis people who were involved in agriculture, business, or the trades had a higher social status than those who hunted buffalo. In turn, the buffalo hunters had a higher social status than the Winter Rovers, who trapped and fished and only seasonally came into the settlement.

Red River's Métis community had their own social ranking system and generally held the buffalo hunters in high regard.

Winter Rovers originated in the Red River area, but did not feel comfortable in the settlement as it grew more agricultural over time. Many left and moved farther west. Some of these Winter Rovers and their descendants later founded Alberta's Métis Settlements. The Métis Settlements were created in 1938 to give Alberta's Métis population a land base. You will learn more about these communities in Chapter Six.

The Métis at Red River attended church and developed courts of justice similar to their paternal ancestors. This painting shows St. Boniface Church, which was built by Reverend Joseph Norbert Provencher, the first bishop of Red River.

MICHIF

One distinct way in which Métis people combined European and First Nations cultural traits was in the development of unique languages: Bungi, Patois, and Michif. Bungi is a mixture of Orkney Scottish and Cree. Patois is classified as a French variant and is considered to be French with a First Nations influence. Michif is considered a language on its own, a mixture of French, Cree, Anishinabé and English. The following excerpt is taken from a series of ten Michif lessons offered by the Métis Language Resource Centre. Visit the site at *www.metisresourcecentre.mb.ca/language/* to hear audio pronunciation recordings.

My mother is baking bannock.	*Ni mámá késhishew la gallet.*
My father ate it all.	*Ni pápá kakéyaw ki mówew.*
My brother and my sister ate grandma's bannock.	*Moñ frayr pi ma soeur ki mówewak kókom sa gallet.*
My grandfather chopped wood.	*Ni moshóm ké nikótew li bwá.*
Her grandmother made supper.	*Ókoma ké li soupékeyiwa.*

The Métis Nation emerged as a distinct cultural group by blending elements of European and First Nations cultures in creative ways. This ability to combine useful elements of both cultures made the Métis an enormous asset in the fur trade. With the exception of those living in or near Red River, most Métis people tended to live close to fur trading posts. Pages 148–149 include many examples of Métis cultural innovations.

Métis women used the leather skills of their First Nations ancestors to make clothing patterned on European styles. They then decorated this clothing with elaborate beadwork, such as the pattern seen here on Louis Riel's deerskin jacket.

Beadwork

For centuries First Nations and Inuit women had used natural materials, such as porcupine quills and moose or caribou hair to decorate clothing and other objects. When they received European glass beads, women added them to decorate their moccasins, leggings, bags, and jackets. Some Métis women began to incorporate European women's embroidered floral designs into their beadwork. These Métis women became so well known for their beaded flowers that some First Nations called them Flower Beadwork People.

The Métis Sash

The Métis are also known for their finger-woven sashes that were tied around the waist with the fringes hanging down. Although today the sash has mainly symbolic value, it once had highly practical uses. It was used to carry heavy objects, as a key holder, a first aid kit, a washcloth and towel, and an emergency horse blanket or bridle. Even the fringes were sometimes used to supply a sewing kit on hunts. The sash is still worn by some Métis people on ceremonial occasions. Its colours are traditionally red, blue, green, black, and yellow.

The Red River Jig

Whenever groups of Métis people met at summer or winter camps, there was always singing, storytelling, and feasting. Dancing was and continues to be a favourite form of entertainment for many Métis people. Although they have many forms of traditional dances, the Métis are most famous for the Red River jig. This dance combines the intricate footwork of First Nations

Métis dances, such as this one performed by the Edmonton Métis Cultural Dancers, are a way many people reinforce their common bond and cultural identity.

dancing with the music of European reels and square dances. Traditionally, a jig would start in the early evening and not finish until dawn. The Scottish fiddle became a favourite Métis instrument. Most people could not afford to buy expensive imports, so they made their own out of maple and birch wood.

The York Boat

The York boat is another Métis innovation. Developed by William Sinclair in 1835, the York boat replaced the birchbark canoe as the preferred mode of travel in the fur trade in some regions. The canoe was valued for its speed, but it lacked the strength and durability needed to handle thousands of kilograms of freight over rough water. As the fur trade expanded, so did the need for a stronger method of transportation. The York boat took its name from the Hudson's Bay Company's toughest trade route between York Factory and Norway House, Manitoba, where it was first used. The heavy York boat could be rowed or sailed, but it had to be dragged over portages, which earned it the nickname "the man killer" by those who had to do the work.

The Red River Cart

One of the best-known symbols of Métis culture is the Red River cart, which was used to haul belongings or meat and hides back from buffalo hunts. The design of the cart was similar to those used in the Scottish Highlands and some parts of Quebec. The Métis version was made entirely of wood so it was easy to repair. The large, spoked wheels were fashioned so they would not sink into soft mud. Grease was not used on the axles because dirt would stick and seize the wheels. The carts became known for the high-pitched sound they made as they travelled.

The Red River cart doubled as a raft when the wheels were taken off.

LOOKING BACK

In the early years of the fur trade, First Nations found the relationship with Europeans to be beneficial. New trade goods affected their quality of life in many positive ways. In addition, First Nations populations far outnumbered even the most populated European settlements and trading posts. If the relationship had not been positive, they could have easily turned the foreigners out or refused to assist them. Europeans needed First Nations help, so this refusal would have likely meant their death or quick return to their homelands.

However, over time, the changes experienced by First Nations were less positive. In small groups or as a class, discuss why First Nations did not end trade with Europeans and drive them away as soon as negative effects were apparent. In your answer, consider issues such as growing First Nations dependence on trade goods, kinship bonds between First Nations and Métis peoples and changing attitudes. Review pages 140–149 to find other ideas for your discussion.

Expansion West and North

BEFORE YOU READ

On pages 134–139 you learned how and why the French and British established themselves in North America. On pages 140–149 you learned some of the ways that First Nations and European cultures influenced and adapted to one another. In this section, you will learn how the fur trade reached its peak during the second half of the eighteenth century. It was a period of rapid expansion and intense competition. Some First Nations found themselves drawn into the fur trade for the first time, others saw their roles change significantly, and the Métis people defined themselves as a nation.

In 1760, the Seven Years' War between France and England ended with the defeat of France in Quebec on the Plains of Abraham. This led to a significant shift in both the fur trade and First Nations–European relations in Canada.

Until that point, British settlement in Canada had been limited. In 1749, they established Chebucto (soon renamed Halifax), their first major settlement. It was not a promising start. In the first winter, nearly 1000 of the 2500 settlers perished. Those who survived faced increasing hostility from the Mi'kmaq, who were alarmed at the permanent settlement in their territory.

With the fall of New France, settlement grew rapidly. Thousands of New Englanders arrived in Nova Scotia in the 1760s, followed by other immigrants from Ireland, England, and Scotland. After the American War of Independence, waves of settlers who wished to remain in British territory flooded north. About 20 000 of them settled in Nova Scotia in 1783 and 1784.

The British settlers were entirely different from the French fur traders. They wanted land and lots of it. Agriculture needed a system of land ownership, fences, roads, railways, supplies, and towns. Whereas the fur trade economy depended on First Nations maintaining at least some parts of their traditional ways of life, such as their mobility, agriculture was completely opposed to this lifestyle.

It was a turning point in the history of First Nations and Europeans. Once by far the majority of the population, some First Nations found themselves increasingly in the minority. In addition, disease drastically reduced their populations, weakening their ability to resist the changes overtaking their territories.

Loyalists — settlers who left the United States after the American War of Independence — drew lots for land in Canada, assuming the land was theirs to be taken.

Particularly in the east, where most of the settlers moved, many First Nations found themselves in conflict with settlements and sometimes were displaced from their traditional lands. **Displacement** occurs when people are forced to move from their homelands.

THE WESTERN TRADE

When English forces defeated the French and took control of Canada, the Hudson's Bay Company (HBC) looked forward to growing profits. After decades of competing with French traders, they hoped to now have a monopoly on the fur market.

The fur trade based in Montreal continued to flourish, however. The voyageurs and the Métis continued to travel the rivers heading west from the Great Lakes. By now, their contacts with First Nations extended as far as the prairies.

Independent Scottish traders began to take control of French trading posts, competing with each other as well as with the HBC. As they pushed westward, the HBC had little choice but to do the same. Until then, they had been content to stay in their posts by Hudson Bay, conducting most of their trade through middlemen.

In 1774, the HBC established its first inland post, Cumberland House, on the lower Saskatchewan River. In the face of this challenge, the Scottish traders decided to pool their resources. The North West Company was born.

In the decades that followed, the Nor'Westers (as they came to

This illustration shows a trading party from the Blackfoot Confederacy around 1875. The Blackfoot nations began trading directly with the Europeans almost one hundred years earlier. They called the traders Naapiikoan, *because the Europeans reminded them of Naapi, the Old Man from the Blackfoot oral tradition. Naapi has a habit of acting inappropriately and causing chaos. What does this nickname suggest about the confederacy's initial perception of Europeans?*

be known) and the HBC leapfrogged each other, establishing posts farther and farther west. Fort Chipewyan, established in 1788 by the North West Company, was a significant post in the western and northern expansion of the fur trade.

For decades, members of the Blackfoot Confederacy had only traded indirectly with the Europeans. To make the long journey to the trading posts, they would have had to cross Cree and Nakoda territory. In addition, the trip would have interfered with their fall buffalo hunt.

That changed when Rocky Mountain House opened in 1799 and the American Fur Trading Company built their first trading post (in what is now Montana) in 1831. The new posts were within ten days' travel. For the next four decades, members of the Blackfoot Confederacy pitted the British against the Americans, always holding out for the best price and taking their buffalo robes, dried meat, and

Once the Hudson's Bay Company (HBC) was firmly established in the territory south and west of Hudson Bay, the company cast its eyes north. Beginning in the mid-eighteenth century, they made repeated attempts to establish trade with Inuit peoples. For decades they did not succeed.

Then, in 1839, they sent an Inuk employee north from Fort George in search of trade. That first summer, he brought a single family back, but the next year he returned with about thirty families with furs and skins for trade.

After that, Fort George enjoyed regular trade with Inuit peoples. In 1851, the HBC opened a northern post at Little Whale River in order to expand the northern trade. The post operated for the next forty years.

Seal pelts and sealskin clothing made up a good portion of the Inuit trade goods. Skins were most valuable when their layers of blubber were left intact. There was a growing shortage of whale oil, used in lamps and candles, and seal oil made from blubber was an excellent substitute.

This young girl is holding Arctic furs for trade near Hudson Bay. Demand for such furs rose briefly as demand declined for beaver and buffalo. What furs are in demand today?

furs to the company that offered the widest range of trade goods.

Around this time, alcohol began to play a larger role in the fur trade. The HBC and the North West Company were eager to maintain the flow of furs. They realized that First Nations had little incentive to keep hunting and trapping for furs once they had all the trade goods they needed.

Alcohol, however, was a different story. It could be consumed on the spot so that people would always be eager to trade for more. It could be transported more cheaply and easily than many conventional trade goods, such as metal pots and tools. It was also addictive.

Before long, alcohol became one of the most important trade items for both the HBC and the North West Company, with often disastrous consequences for First Nations communities.

It would be interesting to bring back a true picture of the very first drink of firewater that the white man ever gave to the native. What prompted the action? Was this drink given in terms of friendship? Was it a simple speculation of what one drink would do? And what of the Indian? It is safe to assume that he never swallowed that first mouthful. He must have sputtered out all he could and when he was able to talk he undoubtedly hollered "Fire!"

— Joseph F. Dion, Kehewin First Nation, *My Tribe the Crees*

■ REFLECTION

1. Re-read "How the People Hunted the Moose" on pages 2–3, as well page 68, which describes traditional First Nations and Inuit spiritual aspects of the hunt. Write a description of hunting from a First Nations and Inuit perspective. How is the hunt a political, economic, social, and spiritual part of traditional First Nations and Inuit cultures?

2. With a partner, research the work of environmental groups in the late twentieth century to end the seal trade. How do these groups view hunting?

3. What is your position on the issue? Have your studies in this course influenced your ideas? Debate this topic as a class or in a small group.

THE BUFFALO TRADE

By the mid- to late-eighteenth century, the North West Company and HBC had extended their trade far into the interior. The new posts were far from the eastern ports to Europe and the companies faced a huge challenge shipping supplies and trading goods in, and transporting furs out. Crews often spent months paddling canoes and needed a portable, concentrated food source to sustain them.

In 1779, Nor'Wester trader Peter Pond brought back pemmican from a trip he made to the Athabasca River. Pemmican is made by drying buffalo meat, grinding it into a powder, and mixing it with melted fat. Sometimes berries are added for flavour and extra nutritional value. Pemmican had been a staple food among First Nations for centuries.

Pemmican kept indefinitely and provided huge amounts of food energy for very little weight. In short, it was the perfect food for travelling fur traders. Before long, both the North West Company and the HBC had set up posts along western rivers aimed specifically at the pemmican trade. The demand from the competing fur-trading companies for pemmican, newly popular buffalo robes, and dried buffalo tongues gave birth to a new economic opportunity for both First Nations and Métis peoples.

During their fall hunt, First Nations used buffalo jumps or buffalo pounds to kill large numbers of buffalo at once. They quickly dried most of the meat in order to preserve it for the winter. They pounded it into pemmican and then sewed it into buffalo-hide sacks. This traditional part of their way of life was easily and profitably expanded to supply fur traders.

As early as 1811, the Hudson's Bay Company at Red River used horses to haul furs, buffalo hides, and pemmican up and down the Red River trade routes between Manitoba, North and South Dakota, Minnesota, and the area that would become Alberta and Saskatchewan.

Métis people along this route started to play a large role in the buffalo trade, competing with some First Nations. First Nations and Métis hunters began killing more and more buffalo to feed the fur trade. Companies also hired Métis people as freighters to ship hides and supplies between the various trading posts and recently established towns.

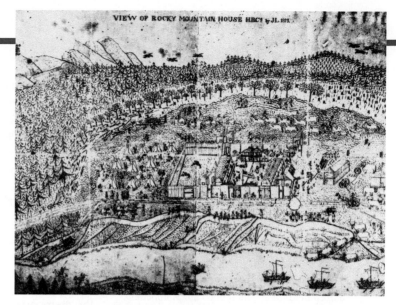

VIEW OF ROCKY MOUNTAIN HOUSE HBC? ♦ JL. 1871

Notice the river in the foreground of this 1873 illustration of Rocky Mountain House. Most trading posts were established on rivers to be near transportation routes and near locations visited frequently by First Nations.

THE BUFFALO JUMP

A low rumble, like approaching thunder, rolls across the prairie. The buffalo are stampeding. Tightly packed together, the massive, shaggy beasts move as one, united in their frantic flight. Hundreds of huge hooves, the largest bearing as much as one tonne in weight, pummel the tall grasses, and the earth begins to shake.

Suddenly the leader spots the precipice, where the land abruptly drops. Bellowing her anger and distress, she desperately attempts to turn, but it's impossible to stop the momentum of the panicked animals behind. Like a roaring freight train, they slam into her at 50 kilometres per hour. Hundreds of animals spill over the cliff, crashing down to their deaths.

For thousands of years, Plains First Nations had hunted buffalo, their primary food source. The buffalo also provided clothing, tools, and shelter. First Nations used various hunting methods, the most sophisticated being the buffalo jump.

First Nations hunters took advantage of the buffalo's instinct to stampede when faced with danger. They searched for sites where cliffs occurred without warning, and they devised a way to channel the stampeding herd over the cliff.

Buffalo jump sites exist in Canada and the United States, but the oldest and best-preserved site is Head-Smashed-In, in southern Alberta. The name arose after a curious young man, who wanted a close-up look at the stampede, had his skull crushed by falling buffalo.

The enormous site has four distinct components. The **gathering basin**, 40 square kilometres of grazing area, attracted herds late into fall. Hunters disguised in buffalo robes lured the herd, imitating bleating calves, towards the **drive lanes**. As the herd moved closer, the hunters circled behind, shouting and waving robes to frighten the herd into a stampede. Thirty different lanes, lined with 20 000 cairns, directed stampeding herds towards the **cliff site**.

Below the cliff site was the **processing area**, where groups camped while butchering the buffalo, sun-drying the meat for pemmican, and cleaning the skins. Every part of the buffalo was used. Such a huge operation required the cooperation of many groups that separated again after the hunt.

▌ REFLECTION

Head-Smashed-In Buffalo Jump was named a United Nations Educational Scientific and Cultural Organization (UNESCO) World Heritage Site in 1981. This means it joins places such as the Egyptian pyramids and Stonehenge for its great significance to the world's cultural heritage. Working alone, with a partner, or with a small group, celebrate this important location. Some ideas for projects include the following:

- building an architectural model of the interpretive centre itself, which is built into the side of the ancient cliff so that it blends into the surrounding environment

- writing a story about the hunt told from the perspective of a young person joining the hunt for the first time
- writing a poem that evokes the emotions of the site or the hunt
- performing a dance, song, play, or skit highlighting some aspect of the hunt or culture of the people who used the jump
- creating a drawing, picture, sculpture, video, or diorama that portrays the drama of the hunt.

If you can, visit the site before you begin your project. To learn more about Head-Smashed-In, visit the Web site at *www.head-smashed-in.com.*

THE MÉTIS BUFFALO HUNT

The buffalo hunt helped shape the Métis people into a cohesive nation. It took military precision to organize hundreds of men, women, children, horses, oxen, and Red River carts for a trek hundreds of kilometres to where the buffalo herds were. The hunt was a prominent feature of life at Red River by 1820. It contributed to the development of the distinct Métis way of life and sense of nationhood.

The hunting technique used by the Métis differed from that of their First Nations ancestors. Instead of driving buffalo over cliffs or into enclosures, and killing them with spears and arrows, the Métis used

guns and horses called buffalo runners in a technique called "running the herd."

At the beginning of the hunt, scouts were sent to locate the herd. When it was spotted, the hunting group rode forward in single-line formation. At a signal from the captain of the hunt, the riders charged the buffalo, causing them to stampede. The riders would then gallop into the herd, select an animal, and fire at point-blank range from their galloping horses.

An experienced hunter on a trained horse could kill ten to twelve buffalo in a two-hour period. When the hunters were finished, the women and children moved in to skin and butcher the carcasses.

THE 1840 BUFFALO HUNT

The 1840 buffalo hunt occurred at the peak of the buffalo trade. The hunting party left its organization camp near the Red River in early June. It included

- 620 men
- 650 women
- 360 children
- 586 oxen
- 503 horses
- 1240 Red River carts.

They travelled 402 kilometres in nineteen days before the first buffalo were spotted. When the hunt ended on August 17, the party had over 454 000 kilograms of meat and hides to transport back to Red River.

Indigenous Knowledge

The buffalo hunt was a significant part of both Métis and Plains First Nations cultures. Using instructions from your teacher, create a shield that celebrates the buffalo hunt. Select a specific First Nations or Métis group and research appropriate symbols and colour to use on your shield. Use traditional symbols and techniques for your shield or be creative in devising your own approach — turn back to page 133 to look at Ron Noganosh's shield for ideas.

VICTORIA CALLIHOO
Lac Ste Anne

Victoria Callihoo is seen here sitting on a buffalo robe she won dancing the Red River jig at the age of ninety-eight.

Victoria Callihoo was filled with excitement as she boarded a Red River cart to participate in her first buffalo hunt. She was thirteen years old. The year was 1874 and her mother, Kininawis, a Cree medicine woman, had chosen Victoria, the most enterprising of all her children, to ride out with her on a group hunting expedition.

Kininawis, whose name means "one of tall stature" in Cree, was a physically powerful woman who stood 1.8 metres tall. Every spring, she left her husband tending the family farm while she joined a buffalo hunt. Leaving Lac Ste Anne and crossing the North Saskatchewan River near Fort Edmonton, Kininawis hunted on the plains north of Red Deer almost all summer long. She returned in the fall, her cart laden with dried meat, pemmican, hides, and sinew.

Over the years Kininawis had come to be recognized by her people as a medicine woman, and was kept busy attending to the sick and injured. Her pharmacy included parts of plants and animals that were used in medicines to treat illness. She also set broken bones and helped to birth many babies. When Victoria attended her first buffalo hunt, she kept the meat-smoking fires going while her mother was busy with the sick and injured.

Both Kininawis and her daughter Victoria joined many communal hunts over the years. After the buffalo became scarce and Kininawis died, Victoria carried on in her mother's footsteps as Lac Ste Anne's resident medicine woman. She died peacefully in her sleep in 1966 at the age of 105. Her life had been a bridge between the days of travelling with a travois to the time of airplanes.

▌ REFLECTION

Working in small groups of four or five students, complete the following activity:

1. What are some of the roles First Nations, Métis, and Inuit women played in the fur trade?

2. List roles women play in contemporary Aboriginal communities. Compare your lists.

3. In your opinion, how do women's lives today compare with those of the past? What reasons can you give to support your answer?

4. Create a performance that highlights women's roles in historical or contemporary Aboriginal communities. Your performance could involve song, music, speech, acting, video, dance, or a combination of presentation forms. To prepare, you might interview Elders or other members of the community, or you might use books or the Internet to research your topic. Keep your presentation under five minutes long.

TRADITIONAL MÉTIS GOVERNANCE

Before the Red River Métis began their annual buffalo hunt, they formed a government to organize the massive operation. Like other aspects of their culture, the government was a mixture of First Nations and European cultures.

Men of the camp elected a captain, usually an Elder, to lead the hunt. The captain was selected for his ability as a hunter and for qualities such as honesty and fairness. A council of lieutenants was also elected, with one lieutenant elected for every ten hunters. These officers met together to determine the time, place, and direction of the hunt. They were also responsible for deciding the number of animals to be killed. Results of the hunt were divided among all the people.

A public crier was elected to inform the people of the rules and orders of the council. Every hunt followed certain rules, which were never written down, but which everyone was expected to know and obey. Any person who did not follow the rules of the hunt could be severely punished.

The rules became known as the laws of the prairie and hunting. For example, no hunting was allowed on Sunday and no person could start to hunt buffalo before the general order was given. Crimes of theft were not tolerated, with the guilty person shamed in front of the entire camp.

Later Métis governments reflected a similar blend of cultures. When the Métis established a provisional government at Fort Garry in 1869, it followed the principles of the buffalo hunt. All men of the settlement over the age of twenty-one elected a council of Elders. The council in turn elected a president and secretary. When an issue affecting the whole community came up for debate, it was referred to the community for discussion. All elected leaders of the provisional government were expected to be accountable to the community and could be removed if the community believed they were incapable of governing.

LOOKING BACK

Until 1760, the French were the dominant European cultural force in the territory now called Canada. French interests in Canada, although they involved some settlements and agriculture, were mainly focused on the fur trade, which was more in tune with traditional First Nations ways of life. Pages 150–157 discussed significant changes in North America following the defeat of French interests in the continent. Among these changes were the growth of the buffalo trade, rising demands for agricultural land, and the rise of the Métis Nation. Check your timeline notes to be sure you included these events.

Decline of the Trade

AS YOU READ

In the mid-eighteenth century, the fur trade was at its peak. Ironically, it also stood at the brink of its demise. By the end of the nineteenth century, the Canadian fur trade was almost over. In four centuries, the trade had transformed the lives of First Nations and Inuit peoples. As you read pages 158–165, make notes about why the trade began to decline. What consequences did the reduction in trade have for each Aboriginal group involved?

BY THE EARLY NINETEENTH CENTURY, THE FUR TRADE WAS IN DECLINE. PART OF THE TROUBLE LAY IN EUROPE. THE NAPOLEONIC WARS BETWEEN ENGLAND AND FRANCE DRASTICALLY REDUCED THE DEMAND FOR FURS AND MADE IT more difficult for fur trade companies to attract European workers.

At the same time, relentless competition between the Hudson's Bay Company (HBC) and the North West Company virtually wiped out fur and game animals in

These buffalo bones, gathered from the prairies between 1880 and 1890, are proof of the slaughter and waste that took place during these years. Canadian, American, and European buffalo hunters shot hundreds of animals that were already almost at the point of extinction. Most were left to rot on the prairie.

Manitoba and Saskatchewan, and depleted them elsewhere across the prairies. Buffalo herds that once blanketed the land in herds of fifty to seventy-five million were now a fraction of their original size.

In 1821, the North West Company was absorbed into the HBC, ending four decades of competition in western Canada. First Nations and Métis peoples lost the advantages of dealing with two competing companies and became increasingly dependent on the HBC.

The situation grew worse as the nineteenth century progressed. Silk replaced beaver as the favoured material for making hats. In any case, the beaver had been all but trapped out in most parts of the country. The buffalo, which had become the new engine of the trade, was also in decline. By 1870, the animal was almost extinct.

Both the American and Canadian federal governments encouraged the slaughter of buffalo herds to make way for more settlements and agriculture.

At the same time, American traders had begun setting up posts along the southern fringes of the Canadian prairies in an attempt to wring the last few dollars from the trade. Infamous whiskey-trading posts, such as Fort Whoop-Up near Lethbridge, Alberta, caused social problems among many communities.

For Plains First Nations, the loss of the buffalo was devastating. Their way of life had for centuries revolved around the buffalo, which sat at the centre of their traditional political, economic, and spiritual institutions.

Changes in fashion resulted in more demand for mink and marten in the early twentieth century, so trading posts expanded rapidly in the Arctic. After reaching a peak in the 1920s, the northern trade suffered during the Great Depression and rapidly declined. By the 1950s, few northerners could make a living from the fur trade.

Within a few hundred years, the fur trade transformed the lives of Aboriginal peoples from coast to coast. As the fur trade ended, it left the First Nations, Métis, and Inuit peoples facing a difficult and uncertain future.

IMPORTED DISEASES

Early records of European contact with First Nations in North America mention a rapid decline in the First Nations population. Unwittingly, European visitors brought foreign bacteria and viruses along with goods for trade. Diseases such as typhoid, diphtheria, colds, influenza, measles, chicken pox, whooping cough, tuberculosis, yellow fever, scarlet fever, gonorrhea, syphilis, and smallpox had never been in North America before.

North, South, and Central America are separated from the world's other continents by large oceans. Until the late fifteenth century, this separation ensured that people in the Americas had little or no contact with the rest of

Issues for Investigation

RESEARCHING THE DECLINE OF THE BUFFALO

Competition to supply the fur trade was only one cause of the buffalo's decline. Railway construction, the growth of the cattle industry, more accurate rifles, government policy, and European, Canadian, and American buffalo hunters all contributed to this tragedy.

What factors led to the decline of the great buffalo herds?

WHAT TO DO

1. In small groups, assign each student one cause of the buffalo decline listed in the introduction to this activity.

2. Research your topic. Prepare notes with main ideas clearly indicated. Exchange notes with your group so that you each have a full set.

3. Choose one of the following projects to make use of your notes:

Project A: Work with a partner to design a Web site that describes the decline of the buffalo. If possible, use an electronic program such as Front Page™ to publish your site.

Project B: Work alone to create visual art that incorporates various causes of the buffalo's decline. Some mediums might include sculpture, painting, collage, diorama, or beadwork.

This common grave, at Graveyard Lake in present-day British Columbia, is for members of the Blackwater Tribe, who were virtually wiped out by smallpox.

In *My Tribe the Crees*, Joseph F. Dion shares a story told to him by Antoine Jibeau, who was the only member of his family to survive the smallpox epidemic of 1869–1870. Jibeau's story begins:

I was only eight years old at the time of the smallpox yet I remember certain incidents as if they took place but yesterday. My home was at the south-east end of Moose Lake, near where the town of Bonnyville is today. My first recollection of the epidemic was that of my oldest brother and a younger sister being sick; these two died in one night, with my father following soon afterwards.

I watched my mother place the bodies of my brother and sister in the cellar. She then fixed up a place in one corner of the house where we laid my father's body. That done, mother took us out to the edge of the woods where she said we would have to camp as it wouldn't do for us to stay in the house any longer. ...Just before I fell off to sleep I heard my mother express the fear that she would not see another day. "What will happen to my little children?" she said.

That was the last time I ever heard her speak.

the world. They did not experience the infections that periodically swept through other places and had no natural immunities to them.

The first epidemics in Canada may have occurred in the early 1500s, when the first European fishers traded with Mi'kmaq peoples. Jacques Cartier reported an epidemic in December 1535 among the Ouendat nations. These outbreaks are called **virgin soil epidemics**, which are diseases that spread among populations that have little or no acquired immunity to the infection. Virgin soil epidemics tend to affect everyone in the community to the extent that few are healthy enough to care for the sick and provide food and protection. As a result, more than half of the population dies from the disease.

Epidemics spread first in eastern Canada, killing thousands during the seventeenth century. Between these epidemics and armed conflict, the once-powerful Ouendat Confederacy was destroyed by 1649. Survivors dispersed to live with other First Nations. Epidemics spread mainly as a result of contact with trade blankets and clothing contaminated with diseases. In many cases, diseases reached populations that had never been in direct contact with Europeans. The diseases spread from First Nation to First Nation throughout the continent during normal trading relationships.

In 1780, a major smallpox — called *omikewin* in Cree, which literally means "scabbing" — epidemic spread across western Canada, killing thousands. Its source may have been contact with a single infected fur trader. In the years that followed, western First Nations experienced epidemics of measles, whooping cough, influenza, and tuberculosis, which the Dené Tha' call *kedzowoti'hi*, which means "sickness of the chest."

In 1837, during a smallpox epidemic, the Hudson's Bay Company began to vaccinate some First Nations people — generally the homeguard who lived around their posts. The company hoped to slow the spread of the disease and save the fur trade from collapse. The vaccines helped save some, but were not widely available.

Traditional healing methods and medicines did not cure the new illnesses and thousands of First Nations people died. In addition, the diseases killed many Elders. With them died knowledge that could never be recovered by those who survived.

Diseases weakened First Nations so much that they were unable, in many cases, to provide for themselves. Populations were so depleted that the kinship networks that were the basis of their social support systems were in many cases wiped out. And so it was in this state — depleted politically, economically and socially — that western First Nations faced the growing demands of Canadian settlement.

1616	First smallpox epidemic in Canada brought by infected French settlers. It quickly spreads to First Nations in the Maritimes, James Bay, and Great Lakes regions.	1600 1620
1634–1641	Smallpox spreads throughout the St. Lawrence–Great Lakes region, beginning first among the Innu in 1634.	1640
1662–1663	Smallpox spreads throughout New France and afflicts thousands of First Nations peoples in the area.	1660 1680
1736–1738	Smallpox spreads across western Canada among the Nakoda and Cree.	1700
1746	Typhoid afflicts the Mi'kmaq in Nova Scotia, killing more than one-third of the population.	1720
1780–1784	Major smallpox epidemic spreads throughout western Canada. The epidemic kills many among the Nakoda, Anishinabé, and Cree of the northern Plains.	1740 1760
1819–1823	Major measles and whooping cough epidemic spreads throughout western Canada. It afflicts many Cree and Nakoda.	1780
1837–1838	Smallpox spreads throughout the northern Plains as a result of contact with infected traders from the United States. The Anishinabé and Nakoda are the worst affected. The Hudson's Bay Company introduces vaccines to some groups to curb the spread of the disease.	1800 1820 1840
1869–1870	Smallpox ravages the Cree, Nakoda, Blackfoot Confederacy, and Anishinabé of the northern Plains. Its origin is the United States.	1860
1891–1901	Tuberculosis strikes the Cree, Nakoda, and Anishinabé of what is now central Alberta.	1880 1900

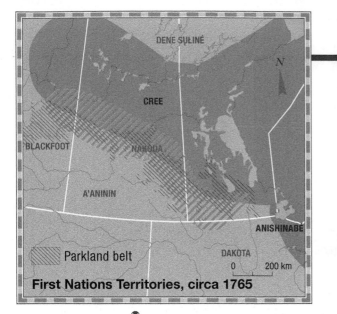

First Nations Territories, circa 1765

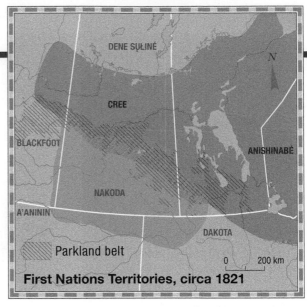

First Nations Territories, circa 1821

These three maps demonstrate the general movement of nations on the Plains from the peak of the fur trade to the beginning of the decline. What pattern can you see?

SHIFTING TERRITORIES

From the seventeenth until the mid-nineteenth centuries, First Nations along the eastern coast and shores of the Great Lakes had many incentives to travel farther and farther from their traditional territories. These movements were at first as **entrepreneurs** — many First Nations people worked independently to profit from the trade. As middlemen, they travelled back and forth from their traditional lands in order to trade with inland groups. Some even moved inland to take advantage of the changing economic opportunities that trade with Europeans offered.

For example, over 300 Haudenosaunee people came west with the North West Company. Many intermarried with other First Nations and Métis peoples and settled in the Athabasca, Grande Cache, and Peace River regions in Alberta.

However, by the nineteenth century, the fur trade was in decline and offered fewer economic opportunities. Excessive hunting and trapping had made traditional ways of life difficult or impossible in some regions. Nations now moved in an attempt to find some way to make a living. As they did so, they came into increasing conflict with other nations who had similar needs. A brief look at the migrations of the Cree and Nakoda, as well as some Métis communities, demonstrates these territorial shifts.

Cree and Nakoda

As the western fur trade expanded, the Cree and Nakoda peoples formed an alliance, working together to supply the trade. Some provided food for the posts and others were middlemen for both French and British traders. They grew prosperous and strong and were successful in expanding their territory.

However, in 1821, when competition between the Hudson's Bay Company (HBC) and North West Company ended, fewer middlemen

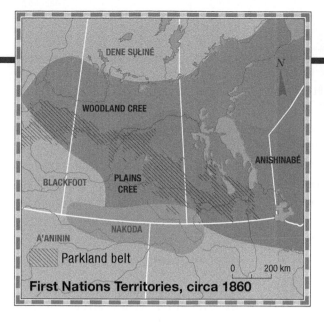

DENE SUŁINÉ

WOODLAND CREE

ANISHINABÉ

BLACKFOOT

PLAINS
CREE

N

NAKODA

A'ANININ

Parkland belt

0   200 km

First Nations Territories, circa 1860

Métis peoples were already living in the region as farmers, fishers, and in various roles in the fur trade.

Like First Nations in the late nineteenth century, Métis hunters found they had to travel farther and farther west to find the buffalo herds each summer. By the 1850s and 1860s, buffalo hunts were being organized from settlements in the Cypress Hills area, the St. Albert–Edmonton area, and near Batoche. First Nations also depended on buffalo for their livelihood and as the herds declined and more Métis hunters appeared, conflict erupted between some First Nations and Métis peoples.

In the mid-1840s and in 1859, Métis hunters fought Dakota hunters for control of the hunt in what is now North Dakota. The Dakota people defended their territory by setting prairie fires that drove the buffalo away and kept Métis people out. The two nations eventually reached a peace treaty.

Métis also battled Cree over the right to hunt buffalo in the Qu'Appelle Valley in present-day Saskatchewan. The Métis people were successful and by the end of the 1860s, completely dominated the dwindling pemmican market as suppliers for the HBC.

were needed. At the same time, some groups found that they could no longer support themselves in the northern forests. Prey were now scarce where they were once plentiful. For a time, the trade in buffalo products provided new opportunities. The Nakoda and Plains Cree moved south to take advantage of the change. However, as buffalo populations also began to decline, the Nakoda and Cree ran into increasing conflict with the Blackfoot Confederacy, which was having a hard time finding buffalo for its own needs.

Métis

Métis communities developed first along the north and south coasts of the Great Lakes as the French moved their posts inland. After the War of 1812, Americans took control of the fur trade in the Great Lakes area. Many Métis people were displaced. Some went north towards the Red River. French and

SOVEREIGN NATIONS

Fur trade history in Canada is also the history of European–Canadian and Aboriginal relations in this country. Understanding this history provides a basis for understanding contemporary Aboriginal political, economic, and social movements. Most of these movements make a claim for some degree of sovereignty.

Sovereignty means independence from the influence or interference of other nations. A sovereign nation is free to conduct its internal and foreign affairs as it sees fit. A nation with less sovereignty might be a colony that enjoys some independence, but is still subject to **colonial governance**, the rules or decisions of a more powerful country. A country with no sovereignty might be one that is attacked and occupied, completely losing its independence.

Before contact, First Nations were sovereign communities, each its own system of political, economic, social, and spiritual organization. Sometimes they fought and sometimes they cooperated, but they generally regarded one another as more or less equal.

Treaties

In the early years after contact, interactions between the Europeans and First Nations were as sovereign nations. For the most part, this relationship was mutually beneficial. The Europeans and First Nations negotiated many military alliances, trade agreements, and exchanges. Cautious cooperation was the basis on which each side concluded treaties.

Treaty making had been an important activity among First Nations long before the arrival of Europeans to the Americas. Treaties had been used between First Nations to establish peace, regulate trade, organize the use of resources, and arrange defence. First Nations approached treaties with Europeans in the same light.

At first, Europeans negotiated treaties with First Nations to ensure friendly relationships as they explored and began to exploit the land's resources. First Nations people far outnumbered the Europeans, who needed First Nations co-operation and assistance to survive. Later, treaties with First Nations were formed for defence

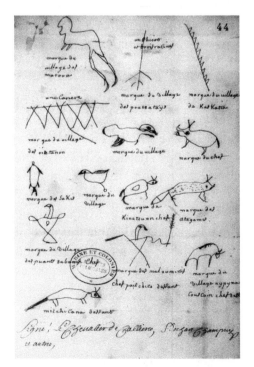

This treaty was signed in 1701 between the French and First Nations in the Great Lakes region. The Europeans and First Nations, in signing such a document, recognized one another as mutually sovereign nations. The First Nations signed with symbols of their clans. How is signing a document with a symbol of a clan symbolically different from signing with an individual's name?

and to ensure allies in wars with other European powers in North America.

Treaty terms were written down by European negotiators and ratified by First Nations ceremonies. First Nations viewed these treaties as sacred oaths.

The British government signed many treaties with First Nations during the eighteenth century. From the British perspective, the treaties recognized both First Nations independence and First Nations agreement to cede large areas of land for British control and future colonization. The British also wanted to protect this land from seizure by other European powers and later by the United States.

From First Nations perspectives, however, the treaties meant something quite different. In First Nations worldviews, it would not be possible to give land to another government or person because no one can own the land in the first place. In the eyes of those who signed the treaties, therefore, the agreements established peaceful coexistence, not a sale or gift of land.

The Royal Proclamation of 1763 recognized the independence of the "Nations and Tribes of Indians" in North America who were under the protection of the British Crown — those whose territories were in the area now known as Canada. With this proclamation, Britain recognized First Nations as independent, sovereign groups with distinct territories.

Today many First Nations leaders argue that their nations should continue to have some degree of sovereignty and independence.

The proclamation arranged for First Nations and Euro-Canadian settlers to share the lands that would eventually become Canada. This document became the basis upon which First Nations and Canadian peoples would conclude other treaties in the nineteenth century.

This illustration is from a 1777 "Map of the Inhabited Part of Canada." What does this title imply about the portions of Canada not on the map? What does this implication say about European attitudes about territorial occupation?

LOOKING BACK

Look back to the timeline notes that you started on page 135. Work with a partner to prepare a final timeline of events in this chapter. Be sure that your timeline is to scale. Include as many events as possible and be sure you include notes or explanations for events you think are most significant. You might choose to create your timeline on a computer. If you do, consider including photographs or other illustrations to highlight significant points.

Chapter Five Review

Check Your Understanding

1. What did Europeans gain from their early relationships with First Nations? What did First Nations gain from their early relationships with Europeans? Answer with a list, concept map, or paragraph giving specific examples.

2. Describe the early relationship between Europeans and First Nations using the following concepts: adaptation, innovation, mutual benefit, and sovereignty.

3. Write a paragraph or series of paragraphs that begins with the following topic sentence:

   > First Nations were entrepreneurs in the western fur trade.

4. Describe four ways that Métis people combined elements of First Nations and European cultures.

5. How did marriages with First Nations women help European traders?

6. Copy the terms that follow and describe how each was significant in the history of First Nations–European relationships.

   List as many ideas as you can for each term.

   > beaver
   > buffalo
   > competition
   > *coureurs des bois*
   > disease
   > explorers
   > guns
   > homeguard
   > Hudson's Bay Company
   > *mariage à la façon du pays*
   > middleman
   > missionaries
   > pemmican
   > North West Company
   > virgin soil epidemics

7. List two factors that led to the decline of the fur trade and explain how at least two specific First Nations, Métis, or Inuit groups were affected.

8. List at least four factors that led to the decline of the buffalo populations on the prairies.

Reading and Writing

9. Read the quotations on page 167. All are from the perspective of someone looking back in time. Imagine that you can go back in time to the period before Europeans began trading regularly with First Nations in North America. Choose a specific First Nation that you will approach. What would you tell them about the future? Write a speech or short story as your answer. Consider the worldview of your audience and try to explain your points in ways that would make sense to them.

10. First Nations traditional knowledge helped Europeans learn how to survive in North America. Write an essay that supports the following sentence with examples from a First Nations's oral tradition and traditional way of life:

    > First Nations traditional knowledge is of relevance to the wise management of Canada's natural resources today.

Viewing and Representing

11. Working with a small group, prepare a series of maps that convey the history of First Nations and Europeans from the fifteenth to the nineteenth centuries. Use online or print map sources, such as the *Atlas of Canada (www.atlas.gc.ca/)* or the *Historical Atlas of Canada*.

12. The illustrations and paintings in this chapter are generally from a European perspective. Choose one to redraw or repaint from a First Nations, Métis, or Inuit perspective.

Going Further

13. How did the lives of First Nations women change after marrying European men? Research this topic with a partner and prepare a dramatic dialogue that makes use of your information.

14. Visit a museum that has exhibits about the fur trade era. Note any positive elements of the exhibit and any that you feel misrepresent First Nations, Métis, or Inuit peoples or their roles in the trade. Write a letter to the museum noting specific aspects of the display that were done well.

    If you believe there are problems with the exhibit, note these in your letter with evidence supporting your viewpoint. Keep your letter polite and specific in your critique. If you note a problem, explain exactly where the problem lies, what the problem is, and how it might be improved or corrected.

15. Research the symptoms and effects of one virgin soil epidemic. Find out how the disease affected a specific First Nation or region of the country. Work with a group of students who researched a different disease to exchange information. Within your group, discuss the political, economic, social, and spiritual effects that European diseases had on traditional First Nations ways of life.

LOOKING BACK

Re-read George Blondin's story on pages 132–133, noting connections between the Sahtú Dene way of life and other Aboriginal peoples. What generalizations can you make about how the fur trade affected First Nations? List these with a few supporting points.

Trade goods were like candy; people knew they could live quite well off the land by fishing or hunting moose, woodland caribou, beaver, and spruce grouse, but tea, tobacco, and sugar made life more enjoyable.

— Joe Mackenzie, Behcho Ko (Fort Rae), *Yamoria the Lawmaker: Stories of the Dene*

The blankets we needed; they were a good substitute for the cumbersome buffalo robes and besides, their many bright colours fascinated us. A new blanket over our shoulders was something to be proud of. The knife was essential, therefore we bought it at a high price. And we never dreamed that the gun, which we were so anxious to own, would be the means of ultimate extermination of our main source of livelihood, the buffalo.

— Joseph F. Dion, Kehewin First Nation, *My Tribe the Crees*

There is a common saying among Indians today: "Before the whiteman came we had the land, they had the Bible. Now, we Indians have the Bible, they have the land."

Sometimes I think the entire history of Indian–non-Indian relations on this continent is summed up in that short statement. When the Europeans first came to the eastern shores of this Great Island, we — members of the huge intertribal society that occupied this land — welcomed them and helped them survive. We taught them what we knew and eased their period of adjustment to the Great Island considerably.

— Chief John Snow, Nakoda, *These Mountains Are Our Sacred Places*

CHAPTER SIX
Today and the Future

AS YOU READ

First Nations, Métis, and Inuit peoples in Canada today face numerous challenges that range from the protection of treaty rights and land claims to the move towards self-government and greater economic self-sufficiency. In general, most Aboriginal leaders are guiding their communities towards a balance between traditional ways and improved quality of life.

Georges Erasmus has dedicated his life to helping Aboriginal peoples across Canada achieve greater self-sufficiency. He has served as president of the Dene Nation, was national chief of the Assembly of First Nations for two terms, and was co-chair of the Royal Commission on Aboriginal Peoples from 1991–1996. In 2002, he delivered the LaFontaine–Baldwin lecture, an annual speech to stimulate debate about the history and future of Canada. An excerpt from his speech follows on pages 168–169.

As you read this chapter, consider these questions:

▲ How did the relationship between Aboriginal peoples and the Canadian government change in the years following the decline of the fur trade?

▲ What have been some of the lasting effects of government policy and legislation on Aboriginal individuals and communities?

▲ Why did Aboriginal peoples form organizations and alliances to negotiate with federal and provincial governments?

▲ What issues do Aboriginal political organizations work to address today?

▲ How have First Nations and Métis peoples in Alberta improved their quality of life through entrepreneurship?

Canada in the Twenty-first Century

Excerpt from a speech by Georges Erasmus

...To paint a picture of the Canada that Aboriginal people envision I need only turn to the ideals of a good life embedded in Aboriginal languages and traditional teachings. The Anishinabé seek the spiritual gift of *pimatziwin* — long life and well-being — which enable a person to gain wisdom. The Cree of the northern prairies value *miyowicehowin* — having good relations. The Iroquois Great Law sets out rules for maintaining peace between peoples — *skennen kowa* — going beyond resolving conflicts to actively caring for each other's welfare. Aboriginal peoples across Canada and around the world speak of their relationship with the natural world and the responsibility of human beings to maintain balance in the natural order. Rituals in which we give something back in return for the gifts that we receive from Mother Earth reinforce that sense of responsibility.

I would guess that most Canadians subscribe to these same goals: long life, health, and wisdom for self and family; a harmonious and cohesive society; peace between peoples of different origins and territories; and a sustainable relationship with the natural environment. Canadians would probably also agree in principle with the traditional Aboriginal ethic that our actions today should not jeopardize the health, peace, and well-being of generations yet unborn.

If there is such a convergence of basic values between Aboriginal and non-Aboriginal peoples, why is communication between us so difficult, so riddled with misunderstandings and tension? ...

Despite the resurgence in Aboriginal [self-sufficiency] in the past thirty years, the gap between Aboriginal and general Canadian life opportunities remains disturbingly wide. While Canada regularly ranks first on the United Nations index for quality of life, registered Indians living on-reserve would rank sixty-third and registered Indians on- and off-reserve would rank forty-seventh under the U.N. criteria of education, income, and life expectancy. Aboriginal youth are especially vulnerable. They are less likely than mature adults to attain academic and vocational credentials and they are hit hardest by unemployment. Moving from a reserve or rural settlement to the city improves income and employment prospects, but only marginally.

Strategies for [addressing these gaps] have been set out in the Royal Commission on Aboriginal Peoples Report and in subsequent forums. They include supporting community-led initiatives that mobilize Aboriginal peoples in diverse situations to deal with their own issues; creating space for Aboriginal institutions that provide sustained, effective leadership in accord with the culture of the community; promoting partnerships and collaboration between Aboriginal people, the private sector, and

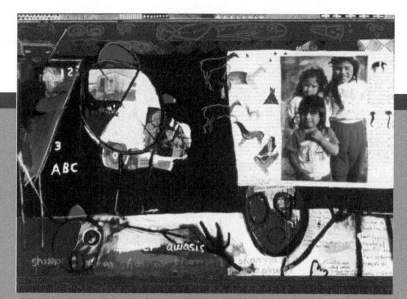

Artist Jane Ash Poitras, from Fort Chipewyan, Alberta, created In Our Dreams the Spirits Tell Us Things *in 1993. Most of Poitras's work focuses on the impact of colonization on Aboriginal peoples. Look closely at each element of her painting and discuss with a partner what her message might be. Research information about Poitras's life experiences. Discuss with a partner whether you see her personal experiences reflected in her work and if so, how.*

public institutions to break down isolation and barriers to productive relationships; and recognizing the authority of Aboriginal nations to negotiate the continuing place of Aboriginal peoples in Canadian society, whether on their traditional lands or in the city.

■ REFLECTION

In his lecture, Georges Erasmus looks to the traditional beliefs and values of various First Nations across Canada to discuss goals for Aboriginal peoples in the twenty-first century. These values include a long life, good relationships, peace, balance with nature, and responsibility. How do you think **standard of living** fits into these goals? Is standard of living related to quality of life?

What do you envision for your life and your community in the twenty-first century? Reflect on five things you would like to see improved in your life, concentrating on mental, emotional, physical, and spiritual growth. Next, reflect on five ideas that you believe would elevate life for all people living in Canada. Write your ideas in your journal and discuss them with a partner.

Shifting Relationships

Relations between Aboriginal peoples and people of other nations who settled in North America, beginning with Europeans, have undergone many changes over the past 500 years.

Between 1500 and 1812, Aboriginal peoples and Europeans established many mutually beneficial political, economic, and social bonds. In this period, for the most part, Aboriginal peoples and Europeans viewed each other as sovereign nations. As you learned on pages 164–165, this view of the relationship was set forth in many treaties and the Royal Proclamation of 1763.

As the fur trade declined, however, European priorities in North America began to change and so did their approach to their historic relationship with Aboriginal peoples.

Chapter Six describes the period of enormous change from the early nineteenth century to the present day. On pages 170–175, you will study how and why the relationship between Aboriginal peoples and the British and then Canadian governments changed from one of partnership to one of domination.

IN THE EARLY NINETEENTH CENTURY, THE RELATIONSHIP BETWEEN ABORIGINAL AND EURO-CANADIAN PEOPLES BEGAN TO CHANGE DRAMATICALLY. THERE ARE SEVERAL REASONS FOR THIS CHANGE. ONE IS THAT EUROPEAN, MAINLY British, settlers were flooding into eastern Canada. They came in search of farmland and new beginnings.

The British government responded to the changes in its colonies by concluding treaties with First Nations to open up lands to European settlement. These treaties were negotiated on the basis of the Royal Proclamation of 1763, which you learned about on page 165. After Confederation in 1867, the Canadian government continued signing treaties with western First Nations. Their goal was the same: prepare the way for future settlement.

At the same time that the Euro-Canadian population grew rapidly, the First Nations population was declining just as fast because of disease. In addition, the spread of agriculture changed the environment in many regions. Food shortages appeared among some First Nations who relied on hunting and trapping for income and food.

Meanwhile, the fur trade that had become an economic mainstay for many First Nations, Métis, and Inuit communities was drawing to a close. The decline of the buffalo was a disaster for Métis peoples and First Nations in western Canada. Many were brought to the edge of starvation.

Increasingly, the British and then Canadian governments no longer needed the First Nations as allies and economic partners. They began to believe that all Aboriginal peoples should adopt European customs, religions, and ways of life. Traditional Aboriginal ways of life had been essential for the fur trade, but now that the trade was no longer a driving force in the colonies, Euro-Canadian acceptance of Aboriginal traditions disappeared.

The next few pages will explore this time of turbulent change overtaking Aboriginal peoples and their relationships with the Canadian government.

FIRST NATIONS AND GOVERNMENT POLICY

As British and then Canadian (in 1867) government priorities changed from the fur trade to settlement and agriculture, their attitudes towards First Nations people changed as well.

In 1857, the British colonial government adopted the Gradual Civilization Act. This was the first step in a policy of assimilation that would last over 100 years. **Assimilation** policies pressured First Nations to adopt the values, beliefs, ways of life, and practices of Euro-Canadian cultures.

According to government thinking at the time, assimilation would be beneficial for and welcomed by First Nations. The act offered incentives to First Nations people in exchange for giving up their culture and adopting Euro-Canadian culture.

First Nations people unanimously rejected policies of assimilation. This response led to more legislation and even more controls over First Nations **rights** and ways of life. Government incentives had turned to government control.

Almost all legislation dealing with First Nations following 1857 had assimilation as its ultimate goal. For example, the Indian Act, adopted in 1876, was supposed to help the federal government implement the terms of treaties signed with First Nations. In effect, however, the Indian Act gave the government enormous power over First Nations peoples living on reserves.

Early relationships between First Nations and European nations were generally beneficial to both peoples. As depicted by this illustration, the different cultures were relatively equal partners. This equality lasted as long as the fur trade was a dominant force in the economy. Why did the decline of the fur trade prompt a change in the relationship?

Among many other changes, the Indian Act imposed a European-style government, called a **band council**, on each nation.

It also refined legislation from the 1850s that defined who was and was not considered an "Indian" under the act. These kinds of definitions, revised many times over the years, began separating First Nations communities with rules that defined who had status under the act and who did not. Today even a single family can include people who are **Status Indians** (registered for benefits under the Indian Act), non-Status Indians, and Métis. In time, the Canadian government imposed other restrictions on First Nations people and banned many traditional customs, ceremonies, and even movements on and off the reserves.

Residential schools run by various Christian churches were set up to educate First Nations children in Euro-Canadian culture, as well as to discourage First Nations traditional customs, languages, and beliefs. Children were sometimes forcibly removed from their homes to live and be educated far from their communities.

Residential schools devastated the social and cultural life of many

Based on what you see in this photograph and what you know of traditional First Nations philosophies about children and education, how would residential schools, such as this one at Hobbema, Alberta, have affected the worldview of First Nations children? Why do you think the government made schools one of their first priorities in implementing its assimilation policy?

First Nations communities. Some children who returned home from residential schools did not remember their First Nation language and were unfamiliar and uncomfortable with traditional ways of life. Some suffered physical and emotional abuse at school.

Communities lost control over traditional territories and were sometimes forced to move to small reserves in unfamiliar areas. For many, the reserve land base allocated to them did not provide an adequate source of economic self-sufficiency. For various reasons, other communities did not receive a reserve at all. Some First Nations fell into deep poverty. By the middle of the twentieth century, First Nations had become isolated from non-Aboriginal Canadian society.

By 1951, when the Indian Act was revised, living standards of First Nations and other Aboriginal peoples were extremely low compared to other people living in Canada.

These problems had grown over time and stemmed from the loss of traditional lands and resources, the destruction of traditional occupations and social institutions, and the denial of First Nations cultural identities by the Canadian government and society. Yet throughout this social disorder, First Nations peoples continued to resist assimilation.

In the 1960s, the Canadian government began to consider major changes to the Indian Act. In 1969, Jean Chretien, then the minister of the federal government's Department of Indian Affairs, brought forward the White Paper. It proposed to end all programs and special legal rights for First Nations people. From the government's point of view, it was the final step in their assimilation policy.

For First Nations, the treaties (even if not honoured completely by the federal government) were the only acknowledgement of the federal government's historic agreements with and obligations to their peoples. Abolishing the Indian Act and the treaties the act was supposed to implement meant losing any opportunity to redeem the promises their ancestors had received. The proposed changes sparked an uproar. First Nations across the country joined forces to fight the proposal. They issued their response as the Red Paper. It was the first of many times that First Nations would work together as a collective to protect their rights.

1763   Royal Proclamation
Recognizes the First Nations right to possess all land in British territories outside established colonies

1857   Gradual Civilization Act
Promotes the assimilation of First Nations peoples into Euro-Canadian society

1867   British North America Act
Unifies the British colonies of Canada, Nova Scotia, and New Brunswick into the Dominion of Canada and gives the Dominion government responsibility over First Nations peoples

1869   Gradual Enfranchisement Act
Outlines a policy of assimilation of First Nations peoples

1869   Red River Resistance
A Métis resistance led by Louis Riel rejects the Canadian government's claim to their land

1870   Manitoba Act
Creates the province of Manitoba and recognizes Métis land title in the province

1871   Treaty Number One
Signed by the federal government with the Anishinabé and Swampy Cree of southern Manitoba

1871   Treaty Number Two
Signed by the federal government with the Anishinabé of southwestern Manitoba

1873   Treaty Number Three
Signed by the federal government with the Anishinabé of northwestern Ontario

1874   Treaty Number Four
Signed by the federal government with the Cree and Anishinabé of southern Saskatchewan

1875   Treaty Number Five
Signed by the federal government with the Anishinabé and Cree of north-central Manitoba

1876   Treaty Number Six
Signed by the federal government with the Plains and Woodland Cree of central Alberta and Saskatchewan

1876   Indian Act
Consolidates all laws relating to First Nations and gives the federal government many political, economic, and social powers over First Nations people

1877   Treaty Number Seven
Signed by the federal government with the Siksika, Kainai, Piikani, Tsuu T'ina and Nakoda of southern Alberta

1883   Residential School Policy
Establishes the first residential schools for First Nations peoples in western Canada

1885   1885 Resistance
Establishes a Métis government at Batoche, which is defeated by federal government forces

1885   Riel's Execution
Riel is tried, found guilty of treason, and hanged

1899   Treaty Number Eight
Signed by the federal government with the Cree, Dunne-za, and Dene Sųłiné of northern Alberta and northeastern British Columbia

1905   Treaty Number Nine
Signed by the federal government with the Dene Sųłiné and Cree of north-central Ontario

1906   Treaty Number Ten
Signed by the federal government with the Dene Sųłiné and Cree of northern Saskatchewan

1921   Treaty Number Eleven
Signed by the federal government with the Dené Tha', Tłįchǫ (Dogrib), Gwich'in (Loucheux), and Hare of the Mackenzie River Valley.

1929–1930 James Bay Treaty Number Nine
Signed by the federal government with the Anishinabé and Cree of northern Ontario

1938   Métis Population Betterment Act
Passed by the Alberta government to establish twelve Métis Settlements to improve living conditions for the province's Métis peoples

1951   Indian Act Revisions
Lift bans on political organizations and the ability of First Nations to sue the government

1960   First Nations Right to Vote
Receive right to vote in federal elections

1969   White Paper
Proposes ending all legal and constitutional rights related to First Nations, abolishing the Indian Act, and ending all federal government programs for First Nations peoples

1970   Red Paper
Consolidates the First Nations' response to the federal government's White Paper; demands that the special legal status of First Nations peoples be retained and all treaty obligations kept

1750
1775
1800
1825
1850
1875
1900
1925
1950
1975

Indigenous Knowledge

With your teacher's help, divide the events listed in the timeline among students in your class. Make each person responsible for expanding their section of the timeline with at least five significant ideas. Take turns typing the points in a file of class notes and give a copy of the notes to each student.

MÉTIS PEOPLES AND CANADIAN POLICY

Throughout their history, Métis peoples have shown themselves ready to defend their culture and rights. Sometimes this has resulted in armed conflict. Other times it has resulted in a war of words.

In general, government policy has tended to ignore Métis claims to land and other rights. Much government legislation that impacted Métis people did not have a specific goal in mind, such as assimilation. It simply did not acknowledge Métis people or their needs, almost as if they didn't exist. In addition, many Métis people were (and continue to be) affected by government legislation for First Nations. All Métis people have First Nations relatives.

In the 1960s, as First Nations organized themselves and encouraged a new kind of leader to step forward, so did the Métis. These leaders insisted that Métis rights and status in the country be acknowledged.

A NATION ASSERTS ITS RIGHTS

As a symbol of nationalism, the Métis flag predates Canada's Maple Leaf flag by 150 years. The flag includes a horizontal figure eight, or infinity symbol, which represents the joining of First Nations and European cultures in a new society that will last forever.

Different stories describe the origin of the flag, but no version has been declared the official history. The first recorded sighting of the flag was on June 1, 1816, when a group of Métis people, led by Cuthbert Grant, erected the flag at a Hudson's Bay Company trading post at Brandon House. The group then took — by force — stores of pemmican back to Red River. Their action was provoked by the company's growing restrictions upon their livelihood — the pemmican trade.

The incident at Brandon House was one of the first recorded Métis acts of unity against an attempt to restrict their independence as a nation. It would not be the last.

▉ REFLECTION

This first sighting of the Métis flag foreshadows many later events in the history of the Métis Nation, such as the Battle of Seven Oaks, which occurred just days after the events at Brandon House. Research the Battle of Seven Oaks and write a paragraph describing how it contributed to a Métis sense of nationhood.

INUIT PEOPLES AND CANADIAN POLICY

Inuit peoples have had a significantly different experience with the Canadian government than First Nations or Métis peoples have had. Inuit peoples were brought under Canadian jurisdiction as ordinary citizens. No treaties were signed with any Inuit groups and there has never been a national registry for people with Inuit heritage, as there is for First Nations people.

These policy differences sometimes caused administrative confusion. The Royal Canadian Mounted Police, who were the main presence of the Canadian government in the Arctic until the 1950s, often treated Inuit peoples the same way they did First Nations, especially regarding liquor laws.

To deal with this confusion, the Indian Act was amended in 1924 to include Inuit peoples, although Inuit programs and policies were always administered separately from those for First Nations.

In the 1920s, the Arctic experienced a serious decline in many of the animals that were part of traditional Inuit livelihoods. In 1929, the federal government purchased a herd of 3000 reindeer from Alaska, where herds had been introduced successfully in the 1890s. The government hoped these animals would take the place of declining game animals. This program has been reasonably successful. Some Inuvialuit in the eastern Mackenzie Delta still raise reindeer for meat, hides, and antlers for export.

During the 1930s, the fur trade almost disappeared and many communities faced starvation. The government responded in 1934 with a relocation program. Inuit peoples were moved to permanent communities, where the government could more easily provide services for them.

The relocations were a failure. The federal government had not understood how closely Inuit people's identity and culture were tied to specific territories and resources. In some cases, people were moved to regions where ice patterns in the winter made hunting and trapping impossible. In one case, Inuit peoples were given nets to fish in a nearby lake, even though the people had a cultural taboo against eating fish that died by

drowning. More hardship ensued. In the late 1970s, the relocation program was finally discontinued.

In the meantime, Inuit peoples had made some political gains. In 1950, Inuit peoples gained the right to vote, a full ten years before First Nations people received the same right. In 1951, during a major Indian Act revision, Inuit peoples were specifically excluded from its provisions. A new kind of Inuit leader emerged during the 1950s and 1960s. These leaders began to articulate an Inuit vision of the future that included **self-determination** and cultural preservation alongside adaptation to the modern world.

In 1929, 3000 reindeer left Alaska for the Canadian Arctic. The herd was part of a federal government plan to help Inuit peoples survive a decline in traditional game. It took five years to herd the animals 3200 kilometres from Alaska to Kittigazuit in the eastern Mackenzie Delta.

LOOKING BACK

Before moving on to the next section, be sure you can answer the questions that follow. What significant changes occurred at the beginning of the nineteenth century that affected government policy and Aboriginal peoples' lives? Compare how shifting government policy differed for First Nations, Métis, and Inuit peoples.

Politics and Government

AS YOU READ

One of the biggest challenges for Aboriginal political organizations is finding a balance between the power of a unified voice and the need to represent diverse needs and perspectives. Why is there power in a unified voice? Why is it unlikely that any single political organization could speak for all Aboriginal peoples? Discuss these questions before you read pages 176–187, about some of the Aboriginal political organizations most active today.

BEFORE 1969, ABORIGINAL PEOPLES HAD MADE SEVERAL ATTEMPTS TO ORGANIZE A NATIONAL POLITICAL ORGANIZATION. EACH ORGANIZATION FAILED, GENERALLY BECAUSE OF LACK OF GOVERNMENT SUPPORT OR ATTENTION.

These included the League of Indians after World War I, the North American Indian Brotherhood after World War II, and the National Indian Council (NIC) in 1961. The NIC's goal was to promote unity among all its constituents — in this case, Status Indians, non-Status Indians, First Nations that had signed treaties, and Métis peoples. The NIC failed partly because it was too difficult to develop a single voice that could speak for the needs of all its members.

After the NIC broke up, Métis people and non-Status Indians formed the Native Council of

NATIONAL ABORIGINAL POLITICAL ORGANIZATIONS

- Assembly of First Nations *(www.afn.ca)*
- Congress of Aboriginal Peoples *(www.abo-peoples.org)*
- Inuit Tapiriit Kanatami *(www.tapirisat.ca)*
- Métis National Council *(www.metisnation.ca)*
- Native Women's Association of Canada *(www.nwac.hq.org)*

Canada. Status Indians formed the National Indian Brotherhood (NIB).

Soon after the NIB was formed in 1968, the federal government announced its White Paper. The NIB led the outcry from First Nations across the country. As a result, the White Paper proposal was dropped and the NIB had found a foothold as a national organization. It had gained experience in dealing with the federal government and it now had support in First Nations across the country.

None of the national Aboriginal political organizations that you read about in this section have official political power. The Assembly of First Nations does not, for example, represent its constituents in the House of Commons as an elected Member of Parliament does. Instead, national Aboriginal political organizations lobby the federal government on behalf of their communities' interests.

The federal government generally includes leaders from Aboriginal political organizations in meetings about policies that affect Aboriginal peoples. However, this inclusion does not always happen, or it does not always include all groups who believe they should have a voice in negotiations. This is why most Aboriginal leaders want self-government for their communities. **Self-government** would give communities the ability to govern themselves without relying upon an invitation to another government's negotiating table.

ASSEMBLY OF FIRST NATIONS

The National Indian Brotherhood changed its name to the Assembly of First Nations in 1982. The Assembly of First Nations (AFN) represents the interests of over 630 First Nations in Canada to the federal and provincial governments. The AFN's mandate is to restore and enhance the historical relationship between First Nations and the Canadian government.

Where one nation speaking out might not receive the attention it needs, the AFN is highly influential because it speaks for so many member nations.

The organization works to present unified views on issues affecting First Nations peoples, such as Aboriginal rights, economic development, education, environment, health, housing, justice, language and literacy, social development, taxation, and treaty rights. **Treaty rights** are special rights to land and other benefits due to the people who signed a treaty and the descendants of those people. The AFN also acts as a forum for various First Nations

NATIONAL CHIEFS OF THE ASSEMBLY OF FIRST NATIONS

David Ahenakew	(1982–1985)
Georges Erasmus	(1985–1991)
Ovide Mercredi	(1991–1997)
Phil Fontaine	(1997–2000)
Matthew Coon Come	(2000–2003)
Phil Fontaine	(2003–)

ORGANIZATION OF THE ASSEMBLY OF FIRST NATIONS

The Assembly of First Nations' organizational structure evolves often as it adapts to the needs of its member nations. Its main decision making bodies are currently the First Nations-in-Assembly, the Confederacy of Nations, and the Executive Committee.

National Chief of the Assembly of First Nations Phil Fontaine is often contacted by news media who want a First Nations perspective on issues.

First Nations-in-Assembly

The First Nations-in-Assembly make decisions on issues brought forward by member First Nations. Each First Nation is represented in the assembly by its chief or another representative from its band council. The assembly meets annually to set national policy and pass resolutions. Each representative has one vote on resolutions, no matter how large their reserve is or how many people they represent.

Confederacy of Nations

When the First Nations-in-Assembly is not in session, the Confederacy of Nations is responsible for making decisions. The confederacy meets every three or four months to monitor and examine AFN policies and programs. The Confederacy of Nations includes the national chief and ten regional vice-chiefs.

Executive Committee

The AFN's Executive Committee consists of the national chief, the regional vice-chiefs, and the chairs of the Elders Council, the Women's Council, and the National Youth Council. The AFN national chief is elected by the First Nations-in-Assembly for a three-year term. To be elected national chief, a candidate needs to win 60 per cent of the vote. The national chief represents the AFN at federal-provincial conferences, in meetings with government officials, and at international conferences. On the Executive Committee, the national chief is a member of the collective leadership. The national chief does not assume special authority or power over the other leaders.

to maintain relationships among one another.

The AFN has been successful in helping non-Aboriginal Canadians develop better awareness about First Nations issues and in providing First Nations representation at key government meetings. For example, the AFN was a significant participant in the many meetings to amend Canada's constitution in the 1980s. Today it continues to be an active participant in other government negotiations.

CONGRESS OF ABORIGINAL PEOPLES

Métis people's interests and those of non-Status Indians were first represented nationally by the Native Council of Canada (NCC), which formed in 1971.

The first Métis Nation Cabinet shown here has representation from all the Métis National Council's provincial associations. Back row left to right: Ministers Ed Ducharme, Harley Desjarlais, Tony Belcourt, Wayne Flaathen, David Chartrand. Front row left to right: Ministers Clément Chartier, Audrey Poitras, Gerald Morin, Lisa McCallum, Allan Morin. Research which provincial association each of these ministers represents and how many Métis people are in their region.

During the 1983 constitutional negotiations, a large group of Métis people felt the NCC was not adequately representing their distinct interests. These members included Métis people from the western provinces and northern Ontario. This group was united by a strong connection to their Red River heritage. They broke away from the NCC and formed the Métis National Council.

The NCC changed its name to the Congress of Aboriginal Peoples in 1987 and still represents the interests of many Métis peoples and non-Status Indians in Canada.

MÉTIS NATIONAL COUNCIL

The Métis National Council (MNC)'s goals are to represent and promote the interests of the Métis Nation by restoring Métis lands and resources, achieving full recognition of the historical contributions of the Métis Nation to Canada, developing cooperative relations with Canadian governments, promoting progress among Métis people, and preserving Métis culture.

The MNC today has provincial associations in British Columbia, Alberta, Saskatchewan, Manitoba, and Ontario. The provincial associations are responsible for representing all Métis people in their province. The provincial associations are also responsible for lobbying provincial governments for access to provincial programs and services, and coordinating MNC activities in local Métis communities.

Each provincial association has an elected council and sends representatives to the MNC. The provincial associations are the focus of political activity for the MNC.

Each provincial association has regional councils, each with its own constitution. Although the specifics of regional and provincial associations vary, common to all is the principle that all Métis people be allowed to participate.

Because Métis peoples were not included in the Indian Act or any other federal legislation until the Constitution Act in 1982, they have always been active politically at the provincial level. They have negotiated directly with provincial governments to achieve land and self-government for Métis people, with considerable success in Alberta.

A board of governors oversees MNC activities. The board holds meetings every two months. A general assembly is held once a year and is attended by the heads of the provincial associations and their elected councils. In 2001, the MNC formed the Métis Nation Cabinet. It is responsible for policy making in areas of culture and heritage, economic development, environment, health, international affairs, social development, women's issues, and youth.

Métis Nation of Alberta

The Métis Nation of Alberta (MNA) was formed in 1932 to represent the interests of landless Métis people in Alberta. Its main goal was to re-establish a land and resource base

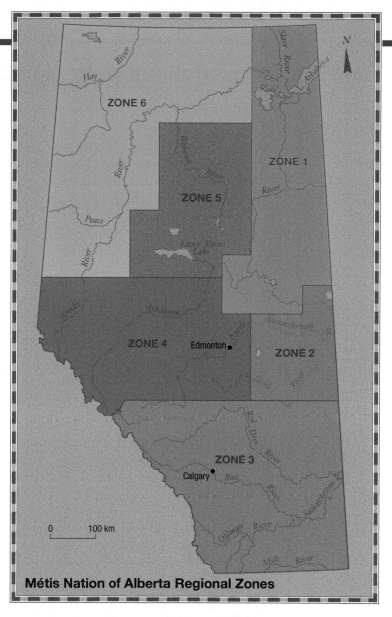

Métis Nation of Alberta Regional Zones

for Métis people in Alberta. In 1938, they were successful. That year the Alberta government created twelve Métis Settlements in the north-central part of the province.

Today the MNA represents the interests of all Métis people in Alberta, including the many Métis people who do not live on one of the Métis Settlements. It has programs that further Métis people's political, economic, social, educational, and cultural development.

Which regional zone is your school in, according to this map?

Audrey Poitras

AUDREY POITRAS
Métis Nation of Alberta President

The Métis Nation of Alberta (MNA) was started in 1932 by a group of five — Joseph Dion, Jim Brady, Malcolm Norris, Peter Tomkins, and Felix Callihoo. It has come a long way in bringing positive political support and economic change for Métis people in Alberta. But as the MNA moved towards the twenty-first century, its organization faced serious instability. The Métis peoples of Alberta came forth to show they were ready for a shift of a different kind.

In 1996, the MNA's director of finance was visiting offices across the province as part of her job. Everywhere she went, people encouraged her to run for the leadership of the association. With elections quickly approaching, Audrey Poitras considered their requests.

"I thought about it, then took a six-week leave of absence to travel from one end of the province to the other, talking to people and campaigning full time," says Poitras. "Everywhere I went, people gave their support."

After winning by a landslide, Poitras has capably served her people for seven years. Under her farsighted leadership, the MNA has not only continued to preserve and promote Métis culture, it has also advanced economic development and employment initiatives. It supports and invests in Métis people to help them attain the skills, jobs, and self-employment that lead to self-sufficiency. The MNA has many economic partnerships with federal and provincial governments to provide programs that support their goals.

Much of the MNA's success stems from how well the organization keeps in touch with people at the grassroots. Poitras insists that "it's the communities and the people that it's all about — not just what goes on in Edmonton or Ottawa."

Poitras continues to visit with constituents, even in the most remote communities, just as she did when she first ran for the presidency. Poitras wants to know the issues from the perspective of her constituents and they appreciate having her attention. Their continued support is proof of that appreciation.

■ REFLECTION

Audrey Poitras demonstrates that listening is key to her success as a leader. As well, her focus on helping Métis people help themselves is essential to the Métis Nation's future success. What programs do the MNA and other Aboriginal political organizations offer for youth? What kinds of opportunities exist for involvement? Research opportunities for youth in the MNA or another political organization.

LOCAL GOVERNMENTS

Although national organizations are important in ensuring the protection of Aboriginal peoples' rights, provincial and local organizations play an equally significant role. The enormous diversity of interests and needs among various communities means that local organizations often have the best sense of community priorities.

In addition, because many needs involve families, language, and **community initiatives**, local organizations will continue to play a significant role in self-determination initiatives. Self-determination includes the rights of self-government, as well as the ability to address local economic and cultural needs.

Métis Settlements

Although twelve Métis Settlements were originally created in 1938, over the years, four of the settlements were dissolved by the Alberta government for a variety of reasons and residents were forced to move.

In the 1970s, the settlements founded the Alberta Federation of Métis Settlements to deal with this issue and others. In 1975, they sued the Alberta government for compensation for natural resources taken from their lands and for more control over their own affairs. In 1988, the provincial government agreed to compensate Métis communities for past use of their natural resources and to increase their powers of self-government.

Issues for Investigation

ROLE PLAYING POLITICAL LEADERS

Numerous political organizations and alliances represent Aboriginal peoples' interests in Canada. Through the Aboriginal Canada Portal Web site (*www.aboriginalcanada.gc.ca*), five national organizations can be contacted: Inuit Tapiriit Kanatami, Assembly of First Nations, Congress of Aboriginal Peoples, Métis National Council, and the Native Women's Association of Canada. Many local and regional organizations also have Web sites, such as the Métis Settlements General Council, at *www. msgc.ca.*

What are the mandates of Aboriginal political organizations?

WHAT TO DO

1. In small groups, choose one Aboriginal political organization discussed in this chapter or choose another with your teacher's approval. Research the group's mandate in terms of improving quality of life, self-government, economic development, and treaty rights.

2. Divide the work up among your group members. For example, one person could research the organization's historical background, one its current mandate and policies, and another some of the issues the organization is actively working on and how it is addressing them.

3. As a class, role play members of your organizations at a social function of political leaders. Circulate around the classroom and introduce yourself and your organization to other leaders. Engage other leaders in a discussion about your own organization and the organization's policies. Your task during the event is to communicate your main ideas in ways that other leaders will remember. Your task following the event is to write a summary of what you learned about at least three other organizations.

Meetings of the Métis Settlement General Council help leaders address common concerns, while each Métis Settlement has autonomy in local decisions. What other systems of government have a similar organizational structure?

The package totalled $310 million over seventeen years and also established self-government for the Métis Settlements. The agreement was approved in a vote by the Métis Settlements in 1989.

In 1990, the Métis Settlements Act amended Alberta's constitution to protect the settlements' land base. The agreement established land ownership rights and local and collective governments. The Métis Settlements General Council was set up to make collective policies for all eight settlements in areas such as residency, use of forest resources, hunting, fishing, trapping, operation of businesses, and spending of settlement funds. Each settlement has its own powers of local government.

Indian Act Band Councils

As mentioned on page 171, the Indian Act abolished traditional systems of governance and set up a band council for each reserve. The Indian Act ruled that band councils would operate according to **hierarchical** Euro-Canadian political systems. Elders were removed from official positions (although their influence in many communities continued unofficially), women were not permitted to participate, and the election process involved a public showing of hands.

An Indian agent, usually a non-Aboriginal person, was a representative of the federal government's power on the reserves. The agent tightly controlled band council meetings, bylaws, and financial matters. The agent could remove chiefs and other leaders from the band council and punish members of the community who did not follow laws. In the end, band councils did not have much authority or power — the federal government could veto any decision they made.

For an act that was supposed to protect First Nations rights enshrined in treaties, it did nothing to reinforce traditional First Nations institutions. Because of this, many nations were slow to accept the changes. However, when financial agreements in the treaties became tied to acceptance of the Euro-Canadian government system, First Nations had little choice. Most began to work with the unfamiliar systems.

Band Councils Today

Although the Indian Act still influences how First Nations governments on reserves operate, many revisions to the act since 1951 mean that band councils today have considerable autonomy.

Each band may choose to elect its leaders by rules set up under the Indian Act, or it may follow traditional customs. For many reserves, the restoration of traditional ways of choosing leaders by consensus and kinship ties has led to greater public participation in reserve politics. On other reserves, the change to traditional ways has created tension between groups who support traditional methods and those who prefer elected leaders. Several bands use a combination of custom and Indian Act procedures.

In 2000, the right to vote in referenda and band council elections was extended to band members living off-reserve. This change may help communities maintain ties with individuals who move away from the reserve to pursue economic or educational opportunities.

Band councils pass bylaws called Band Council Resolutions. Although these bylaws must receive federal approval, fewer are overturned by the government than in the past. Band councils must hold a community meeting and referendum for some types of resolutions, including decisions to surrender reserve land, changes to membership codes for the band, and changes to alcohol bylaws.

Tribal Councils

Since the early 1980s, First Nations communities have developed many

This 2003 meeting of the Kainai First Nation band council shows, from the bottom left hand side of the photo around the table: Oliver Shouting, Rod First Rider, Kirby Many Fingers, Chief Chris Shade, Randy Bottle, Clement Soop and, from the bottom right, Dolores Day Chief and Franklin Wells. Also on the council, but not visible in this photo, are Jason Goodstriker, Will Long Time Squirrel, Marcel Weasel Head, Ira Tailfeathers, and Dan Mistaken Chief. Research the names of the councillors and chief of a band council near your school. With your teacher's help, contact the council to request a visit from someone to discuss the kinds of issues the council deals with at its meetings.

political institutions to promote self-government and self-determination. One of the most significant is the establishment of tribal councils that operate in communities across the country.

Tribal councils are voluntary groupings of First Nations with common interests. These nations join together to provide advisory or program services to member communities. Tribal councils are accountable to their members, not the federal government. A board of representatives or chiefs from member communities governs each tribal council. The board oversees the delivery of services, although staff carry out the programs.

Most tribal councils provide advisory services for economic development, financial management, community planning, technical services, and band governance. Today

78 tribal councils provide services and deliver programs to 475 First Nations. There are 135 First Nations that are not members of tribal councils. Some of these unaffiliated communities receive funding for similar programs directly from the federal government.

Alberta Tribal Councils

In Alberta, seven tribal councils provide services to thirty-two First Nations. The remaining nations in the province are unaffiliated.

The Confederacy of Treaty Six First Nations was created in 1993. It serves as the united voice of eighteen of the Alberta First Nations that signed Treaty Six in 1876.

Issues for Investigation

COMPARING FORMS OF GOVERNMENT

The 1951 Indian Act revisions began a return to self-government for First Nations. Among the 1951 revisions were the restoration of women's right to participate in government, the implementation of secret ballots rather than a show of hands, the repeal of bans on traditional ceremonies, and changes that gave more autonomy to band councils.

How have band council governments evolved over time?

WHAT TO DO

1. In small groups, choose a First Nation to be the focus of your study. You may want to choose a local group so that you have easier access to information about it. Prepare a visual diagram that shows the traditional political and decision making structure of the First Nation. Your teacher may have examples for you to use as references.

2. Prepare a diagram that shows the political structure and decision making process of First Nations as established by the Indian Act in 1876. Using your understanding of traditional First Nations institutions and worldviews, analyze why these changes were so damaging.

3. As much as possible, research the specific political, economic, and social changes to take place in the First Nation you are studying during the nineteenth and twentieth centuries. Prepare a summary of this information using statistics, stories, and any other research you think gives the most complete picture. If specific information is not available,

prepare a summary using general data and infer changes based on your research about the First Nation's culture and institutions.

4. Research how the First Nation governs itself now. You may need to call the band council office to have some of your questions answered. If you do, be sure you have your questions organized before you call. What initiatives has the band council taken to improve the quality of life for its members? Prepare a third visual diagram of the current system of governance.

5. Compare the three stages of change in government. Analyze how this political evolution was accompanied by social and economic changes. Anticipate some of the future needs of the First Nation. What kinds of political changes might be necessary to address these needs?

6. Present your research to the class using oral presentation, posters, PowerPoint™, or other presentation media.

ABORIGINAL PERSPECTIVES

The confederacy has several tasks. The first is to enhance treaty rights. The second is to help member First Nations develop policies and programs for health, social welfare, justice, and economic development.

To achieve these goals, the confederacy uses committees that are advised by councils composed of Elders, men, women, and youth.

The Treaty Seven Tribal Council was formed in 1989 as an advisory organization for the five Alberta First Nations that signed Treaty Seven in 1877. The tribal council offers advice about policy making and lobbying in areas such as education, health, community development, social development, and treaties. The goals of the tribal council are to protect treaty rights, to promote the interests of member First Nations to governments, and to pursue policies that improve the quality of life for members.

Each First Nation is represented on committees set up by the tribal council. The committees help member First Nations develop programs and services. Each First Nation is responsible for delivering its own programs.

Treaty Eight First Nations of Alberta was created in 1997. It ensures the protection and implementation of the terms of Treaty Eight signed by twenty-three Alberta First Nations in 1899.

The organization coordinates lobbying efforts on behalf of its members. The tribal council does not participate in the delivery of any programs and services. Instead, it collects information and develops policies that are reported to member First Nations.

Treaty Eight First Nations of Alberta is involved in several initiatives and projects in education and social development. Education initiatives include scholarship awards, teacher-training programs, and First Nations language instruction. It also works on social development projects related to welfare reform and child benefits.

This meeting of the Lesser Slave Lake Indian Regional Council was held in Jasper, Alberta, in 2004. Left to right: Councillors Bertha L'Hirondelle-Twinn and Ardell Twinn from Sawridge First Nation and Councillor Sydney L. Halcrow from Kapawe'no First Nation. Use the Internet to find out the names of all tribal councils in Alberta today.

FIRST NATIONS INVOLVEMENT IN ALBERTA POLITICS

Historically, First Nations interacted with the federal government rather than provincial or municipal governments. Most First Nations leaders felt some reluctance to develop a provincial government relationship. In dealing only with the federal government, First Nations made a symbolic point. They had the historic right to a nation-to-nation relationship with the federal government, a relationship that was written into treaties.

However, as Canadian federal politics evolved and provincial governments gained more powers, First Nations and their treaty rights were increasingly affected by areas

Indian Association of Alberta delegates are seen here boarding a train at Calgary, Alberta, in 1947. They are on their way to the House of Commons and Senate committee on Indian affairs hearings in Ottawa, Ontario. Left to right back row: David Crowchild, Tsuu T'ina; Joe Bullshield, Kainai; John Laurie, secretary, Calgary, Alberta. Left to right front row: Ed Hunter, Nakoda; Frank Cardinal, Sucker Creek, Alberta; Albert Lightning, Hobbema, Alberta; James Gladstone, Kainai; John Callihoo, Michel Lake, Alberta; Cecil Tallow, Kainai; Mark Steinhauer, Saddle Lake, Alberta.

of provincial jurisdiction. For example, medical care is a provincial responsibility, but under some treaties, Status Indians receive medical care through the federal government. This discrepancy led to wide variations in service and expectations between Status Indians and other provincial residents.

In 1939, First Nations in Alberta formed the Indian Association of Alberta (IAA) to represent their concerns in the provincial and federal capitals. Significantly, the IAA was formed in spite of Indian Act restrictions that banned First Nations people from creating their own political organizations.

At first, the IAA represented the interests of the Nakoda and the Plains Cree of central Alberta. In 1946, the IAA joined forces with southern Alberta First Nations. Following this, the organization became more active in lobbying the Alberta and federal governments for improved social services and financial allowances. It also made recommendations to the federal government about revising the Indian Act.

The Indian Act was revised in 1951, but IAA leadership continued to call for change. They wanted more autonomy for First Nations and protection of treaty rights. In 1958, James Gladstone, a member of the IAA, was appointed to the Senate and became Canada's first senator from a First Nation. As a senator, Gladstone worked tirelessly to express First Nations concerns. His work was essential in getting First Nations people the right to vote in 1960.

The IAA was a strong opponent of the federal government's White Paper. It organized demonstrations, published its views about the federal government's proposal, and was influential in the government's decision to abandon the policy.

In the late 1970s, the IAA and other First Nations political organizations called for First Nations and treaty rights to be recognized in the Canadian constitution. When the federal government announced in 1980 that it intended to patriate the country's constitution from Great Britain, the IAA organized demonstrations in Edmonton in favour of recognizing First Nations rights in the new constitution.

In the late 1980s, the IAA developed several proposals on issues important to First Nations people. These include child welfare, education, health, social services, and local government — all provincial government responsibilities under the constitution. In response, the Alberta government gave First Nations communities more responsibility for child welfare and education.

The IAA began to provide legal assistance to First Nations and to lobby the provincial government on their behalf. In the late 1980s and early 1990s, the IAA, working with other groups, helped the Lubicon Lake First Nation to protect their traditional lands from outside exploitation.

In 1974, the governor-general appointed the Honourable Ralph Steinhauer, a past president of the Indian Association of Alberta, to a five-year term as lieutenant-governor of Alberta. Steinhauer is shown here with his wife, Isabel, who he married in 1928. How does his appointment reflect the significance of the IAA's work?

In the late 1990s, the federal and Alberta governments reduced their funding to the IAA. Despite the drop in funding, the IAA continues to express First Nations concerns, particularly in calls for greater protection of treaty rights in Alberta and Canada.

Indigenous Knowledge

Choose an Aboriginal political leader from Alberta and write a one-page profile of his or her life and contributions. Consider the work of James Brady, Marilyn Buffalo, Pearl Calahasen, Thelma Chalifoux, Joseph Dion, Theresa Gadwa Sr., James Gladstone, Malcolm Norris, or Ralph Steinhauer.

LOOKING BACK

Create a timeline that shows the development of political organizations representing First Nations and Métis peoples in Canada. What are the main accomplishments of each organization? Include this information in point form along your timeline.

Path to Renewal

AS YOU READ

In this chapter, you learned how the federal government's 1969 White Paper sparked a new era in Aboriginal political activism. First Nations leaders became increasingly assertive in their efforts to preserve and strengthen treaty rights. Their work helped usher in a new era in the relationship between the federal government and First Nations.

Since 1969, the federal government has increasingly worked in partnership with Aboriginal political organizations to improve the quality of life for Aboriginal peoples. Pages 188–201 introduce some of the key issues currently facing Aboriginal political leaders. As you read, think about how the issues are interconnected. Try to identify the root problems.

THE ISSUES EACH FIRST NATIONS, MÉTIS, AND INUIT COMMUNITY FACES ARE DIFFERENT. IN ADDITION, THERE ARE ALWAYS INDIVIDUALS WITHIN COMMUNITIES WHO FACE PROBLEMS NOT SHARED BY OTHERS. FIRST NATIONS and Métis peoples who have a land base may exercise inherent rights that are not available to those without a land base. **Inherent rights** are those that a person is born with. They cannot be given or taken away. However, the kind of land base a group has often determines how beneficial these rights

are. Large land bases with natural resources or other economic development potential are preferable to small, resource-poor land bases.

One of the biggest benefits of a good land base is the potential for economic stability. **Economic stability** occurs when a community has the ability to withstand fluctuations of income and expenses. This stability is a quality desired by Aboriginal communities from all regions of the country.

First Nations, Métis, and Inuit people who live in one of Canada's urban areas experience other problems. Cultural differences, stereotypes, **racism**, and the **discrimination** that can result, stem from deeply held attitudes. Changing these attitudes can be a more challenging task than changing government policies.

The next few pages provide a brief look at some of the issues that affect First Nations, Métis, and Inuit peoples as well as ways some of the ways these issues are being addressed.

Wally Desjarlais is a radio announcer with CFWE-FM, hosting The Native Perspective Morning Show. *After age eleven, he grew up in the Buffalo Lake Métis Settlement near Lac La Biche. He began working with CFWE as a high school student while the station was located in Lac La Biche. If the radio station had been located far from his home, do you think he would have had the same career development opportunity? What does this tell you about solving other economic problems for Aboriginal peoples?*

1982   Constitution Act
The British North America Act (1867) is patriated to Canada. The new constitution includes the Charter of Rights and Freedoms and recognizes First Nations, Métis, and Inuit peoples as Aboriginal peoples of Canada.

1984   Cree-Naskapi (Quebec) Act
The act gives the Cree and Innu of northern Quebec self-government and independence from the Indian Act.

1985   Bill C-31
The bill removes sections of the Indian Act that treat First Nations women unfairly. The change allows thousands of First Nations people to regain their Indian status.

1986   Sechelt Band Self-Government Act
The act gives the Salish First Nation of Sechelt self-government and independence from the Indian Act.

1987   Meech Lake Accord
The prime minister and provincial premiers agree on a constitutional reform package to recognize Quebec as a distinct society. Aboriginal leaders criticize the accord for ignoring First Nations, Métis, and Inuit concerns.

1990   Meech Lake Fails
Elijah Harper, a Cree-Anishinabé member of Manitoba's provincial legislature, prevents the passage of the Meech Lake Accord.

1990   Oka Crisis
The Mohawk of Kanehsatake, near Montreal, Quebec, set up a blockade to prevent the town of Oka from building a golf course on traditional burial grounds.

1990   Métis Settlements Act
The act gives title to about half a million hectares of land to the residents of eight Métis Settlements in north-central Alberta.

1991   Royal Commission on Aboriginal Peoples (RCAP)
A royal commission is established to examine the relationship between Canada's Aboriginal and non-Aboriginal peoples and to propose practical solutions to long-term problems.

1992   Charlottetown Accord Fails
The majority of Canadian voters in a nationwide referendum reject the Charlottetown Accord, which would have guaranteed self-government for Aboriginal peoples.

1994   Yukon First Nations Self-Government Act
The act gives Yukon First Nations self-government and control over traditional land rights.

1995   Inherent Right to Self-Government
The federal government recognizes self-government as an inherent Aboriginal right protected under the constitution.

1996   RCAP Report
The *Report of the Royal Commission on Aboriginal Peoples* calls for major changes in the government's relationships with Aboriginal peoples.

1999   Nunavut Territory
Nunavut, considered a homeland for Inuit peoples, is created.

1999   Aboriginal Peoples Television Network
The world's first national Aboriginal television network goes on the air.

2000   Nisga'a Final Agreement Act
The act gives self-government to the Nisga'a First Nation and independence from the Indian Act.

2003   First Nations Governance Act (Bill C-7)
Bill C-7 proposes changes to the Indian Act. It is strongly opposed by the Assembly of First Nations and other Aboriginal organizations and fails before reaching a vote in the House of Commons.

1980

1985

1990

1995

2000

2005

Indigenous Knowledge

The *Report of the Royal Commission on Aboriginal Peoples* is available online at *www.ainc-inac.gc.ca/ch/rcap/index_e.html*. Volume 2 of this report, called Restructuring the Relationship, deals with issues facing Aboriginal peoples as well as proposed solutions. In your class, divide up sections of this part of the report. Read your assigned section and prepare a short oral summary to share with your classmates.

STANDARD OF LIVING

The United Nations Human Development Index consistently rates Canada as having one of the world's highest standards of living. A standard of living includes factors such as the amount of living space per person in a dwelling, the number of major repairs needed on a home, access to good quality water, health care, and education, and so on. The same United Nations index that rates Canada so highly places the standard of living for First Nations living on-reserve at the level of developing countries, such as Botswana and Vietnam. Clearly, First Nations are not sharing equally in Canada's prosperity.

Housing conditions are one indication of standard of living. Statistics Canada defines crowded living conditions as homes with one or more people per room. This means that a home with a kitchen, living room, dining room, and two bedrooms would be considered crowded with five or more people living there.

In statistics Canada's 2001 Aboriginal Peoples Survey, 17 per cent of Aboriginal people living off reserves reported living in crowded conditions. This was down from 22 per cent in the 1996 census. In comparison, 7 per cent of all Canadians reported living in crowded conditions in 2001.

Crowded conditions for Inuit peoples are even more common. In 2001, 53 per cent of Inuit people reported living in crowded conditions. This was down from 61 per cent in 1996, but is still very high compared to other Aboriginal peoples and other Canadians in general.

In addition, 34 per cent of Inuit peoples reported that there were times of year when their drinking water was unsafe. In Nunavik, an Inuit region in northern Quebec, the rate was especially high. Here 73 per cent of Inuit people report contaminated water at certain points of the year.

Some caution in reading these statistics is needed. A standard of living, which is measured by statistics, does not assess quality of

ABORIGINAL PEOPLES SURVEY 2001

Most of the statistical information you find presented on pages 190–198 is from a survey Statistics Canada conducted in 2001. The survey includes information about individuals in Canada who identify themselves as being a member of one or more Aboriginal groups and do not live on a reserve or settlement. The exception to this criteria is the Northwest Territories, for which both on- and off-reserve data are included. According to the 2001 Census, the individuals included in this survey data account for about 70 per cent of the total Aboriginal population in Canada.

Percentage of People Living in Crowded Conditions

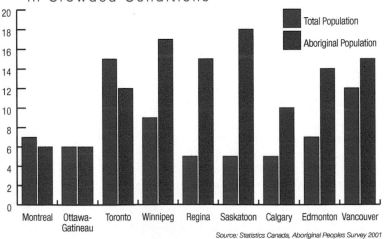

Source: Statistics Canada, Aboriginal Peoples Survey 2001

life, which is a personal measure of satisfaction.

For example, poverty is one factor causing low standards of living. The rate of Aboriginal people living beneath the poverty line is nearly three times higher than that of other Canadians. Yet First Nations people considered poor in comparison to other Canadians might assess their own quality of life as high. The people you learned about on page 29, who left the Hobbema reserve in 1968 to live at Smallboy Camp, lived a life that had a low living standard: tents for homes, fires for warmth in the winter, and an outhouse instead of indoor plumbing. Despite these living conditions, many people at the camp assessed their quality of life as high. They felt connected to nature's rhythms and enjoyed the slow pace of life.

However, for Aboriginal people who aspire to the same material comforts enjoyed by non-Aboriginal Canadians, Aboriginal leaders are working with provincial and federal governments to ensure that they have economic opportunities to pursue this lifestyle.

Government officials and Aboriginal leaders recognize that the causes of poverty must be addressed rather than the symptoms. For example, programs need to address why individuals are unemployed, not provide money to replace employment income.

In some regions, Aboriginal peoples are making significant gains in economic opportunities. In Alberta, the percentage of Aboriginal adults earning $40 000 or more a year increased from 8 to 16 per cent between 1996 and 2001. During the same time period, the number of Aboriginal children living below the poverty line dropped from 56 to 48 per cent.

Aboriginal leaders today seek greater control over their lands and resources, as well as an equitable share of the wealth these resources represent. They see this as an essential first step in re-establishing their people's self-sufficiency, something they enjoyed for thousands of years before European contact.

LAND CLAIMS

Many Aboriginal communities believe that the federal government has failed to provide them with the land that they are rightfully entitled to. In these cases, they launch a land claim. A land claim demands title to territories legitimately belonging to Aboriginal groups based on historical use and occupancy.

The federal government recognizes two main types of land claims. A comprehensive claim is essentially a modern-day treaty. Comprehensive claims arise when a group of Aboriginal peoples has been deprived of its traditional territory without ever having signed a treaty. For example, until recently, most First Nations in British Columbia had never signed treaties, yet the province did not recognize First Nations title to land. Now, the federal and provincial governments

Many First Nations reserves across Canada have trouble getting safe drinking water. Esther Wesley, a resident of the Stoney reserve, is shown here in 1997 hauling water from her rain barrel because she has no water in her house.

On May 26, 2004, the Labrador Final Agreement was signed, making it the fourth and final comprehensive land claim settled by Inuit peoples in Canada. The new region is called Nunatsiavut, which is Inuktitut for Labrador. Other comprehensive land claim agreements Inuit peoples have settled include the James Bay and Northern Quebec Agreement (November 11, 1975, Nunavik); Inuvialuit Final Agreement (June 5, 1984); and the Nunavut Final Agreement (May 27, 1993).

The Nunavut Land Claims Agreement Act (NLCA) is an especially remarkable political achievement that was designed, led, and achieved by Inuit peoples.

However, Nunavut is also an important symbol and inspiration for other people around the world. Indigenous peoples from places as different as South Africa, New Zealand, and South America hope to use the NLCA as a model for their own political and economic goals.

Nunavut's flag includes the colours gold, blue, and red. Using the Internet, research what each colour symbolizes.

Unlike other settled claims, Nunavut is a territory independent of other territories and provinces. It has a public government, which means anyone can run for office or vote. There are no restrictions based on heritage. However, the government's operation is connected to the land claims agreement in several key areas. For example, the NLCA specifies that the number of Inuit people employed in the public service must be directly proportional to the Inuit population.

Nunavut reflects the needs of its Inuit population in many ways. Its territorial government has no political parties. Instead, the legislative assembly operates on the basis of consensus politics. Inuktitut, English, and French are the government's official languages, ensuring that Inuit peoples can receive government services in their Aboriginal language. In addition, Nunavut's government is highly decentralized. It has eleven headquarters divided among its capital, Iqaluit, and ten other regions.

■ REFLECTION

Research the contributions of an Inuit political leader and write a one-page summary. You might consider Rosemarie Kuptana, former leader of the Inuit Tapirisat of Canada, which was formed to negotiate the Nunavut land claim with the federal government, or John Amagoalik, who pushed forward the campaign for the creation of Nunavut.

are negotiating comprehensive land claims with these nations.

Specific claims deal with issues arising from treaties. Specific claims only affect First Nations because only First Nations signed treaties. If a First Nation feels that it never received the land it was entitled to according to treaty, or that the government has unfairly taken away some of its land, it files a specific claim.

Some First Nations object to the term *land claim*. They see land as an inherent right, not something they need to claim. In the Cree language, First Nations were placed on their land *otawâsimisimâwak*, as "children of the Creator." Their land is their birthright.

SELF-GOVERNMENT

In 1995, the federal government officially recognized Aboriginal peoples' inherent right to self-government.

In other words, the government acknowledged that Aboriginal peoples have been denied a birthright: the ability to govern their own lives. Acknowledging this fact has proven easier than putting it into practice. Although several Aboriginal groups now have self-government agreements, most are still in negotiations.

TREATY RIGHTS

The 1969 White Paper downplayed the significance of Canada's historical treaties. It suggested that "a plain reading of the words used in the treaties reveals the limited and minimal promises which were included in them."

First Nations leaders responded strongly. They saw the historical treaties as the foundation of their relationship with Canada. They were appalled that the federal government intended to legislate the treaties out of existence.

The White Paper made First Nations realize that they could not take their treaty rights for granted.

Today the Assembly of First Nations maintains a Treaties and Lands Unit to provide technical advice, research, and administrative support to First Nations that have problems concerning their treaty rights.

In recent years, First Nations have also had the courts on their side. Supreme Court decisions have repeatedly recognized the continued importance of treaty rights.

HEALTH

Health is one of the most important factors in a person's sense of well being. Statistics Canada reports that Aboriginal peoples are one-and-a-half times more likely to have a chronic disease than other Canadians. A chronic disease is one that lasts six months or more. Suicide rates are a staggering three times higher than those in Canada's general population. Life expectancy is a full six years shorter.

In the 2001 Aboriginal Peoples Survey, 56 per cent of Aboriginal people living off-reserves reported

> [D]espite the extension of medical and social services (in some form) to every Aboriginal community, and despite the large sums spent by Canadian governments to provide these services, Aboriginal people still suffer from unacceptable rates of illness and distress. The term crisis is not an exaggeration here.
>
> — *Report of the Royal Commission on Aboriginal Peoples*

"Excellent or very good" health, while 65 per cent of the total Canadian population reported the same. Among fifteen to twenty-four year olds, the gap between Aboriginal and non-Aboriginal populations closed up considerably. Of Aboriginal peoples in this age group, 69 per cent rated their health as "Excellent or very good," compared to 71 percent of non-Aboriginal fifteen to twenty-four year olds.

However, health declines more rapidly in aging Aboriginal populations. After the age of twenty-five, the percentage of Aboriginal people reporting "Fair or poor" health is

Indigenous Knowledge

One controversial treaty right concerns a clause from Treaty Six known widely as the "medicine chest clause." Signed in 1876, Treaty Six contains a clause promising to keep a medicine chest in the home of the Indian Agent for the use of the Treaty Six First Nations people. However, disagreement exists about what the clause means today. Some say it means free medicine, others say free medical care, and still others that it means nothing more than a literal chest of medicine for reserves. Like many disagreements over treaty rights, much rests on interpretations of the intentions and understandings of those involved in the treaty negotiations. To find out more about this complex issue, visit the Web site of the Native Law Centre at the University of Saskatchewan (www.usask.ca.nativelaw.medicine.html).

almost double that of the total Canadian population.

People with chronic conditions are more likely to report their health as poor. The top five chronic conditions reported by Aboriginal peoples, from most frequently

reported to least frequent include arthritis or rheumatism, high blood pressure, asthma, stomach problems or ulcers, and diabetes.

Diabetes is of special concern, particularly when Aboriginal rates of the disease are compared to non-Aboriginal rates. In 2001, 7 per cent of the Aboriginal population reported diabetes, while 2.9 per cent of the total Canadian population in the same age ranges reported the condition. Health Canada has evidence that on-reserve populations have even higher rates of diabetes, which would make this gap even wider.

First Nations and Métis peoples generally report similar levels of each chronic condition, while Inuit peoples report significantly lower levels in each case. These lower

Percentage of Population Reporting
Chronic Health Problems

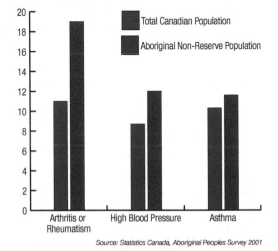

Source: Statistics Canada, Aboriginal Peoples Survey 2001

Issues for Investigation

PRESENTING STATISTICAL INFORMATION

How can statistical information be presented most clearly?

WHAT TO DO

1. Below are data from Statistics Canada's Aboriginal Peoples Survey 2001. The first set of data relates to rates of diabetes reported by various segments of the population. The second set relates to Aboriginal languages use.

   • *Set 1: Percentage of population reporting diabetes: 8.3 per cent First Nations people living off reserve, 5.9 per cent Métis peoples, 2.3 per cent Inuit peoples, 2.9 per cent total Canadian population.*

   • *Set 2: Percentage of Aboriginal population speaking or understanding an Aboriginal language: Adults: First Nations 32 per cent, Métis 16 per cent, Inuit in the Canadian Arctic 90 per cent; Children: First Nations 25 per cent, Métis 11 per cent, Inuit in the Canadian Arctic 90 per cent.*

2. For each set of data, present the information in sentences, in point form bullets, in a chart, and in a bar graph. You might use one of the bar graphs shown in this chapter as an example. Be sure, in each example, that you have identified the original source of the information.

3. Which method presents the information most clearly? How might you use what you learned in this activity to help you study for exams or prepare reports?

percentages may be due to less contact with doctors in the Arctic, which might mean fewer people are diagnosed with chronic complaints.

Poverty plays a role in causing poor health, but it is only part of the problem. Provincial and federal governments have been working with First Nations to improve the health of people in their communities. For example, Alberta's Aboriginal Health Strategy Project Fund supports programs to improve access to health care.

ENVIRONMENT

Traditional First Nations and Inuit worldviews believe that all in creation are interdependent. Humans are not separate from nature, but are part of it. Because of this, First Nations are determined to play a central role in protecting Canada's environment. For example, the Assembly of First Nations maintains an Environment Secretariat, a special department devoted exclusively to environmental issues.

In recent years, First Nations, Métis, and Inuit voices have increasingly been heard whenever industrial development threatens the environment. In response, governments have become more willing

to involve Aboriginal peoples in environmental discussions, and land claims settlements often provide for environmental protection.

ALCOHOL AND OTHER DRUG ABUSE

Alcohol and other drug abuse often go hand-in-hand with poverty and unemployment. They also lead directly to social problems and health issues. In Canada, Aboriginal people are two to six times more likely than other Canadians to have alcohol-related problems.

In 1982, Indian and Northern Affairs launched the National Native Alcohol and Drug Abuse Program (NNADAP). The NNADAP funds

What do you think artist Lawrence Paul Yuxweluptun might be saying about cultural differences in approaches to environmental problems with Red Man Watching White Man Trying to Fix Hole in Sky *(1990)?*

When we walk upon Mother Earth we always plant our feet carefully because we know the faces of our future generations are looking up at us from beneath the ground. We never forget them

— Oren Lyons, Onondaga

My grandmother would often tell of how she had never expected that the land and water would change so rapidly and affect the traditional well-being of her people. My grandmother's teachings and pleas left a very vivid and lasting impression on me and therefore greatly influenced my career choice. I would like to encourage Aboriginal people to use their traditional ecological knowledge and apply sustainable development techniques for their natural resources.

— Kuni Albert, Fond-du-Lac First Nation, University of Calgary student and National Aboriginal Achievement Foundation scholarship recipient fifty-four treatment centres and more than 500 community-based prevention programs. Most of these programs are controlled by Aboriginal communities.

JUSTICE CONFLICTS

Few First Nations languages include the concepts of guilt and sin. A Choctaw–English dictionary compiled in the 1800s defined the verb sin as "to make a mistake" or "to be lost in the wilderness" — meanings quite different from those assigned by today's criminal courts.

Many aspects of First Nations and Inuit cultures are completely opposite to the structured expectations within a courtroom. In some cultures, looking directly at someone is considered rude and disrespectful. In a courtroom, not meeting someone's eyes is sometimes interpreted as an indication of guilt or untrustworthiness.

In traditional ways of handling disputes, First Nations people take responsibility for their actions and do not speak out against others. In Canadian courts, these cultural traditions have often resulted in guilty pleas and refusing to testify. For a First Nations person operating within a traditional worldview, pleading not guilty to an offence that he or she committed would be lying. In the Canadian court system, a not guilty plea is seen as an acceptable beginning to a court proceeding in which a person is innocent until proven guilty. It is not up to individuals to confess guilt and incriminate themselves. It is up to the court to prove they are guilty.

In addition, First Nations people sometimes have trouble fulfilling legal requirements, such as showing up at court or meeting with a parole officer on a specific date. Reasons for this trouble might include not having a car or phone. Today the legal system in some provinces is attempting to accommodate these needs by requiring parole officers to visit First Nations communities when required.

Indigenous Knowledge

The Donald Marshall case has become a touchstone in the work of Aboriginal leaders for changes to Canada's justice system. Marshall was convicted in 1971 for the murder of a young woman in Sydney, Nova Scotia. The case involved a botched police investigation, community pressure and prejudice, and perjured evidence. The end result was Marshall's wrongful conviction and his incarceration for eleven years before he was finally cleared of the crime. Research the details of the Donald Marshall case or another case involving the judicial system in which an Aboriginal person was treated unjustly. If you choose another incident, clear your idea with your teacher before you begin.

Donald Marshall's name has become a symbol of the injustices First Nations, Métis, and Inuit peoples have experienced in the Canadian justice system.

First Nations people represent 65 per cent of federally incarcerated inmates. Inuit offenders remain in prison longer than other Canadians, including First Nations people. Recognizing that cultural contradictions have contributed to this situation, the Canadian justice system is making changes.

Restorative justice programs focus on traditional First Nations, Métis, and Inuit justice priorities, which are restoring harmony and making amends rather than punishment. Restorative justice requires personal commitment on the part of those involved in the situation. Initiatives include the following:

- **Native Youth Justice Committees** consisting of Elders and other community members meet with young offenders and their parents to discuss what happened and how to make amends. Most committees operate in Alberta, where the first one was established in the 1980s at Fort Chipewyan. By 1993, the youth crime rate in that community had decreased by one-third.

- **Sentencing Circles** involve Aboriginal community leaders, Elders, the judge, court workers, the victim, the offender, and his or her family members and other stakeholders. Together they agree upon what is best for the offender. Sentences involve deciding what is best to repair the harm rather than focusing only on punish-ment, such as fines or jail terms.

Though sentences often involve counselling with Elders and community service work, more serious crimes result in different outcomes. For example, in 1996 a

Members of SaskNative Inc. participate in a mock sentencing circle in this photograph from the Native Law Centre at the University of Saskatchewan. Cameras are not permitted in a real sentencing circle.

circle sentenced a Saskatchewan youth to live for one year on an uninhabited island. Traditionally, banishment is one of the most severe punishments that could be given, reserved for the worst troublemakers.

Significantly, some of these initiatives are being adapted for use by non-Aboriginal communities for crimes that do not necessarily involve Aboriginal offenders. More than eighty communities in Canada currently offer some restorative justice programs. The Calgary Community Conferencing Project, for example, arranges meetings between those injured by a crime committed by a teenager and the young person and his or her family. The meeting helps repair the relationship between the perpetrator, those they have harmed, and the community at large.

▣ REFLECTION

Do you support restorative justice programs for young offenders? What about for adult offenders? Do you think these programs should be restricted to only certain crimes or all crimes? Debate these ideas in small groups or as a class.

Percentage of Twenty to Twenty-four Year Olds with Less Than High School Diploma

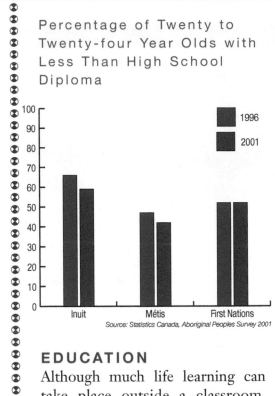

Source: Statistics Canada, Aboriginal Peoples Survey 2001

Percentage of Twenty-four to Thirty-four Year Olds with Post-Secondary Education

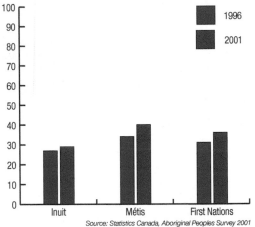

Source: Statistics Canada, Aboriginal Peoples Survey 2001

EDUCATION

Although much life learning can take place outside a classroom, most economic opportunities go to people with formal education.

Education is therefore one of the top priorities for Aboriginal leaders across the country. Since the early 1970s, Aboriginal peoples in many areas have increasingly taken control of their young people's education. Federal and provincial governments have been actively involved in this shift of responsibility and control.

However, many communities still lack the control or funding they need to provide their children with the education they aspire to.

The magnitude of this problem is supported by census data. In 2001, 48 per cent of Aboriginal people ages twenty to twenty-four had not completed high school, compared to 26 per cent of the total Canadian population. Aboriginal peoples aged twenty-five to forty-four who have post secondary education is 39 per cent, compared to 55 per cent for the total Canadian population.

Reasons most often cited for leaving school include boredom, family responsibilities, and needing to get a job.

Indigenous Knowledge

Examine the data presented in the bar graphs on this page carefully. Write a series of sentences that explains the data. Create another bar graph from data on this page that compares Aboriginal rates of school completion with data for the total Canadian population. Explain why the statistics concern Aboriginal leaders.

The top reason Aboriginal students give for leaving high school is boredom. Working in a small group, imagine that you have been hired to film a television commercial aimed at convincing Aboriginal students to stay in school. Using a video camera, film a two-minute commercial that will get your point across.

ANALYZING PROBLEMS AND FINDING SOLUTIONS

What kinds of solutions can you offer for the problems facing Aboriginal peoples?

WHAT TO DO

1. In groups of three or four students, choose to investigate one of the following topics:
   - poverty
   - economic instability
   - land claims
   - self-government
   - treaty rights
   - justice disputes
   - environmental issues
   - drug or alcohol abuse
   - health
   - housing
   - discrimination
   - education

   Try to ensure that each group has a different topic. If you would like to investigate a topic that is not on this list, clear your idea with your teacher first.

2. In your group, divide up the following research areas so that everyone has something to prepare:
   - What is the background or history of the issue?
   - What Aboriginal political organizations are involved in the issue at local and national levels?
   - What kinds of solutions have been proposed or implemented?
   - Which solutions worked? Which did not? Analyze reasons for the success or failure in each case.

3. In your group, discuss each student's findings and brainstorm solutions. At this point, you are just generating ideas. Do not worry too much about the practicality of your suggestions. Be creative.

4. Among your group, reach a consensus as to which solutions appear the best. Consider whether the problem is one that can be fixed quickly or whether a long-term approach is necessary. Your goal is to get to the root of the problem in order to see long-term change.

5. Write out the steps that would be needed to achieve your goal. Estimate a time frame. Establish the organizations and governments that would need to be involved. How would an agreement be achieved? Anticipate the roadblocks to consensus and come up with solutions.

6. Prepare a concise presentation on your topic. You might provide other students with a worksheet to guide their notes on your project as you present.

7. Set up your presentation in the following way:
   - Introduce your topic. Provide background information or history. Do not overload your classmates with details, but be sure they understand the essential points.
   - Using PowerPoint™ or another presentation medium, such as video, audio, photographs, or interview tapes, present your solution. Include the steps needed, the organizations involved, potential problems in negotiations, and your solutions.

8. Answer your classmates' questions. If it is your turn to be an audience member, listen attentively and contribute a thoughtful question when they are done.

You may wish to invite an Elder to facilitate your talking circle. If you do, think about the topic ahead of time and be prepared to share thoughtful ideas.

THE FUTURE

In the past, Aboriginal people's sense of connection to their culture would have been automatic — just part of life. Today Aboriginal peoples have many more cultural influences around them and their situations in life may or may not encourage them to make this connection.

The three stories on pages 200–201 offer different perspectives about what it means to be an Aboriginal person today. The first is a statement from a grade nine student in Edmonton, the second a story about an eighteen-year-old who lost and found his cultural path, and the last a story about a well-known artist who grew up outside his culture, but nevertheless feels a strong sense of connection to it.

In your talking circle, share your own ideas about cultural connection and how this connection might help Aboriginal peoples resolve the issues facing their community.

Rebecca Gadwa

I'm a grade nine student living in the city, but I have lots of family ties to my Kehewin First Nation home. I'm lucky to have an Elder in my life whom I'm very close to — my grandmother. I don't speak my language, which is Cree, but my culture is very important to me because it reminds me that I am different from everyone else in this world. I'm able to hear stories from my grandmother and parents about my culture and how we do things differently, and most importantly, I'm told that I should respect everything on this Earth. I've spoken about my culture in school — in social studies — and my classmates truly seemed interested. On the down side, I've also come across people who have pretty stereotypical views about what an Aboriginal person believes in and how their culture is. I think the things that I learn about my culture throughout my lifetime will matter most when I'm older and a person from the younger generation comes to me to ask about my Cree people — then I'll be able to answer them.

WHAT ROLE MIGHT A CULTURAL CONNECTION PLAY IN THE FUTURE OF ABORIGINAL PEOPLES?

Tony Delaney

Delaney has just turned eighteen, but many of his ideas seem to come from someone much older. He insists he's no different from thousands of other youth who start out life misguided and emotionally abandoned, eventually performing violent acts to gain acceptance into a street gang.

"Yeah, I've been on the dark side. I stole cigarettes and drank alcohol when I was young. For about five years when I was living in the city, I was suicidal. Then I went back to the reserve and started going to Sweat Lodges and other ceremonies. I wanted to get back to my traditional roots and that path has helped me a lot. Without that I don't know where I would be today."

Delaney speaks fondly of the many traditionalists, cultural advisors, and Elders who helped him reconnect to his birthright —

his First Nations culture. What he experienced in the presence of Elders and in ceremonies was too powerful for him to deny "and it's the key to helping other high-risk youth find a better way in life."

Now on a straight, clean path, and informed by his Kainai traditions, Delaney has accepted a role as a spokesperson for the youth of the Blood Tribe. He advises Assembly of First Nations representatives on issues concerning First Nations youth and is regularly asked to speak at conferences and other gatherings. It's a responsibility he doesn't take lightly. He regularly prays and asks his peers and those around him for guidance.

He was especially gratified to help run the Spotted Eagle Calf society in his community, a three-month program that enabled young people to attend ceremonies like the Sundance and receive a name in the Kainai tradition.

"I'm just trying to be like my ancestors. I saw an old black and white pictures of some of the old chiefs and they all looked humble. It must have been around the '40's as Chief Shot Both Sides was in it. They all watched out for the people, visiting them when they were sick or helping them out when they needed food. I just want to be like that," he explains.

George Littlechild Price

Walk into any Aboriginal art gallery, pick the boldest, in-your-face chroma colour canvas, and you'll likely see it is signed by artist George Littlechild Price.

Known for his portrayals of his Plains Cree ancestors that are fused with contemporary vivid colour, George Littlechild is recognized as one of the foremost First Nations artists working in Canada today. He is also the author and illustrator of three children's books, including the award-winning *This Land Is My Land*.

Born in Edmonton, Littlechild Price was encouraged by his foster mother to take art lessons and to pursue his art throughout his school years. She also insisted he go to art college when he graduated. His post-secondary educational achievements include a diploma in Art and Design from Red Deer College, and in 1988 he received a Bachelor of Fine Arts from the Nova Scotia College of Art and Design in Halifax.

Today Littlechild Price devotes much of his time towards working with youth In British Columbia, his adopted province, and has this message for young people:

"Find the spirit within yourself, as you have all the tools necessary to make it in the world. The Creator grants each and every individual with a gift, a gift that once discovered can transform you and place you on your life's journey.

The Creator granted me the gift of art — a very powerful gift that I am most thankful for. My art has provided me with all the things I need and has brought me hope and joy. It has allowed me to create change within myself and the world.

You, too, can make a difference. Each day, thank the Creator for all that you have, even when there are obstacles in the way. Never give up! Each and every one of you is a part of the Creator's plan. Make the ancestors proud of the life you lead and of who you are."

LOOKING BACK

What do you see as the single most important issue facing First Nations, Métis, and Inuit peoples in Canada? How does that issue interact with some of the other issues you have read about in this section? How have Aboriginal peoples, the federal government, and non-Aboriginal Canadian attitudes changed since the federal government released its White Paper? Discuss your answers to these questions in small groups or as a class.

Entrepreneurship

AS YOU READ

Aside from political activities and government negotiations, many First Nations, Métis, and Inuit peoples have used their own initiative to improve the quality of their lives. Many of these entrepreneurs are successfully competing in the local, regional, national, and international marketplaces. Some of the most successful have found ways to integrate traditional values into their businesses. As you read pages 202–207, make notes about the traditional values you see evident in these entrepreneurs' work.

THOUGH IT HAS ONLY BEEN A CENTURY SINCE HER ANCESTORS BARTERED FOX PELTS FOR TEA AND FLOUR AT THE LOCAL HUDSON'S BAY COMPANY, PATRICIA PICHÉ OPERATES IN THE INTERNATIONAL MARKETPLACE AS IF IT were in her blood. The fashion designer creates clothing decorated with bold geometric designs in the traditions of her Cree and Dene Sųłiné heritage. She has broken into the sought-after United States market, selling her line in several popular clothing chains. Piché specializes in contemporary western wear and traditional First Nations clothing.

Piché is joined by a growing number of First Nations, Métis, and Inuit people who own and operate their own businesses. From corporations that employ hundreds of workers to one-person home businesses, the goods and services they offer cross the entire spectrum of the economy — from hotels, banks, and oil and gas services to retail stores, restaurants, and colleges.

According to the Alberta chapter of the Canadian Council for Aboriginal Business, there are 15 000 businesses owned by Aboriginal people in Canada. Half of these are located in urban centres, with the rest located in rural communities or on reserves. Aboriginal self-employment has, over the past fifteen years, grown at three times the average Canadian rate. Today many reserves have a full complement of business, professional, and trades people.

For example, Peace Hills Trust, established in Hobbema, Alberta, now has offices in several major centres across Canada. The company provides financial services primarily to First Nations communities. It has a strong focus on First Nations employees and community development.

Peace Hills Trust has a distinctive corporate logo — a hill — with a deep meaning. It represents the place where the Cree and Blackfoot formed a lasting peace a century ago.

BERT CROWFOOT
Siksika First Nation

Bert Crowfoot has made a career out of building connections between Aboriginal people across the country.

Based in Edmonton, Crowfoot's Aboriginal Multimedia Society is one of Canada's premiere providers of Aboriginal communications. In 1983, the society launched the newspaper *Windspeaker* to cover provincial stories in Alberta. In 1985, with the help of Ray Fox, the *Native Perspective* radio program on CFWE-FM was born.

It seemed the up-and-coming society would flourish, but suddenly the government pulled its funding in the early 1990s. Initially, downsizing and staff cuts seemed imminent. But in a bold move — not to mention strategic planning and hard work — Crowfoot and his staff expanded the organization instead. They moved in to fill the void left by other provincial newspapers disabled by funding cuts across Canada.

"What may look like a stumbling block can turn into a stepping stone," maintains the ever-optimistic Crowfoot. "All you need to do is look for the positives. Challenges can make everything look bad, but just hang in there and you'll find the good, and then you can act on it."

The society now publishes five Aboriginal newspapers and *Windspeaker* has gone national, covering events in Aboriginal communities across Canada. *Windspeaker* links communities in ways that no other news media even tries. The society is also expanding its radio distribution to serve all Alberta First Nations and Métis communities.

Bert Crowfoot

Crowfoot learned the publishing trade by working his way up through the business. He first became a freelance writer for the Edmonton-based *Native People* newspaper, becoming editor in the early 1980s. With the help of his staff and a governing board, the Aboriginal Multimedia Society of Alberta was formed in 1983. The rest is history.

Always one to believe in and promote the potential of his people, Crowfoot generously shares his expertise with other Aboriginal newspapers. His latest innovation includes a training centre for journalism hopefuls who — once they've gained the necessary skills — can move into careers in the society's newspapers and radio station.

Bert Crowfoot expects a future filled with inspired innovations and expansion. He leads the Aboriginal Multimedia Society with the philosophy "Your potential is limited only by your initiative."

◼ REFLECTION

Bert Crowfoot is an innovative entrepreneur using communications media, one of the most powerful forces for change in the world today. Crowfoot also uses his talents to give back to his people. Research the activities of other Aboriginal media enterprises, such as the Aboriginal Peoples Television Network. How can communications media be a tool to help Aboriginal peoples?

GLOBAL BUSINESS

While many on-reserve enterprises focus their businesses on their own communities, a growing number reach out to global customers as well.

The Blood Tribe Agricultural Project (BTAP), which won a 2003 Canada Export Award for excellence, is a good example of a community-owned project with international success. It is the largest irrigation operation in western Canada.

The roots of the company go back to the 1940s, when the Kainai First Nation agreed to surrender land for the development of the St. Mary's Dam and irrigation canal. They did so with the understanding that the government would help the First Nation develop their agricultural abilities at some point in the future.

The BTAP, established in 1991, is a partial fulfillment of this understanding. The operation now

Located on the Kainai reserve in southern Alberta, the Blood Tribe Agricultural Project provides water to approximately 10 000 hectares of farmland. It also produces and exports high-quality hay to places such as Japan, Korea, Taiwan, the Middle East, and the United States.

provides permanent and seasonal employment for many members of the Kainai First Nation. Some people have received education, training, and mentorship through the project. Many people enroll in community colleges so that they can get the skills they need to work for the company.

The Blood Tribe Agricultural Project's 2003 annual report includes a report from a community Elder, reflecting the important place Elders have in the community and business. In the report, Mrs. Irene McHugh reminisced about the farming she and her husband, Leo McHugh, did by the St. Mary's River. Their land was part of the area given up to the government to allow the dam to be built.

In northern Alberta, the Sawridge First Nation not only owns many hotels in popular tourist areas, such as Jasper National Park, but

The Sawridge Inn in Jasper, Alberta, is a four-star resort that caters to tourists and conferences. The Sawridge First Nation also operates hotels in Fort McMurray and Slave Lake, which cater to the oil and gas industry. How might hospitality enterprises reflect traditional values held by First Nations?

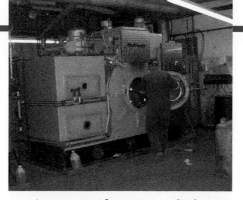

Mahikan Trails, a Canmore-based guiding business, was started by Métis owner Brenda Holder, who was born and raised in Jasper, Alberta. Mahikan is the Plains Cree word for "wolf." Holder is descended from a family of guides who once led European explorer Alexander Mackenzie's trip west.

Profits from the Goodfish Lake Development Corporation's drycleaning business, which employs ninety-one people, go back to its owners, the Whitefish First Nation #128. They put the money back into the company to help it grow and they plan to build a state-of-the-art drycleaning plant to maximize efficiency.

also the largest bottled water plant in Canada. Sawridge Waters, located on Annacis Island, near Vancouver, exports Spirit Water to the United States. The First Nation demonstrates great entrepreneurship and is a role model for many others. The band's objective is to be self-sufficient, providing jobs and a stable economic base that is not dependent on government contributions or on depleting natural resources.

NATURAL RESOURCES

In the past, First Nations people on reserves watched as resource companies extracted oil, gas, and trees from their areas without receiving much or any benefit. Now, through improved community relations and training programs, First Nations and other Aboriginal people often work directly for these companies or provide services to them. One example is the Goodfish Lake Development Corporation.

As a manufacturer and cleaner of protective garments and work camp linens for eastern Alberta's booming oil sands industry for over twenty-six years, the corporation is expanding its sights.

"With another oil sands operation coming on stream, we'll be doubling our workload and staff to keep up with demands," says General Manager George Halfe.

The Cold Lake First Nation has an economic benefits agreement with large resource companies operating near its reserve. The agreement ensures that some of the wealth that companies generate by taking resources from the region will be shared with people on the reserve. With training for band members and improved communication between companies and the First Nation regarding jobs and contracts, employment rates on the reserve are at an all-time high.

The Métis Nation of Alberta (MNA) is also flexing its economic development muscles. The organization now owns three office buildings and is getting into the oil and gas industry. The MNA, like many Aboriginal-owned and operated enterprises, consults with its Elders advisory council on

Revenue from oil wells, such as this one on the Kainai reserve, have helped fund many commmunity projects, such as schools and community centres.

cultural issues, long-term planning, and other matters.

The Métis Settlements Act began a new chapter in the lives of Métis people living at the province's eight settlements. A financial settlement gave many people a chance to pursue on-settlement businesses as individuals and on behalf of their communities.

The development of the natural resources on the settlements is a big part of plans to improve people's quality of life. However, these plans are not shortsighted. Each settlement has short- and long-term goals for sustainable resource harvesting that will help support future generations. Sustainable harvesting means that the companies use environmentally sound practices that allow the environment to continue to function and regenerate.

For example, the Gift Lake Métis Settlement has completed an extensive forest management plan to give an accurate inventory of settlement trees and their potential for logging and regrowth. On the Paddle Prairie Métis Settlement,

several families log with horses to ensure the wildlife habitat is not sacrificed.

In general, natural resources have been a great benefit for many First Nations in Alberta, providing funds for economic development in other industries and community projects. Communities with such revenues have invested in new housing, community centres, arenas, and schools.

Some revenues have been invested in existing businesses and some have been used to start new ones, both on- and off-reserve. These investments have created new wealth for the betterment of individuals and communities.

The disadvantage of being resource-rich, some Elders comment, is that workers must often be apart from their families for long periods, and they sometimes adopt a "work hard, play hard" ethic. This may contribute to social problems that include domestic violence, gambling, drugs, and alcohol. Elders also notice that some young people have become preoccupied with accumulating material wealth and have little time for cultural and spiritual pursuits.

Furthermore, the wealth from resources creates divisions between First Nations that have them and those that do not. For example, differences in standards of living on reserves across Alberta are often dramatic.

STARTING YOUR OWN BUSINESS

Every business starts out with an idea. A business plan helps turn the idea into reality. A business plan is a strategy in words and numbers. It is a way to make step-by-step plans and track progress. A good business plan will discuss marketing (selling and distributing your product or service), operations (managing and running your business), and finances (getting money to start your business and keep it going). Good planning and realistic goals are the keys to a good business.

What kind of planning does it take to be an entrepreneur?

WHAT TO DO

In groups of three, discuss ideas for a business you would like to start. You might consider planning a summer or part-time job. Your task in this activity will be to write a plan for this business. A good business plan will have some or all of the following:

- an introduction (What is the purpose of your business?)
- a description of your product or service (What will your business do? What product or service do you plan to sell to customers?)
- a marketing plan (Are there any competitors selling the same product or service as your business? How will your product or service be different from theirs? What will be the price of your product or service? How will you let potential customers know about your business?)
- an operations plan (What decisions will you need to make in running your business? How will your business make these decisions? Who will do which tasks?)
- a financial plan (Make a budget by anticipating everything that might cost you money, including postage, photo-copying, transportation, equipment, and so on. How much money will you need to start your business? What are your potential sales? What are your potential costs? How much profit will your business earn?)

- a conclusion (What are your long-term goals? How will your business help you achieve your long-term goals?)

In addition to this information, consider how what you have learned in this course about traditional First Nations worldviews might give your business a special quality. It might impact how you run the business or the kind of product or service you offer.

Many books and Web sites are available devoted to writing business plans. Look them over for ideas, but remember that your business and plan do not have to be as long or complex as these examples.

LOOKING BACK

What is an entrepreneur? What kinds of values do Aboriginal entrepreneurs incorporate into their businesses? Make a list in your notes and write a short profile of one Aboriginal-owned business that you admire. In your profile, explain why you admire it.

Chapter Six Review

Check Your Understanding

1. Make a timeline showing the development of Aboriginal political organizations.

2. What significance did the federal government's 1969 White Paper have for Aboriginal peoples?

3. Why are there many political organizations for Aboriginal peoples instead of just one?

4. What role do tribal councils play? Give an example of a tribal council from Alberta and describe the kinds of activities it undertakes.

5. Define *standard of living* and name some criteria that are used to assess it. How is quality of life related?

6. What is the Assembly of First Nations? What factors led to its influence as a national First Nations political organization? How does it incorporate traditional values in its operation and structure? How does it incorporate Euro-Canadian political institutions?

7. What are some of the roles of the Assembly of First Nations' national chief? How do these roles compare to those of a leader such as a prime minister or premier?

8. What political organizations represent Métis people and non-Status Indians?

9. Describe how the political situation for Inuit peoples is different from that of First Nations and Métis peoples. What has this meant in terms of Inuit leaders' priorities?

10. How does having a land base often affect political priorities for Aboriginal peoples?

11. What are the Métis Settlements and what is the significance of their existence?

12. What is the Indian Association of Alberta and what has it achieved?

13. What reasons did the government have for policies of assimilation?

14. How did the Indian Act affect traditional forms of First Nations governance?

15. List at least five issues facing Aboriginal communities today and write a sentence or two for each explaining what the concern is and why.

16. What are the goals of the Métis National Council?

17. Describe at least two examples of Aboriginal entrepreneurship in Alberta and explain how Aboriginal culture is a part of the business.

18. Describe how natural resources can be a benefit and a drawback for Aboriginal peoples in Alberta.

Reading and Writing

19. Research a land claim in your province. Write a timeline of the negotiations, setbacks, and resolution, if it has been settled.

20. Research a settled land claim from somewhere in Canada. Prepare a one-page summary. Based on your research, what recommendations can you make to Alberta First Nations who have outstanding land claims?

21. Investigate a First Nation or Inuit community that is affected by environmental problems. How is the community affected? What has been the response of the community? Write a newspaper editorial from the perspective of a member of the community discussing the issue.

Viewing and Representing

22. Watch a documentary or other film about an Aboriginal political organization, social issue, or event. What point of view does the filmmaker have towards his or her subject? What specific details give you this impression? Did the film change your idea about the topic? If so, describe how.

Write a film review for your teacher describing whether you think the film is of educational value and why. What are the main points that the film conveys? Write three questions that would help the teacher assess a student's understanding of these main ideas. Indicate any problems with the film and whether you would recommend that other classes use it.

23. Draw a diagram showing traditional First Nations forms of governance and one showing band councils under the Indian Act.

24. Research programs that are offered by the federal government and Aboriginal political organizations to help Aboriginal youth improve their employment options. Choose a program that interests you and prepare a poster, pamphlet, or radio announcement that would both promote the program and engage Aboriginal youth.

Speaking and Listening

25. Watch a television program featuring Aboriginal content, such as *Cooking with the Wolfman* on the Aboriginal Peoples Television Network. Do you think such programs can break patterns of thinking such as stereotypes?

    With a partner or small group, think of a new television program that features Aboriginal content of interest to high school students. Your task is to write and present a pitch, or sales talk, about your program to a room of network executives (your class). Your pitch can last no longer than four minutes and should be as exciting and interesting as you can make it.

26. Write a speech from the perspective of a First Nations chief following announcement of the government's White Paper. Give your speech to the class.

Since Cooking with the Wolfman *first aired on the Aboriginal Peoples Television Network in 1999, thousands of viewers have been exposed to First Nations languages, traditional foods, storytelling, and humour as host Chef Professor David Wolfman prepares appetizing meals, such as rabbit parmesan breaded with pine nuts and chick pea flour.*

Going Further

27. Request an interview with the owner or manager of a business owned by an Aboriginal entrepreneur. Research what the business does and prepare a list of questions to ask in your interview.

    Using quotations from your interview, write a newspaper article that describes something newsworthy about the business. What are its biggest accomplishments? Be sure you are accurate in quoting your source. Send the business a copy of your article when it is done.

LOOKING BACK

Re-read Georges Erasmus's speech from pages 168–169. In this book, you've read many statements made by Aboriginal political, economic, and cultural leaders. Incorporate the statements that have the most meaning to you into a collage that illustrates your ideas about the future for Aboriginal peoples in Canada.

CHAPTER SEVEN
Symbolism and Expression

Most First Nations and Inuit peoples' languages do not traditionally have a word for *art*. This does not mean that their lives were historically devoid of beauty or creativity. Instead, every aspect of their daily lives — from clothing to shelter to hunting — was infused with artistic expression. Traditional peoples did not hang their art in museums or galleries. Instead it formed the vivid paintings on the walls of First Nations tipis; it was woven into the sashes worn by Métis fur traders; and it crept up during an Inuit hunt in the guise of a beautifully carved wooden club. This chapter introduces the wide-ranging artistic work that First Nations, Métis, and Inuit peoples practised in the past and continue to practise today.

Marilyn Dumont, a Cree-Métis poet who was born in Olds, Alberta, is a descendant of Gabriel Dumont, a Métis leader during the 1885 Resistance. In her prose poem, "It Crosses My Mind," she asks where Métis people fit within Canadian culture. She questions whether it is only a matter of time before young Métis people become assimilated into non-Aboriginal cultures.

Considering her questions, reflect on your own family's traditions. What traditions would you want your children to keep? How important is it to you that these traditions live on?

As you read this chapter, consider these questions:

▲ What place did artistic expression have in traditional First Nations, Métis, and Inuit communities?

▲ How were spirituality and a relationship to the land expressed in traditional art?

▲ How do the cultures and spiritual ideas of their ancestors affect the work of contemporary Aboriginal artists?

▲ What contributions have Aboriginal artists and writers made to Aboriginal and non-Aboriginal communities?

▲ How do Aboriginal authors express their life experiences in their work?

▲ In what ways does the oral tradition influence the work of Aboriginal authors?

It Crosses My Mind

By Marilyn Dumont

IT CROSSES MY MIND TO WONDER WHERE WE FIT IN THIS "VERTICAL MOSAIC," THIS COLOUR COLONY; THE URBAN PARIAH, THE DISPLACED AND surrendered to apartment blocks, shopping malls, superstores, and giant screens, are we distinct "survivors of white noise," or merely hostages in the enemy camp and the job application asks if I am a Canadian citizen and am I expected to mindlessly check "yes," indifferent to skin colour and the deaths of 1885, or am I actually free to check "no," like the true north strong and free and what will I know of my own kin in my old age, will they still welcome me, share their stew and tea, pass me the bannock like it's mine, will they continue to greet me in the old way, hand me their babies as my own, and send me away with gifts when I leave and what name will I know them by in these multi-cultural intentions, how will I know other than by shape of nose and cheekbone, colour of eyes and hair, and will it matter that we call our-selves Métis, Métisse, mixed blood, or aboriginal, will sovereignty matter or will we just slide off the level playing field turned on its side while the provincial flags slap confidently before me, echoing their self-absorbed anthem in the wind, and what is this game we've played long enough, finders keepers/losers weepers, so how loud and long can the losers weep and the white noise infiltrates my day as easily as the alarm, headlines, and Morningside but "Are you a Canadian citizen?" I sometimes think to answer, yes, by coercion,   yes, but no … there's   more,   but   no   space provided   to write my historical interpretation here, that yes but no, really only means yes because there are no lines for the stories between yes and no and what of the future of my eight-year-old niece, whose mother is Métis but only half as Métis as her grandmother, what will she name herself and will there come a time and can it be measured or predicted when she will stop naming herself and crossing her own mind.

The members of Warparty, from left to right, Thane Saddleback a.k.a. TJ, Rex Smallboy a.k.a. Mic Noble, Cynthia Smallboy a.k.a. Girlie Emcee, are from Hobbema, Alberta. Their music speaks about their experiences of reserve life through the sounds of mainstream rap and underground hip-hop. Other Aboriginal musicians, such as Red Nation, Buffy Sainte-Marie, or Kashtin, also reflect their experiences in their work.

Thousands of artists in Aboriginal communities across Canada work in the traditions of their ancestors, such as this Cree woman from northern Quebec, who is making a snowshoe. These artists create objects of beauty and use, although they might never show their work in a museum or take centre stage at a concert.

■ REFLECTION

1. What prompted Dumont to write her poem?
2. What does the term *white noise* usually mean and how does Dumont use it in her writing?
3. What are the references that Dumont alludes to (i.e., "true north strong and free," "deaths of 1885," "sovereignty," and "Morningside")? Look them up in a dictionary or encyclopedia if there are any you cannot explain. How does each add to the meaning of the poem?
4. What conclusion, if any, does Dumont reach?
5. Contrast the three examples of Aboriginal creative expression shown on pages 210–211. What does the diversity shown here tell you about Aboriginal artists today?

Art and Community

AS YOU READ

Artistic creation and expression served many functions in traditional communities. It recorded history, connected people to the spiritual world, created a sense of community and identity, and reinforced the worldview that makes First Nations, Métis, and Inuit cultures unique. These many functions meant that art was a fundamental part of every aspect of traditional First Nations, Métis, and Inuit lives and cultures. Pages 212–224 explore these traditional functions and various traditional and contemporary artists and art forms. Most contemporary artists reflect their cultures in their work, although some do so using traditional forms of expression and others use new forms and techniques.

IN TRADITIONAL FIRST NATIONS, MÉTIS, AND INUIT COMMUNITIES, ART WAS A HOLISTIC PART OF EVERYDAY LIFE, WHICH MEANS IT WAS SO MUCH A PART OF DAY-TO-DAY LIVING THAT IT COULD NOT BE SEPARATED AS A DISTINCT activity. In other words, creativity was not an activity carried out by a segment of the community who called themselves artists. Everyone expressed themselves through song, dance, and the tasks of everyday life. There were, of course, individuals with certain gifts — a good ivory carver, for example — but every individual was an artist of one kind or another.

As you learned in previous chapters, people in traditional communities worked hard to provide for themselves and their families. Yet they also took time to create objects or experiences of beauty and celebration.

Among traditional Woodland Cree communities, for example, fine quillwork, and later beadwork and embroidery, decorated clothing. An individual with beautiful decoration on his or her clothing had prestige. Its presence meant the person's family was well equipped with the necessities of life and had the time to pursue such creative expression. It spoke to the talent and skills of the whole family.

People from all cultures feel pleasure listening to music, watching dance, or looking upon a painting or other work of art that stirs their emotions. Such feelings can make them feel connected to the world. This sense of connection, especially when shared with other people, gives individuals a sense of being part of a community.

People of all cultures often express great pleasure in the act of

In traditional Aboriginal communities, everyday items, such as moccasins, were created with great care and creative expression. These moccasins were made by a member of the Blackfoot Confederacy around 1875. Different First Nations had distinctive styles of moccasin construction and decoration. What other useful items have you seen in photographs in this textbook that show similar attention to creative expression?

creating art. Many explain that moments of creation draw them closer to the Creator or another spiritual force. Participation in community dances and songs, for example, builds and reinforces a sense of connection to other people and to the Creator.

Seen in this way, the act of creating something beautiful can be a spiritual pursuit, like a prayer. Using the Earth's gifts to create beauty honours Mother Earth's beauty. In First Nations traditions, artwork takes from the Earth, but gives thanks at the same time. It is part of the reciprocal relationship of giving and receiving that is part of First Nations cultural traditions.

In traditional First Nations and Inuit communities, art was also important because it recorded past events and visions of the future. It helped transmit culture and knowledge from one generation to the next. On the Plains, for example, buffalo hides were often painted to relay the story of a great battle, hunt, or act of heroism. Such paintings served as a support for the oral tradition — acting as memory aids for those who know the oral history.

Dances and songs often served similar purposes among traditional peoples. They helped record ideas, prayers, and traditions. Many traditional songs repeat phrases, refrains, or rhythms to make them easier to learn, share, and remember.

SYMBOLISM

First Nations, Métis, and Inuit peoples have many traditional symbols that reflect their spirituality and relationship with the environment.

Among traditional Plains First Nations, every object, from clothing to buffalo hides covering tipis to ceremonial tobacco pipes, was adorned with symbolic designs. These designs made the objects beautiful and told stories. Symbols sometimes represented spiritual journeys, important events, and accomplishments of the people who created them.

Particularly powerful symbols were repeated often on many different objects. Through repetition, the symbolic meaning of each design formed a visual language that was understood by members of a community. Among the nations of the Blackfoot Confederacy, for example, the circle represents the interconnectedness of all aspects of life. As you learned on pages 87–88, most other First Nations use the circle to represent similar meanings. Many First Nations, Métis, and

The powwow is the oldest surviving public festival in North America. Many forms of First Nations cultural expression are part of it. Powwows include singing, dancing, drumming, and visual symbolism on the elaborate regalia worn by participants. This powwow photograph was taken in Wetaskiwin, Alberta, in 2003. (Names of those pictured are unavailable.)

Indigenous Knowledge

Symbolism is employed when an artist uses a person, place, object, or event to represent something else. Some symbols are considered universal, such as the cross as a symbol of Christianity. Other symbols can have meaning for a single community or individual. Bring an object to class that has symbolic meaning to you. Share the significance of the object with your classmates.

Inuit artists practising today continue to use traditional symbols. For many, the symbols are as powerful now as they once were.

Symbols are often rooted in the spiritual beliefs of a community. Creative expression was traditionally a way of connecting with and honouring the spiritual world. For example, symbolically adorned tobacco pipes and drums are an integral part of many First Nations spiritual ceremonies. Use of these objects is seen as a form of prayer or other communication with the Creator.

The symbols found in traditional works of art are as varied as the cultures and lifestyles of the people who created them. However, because the natural environment played such a central role in the spirituality of traditional First Nations and Inuit societies, the source of many cultural symbols can be found in the natural world.

Traditional stories and objects depicted animals or elements of nature that held sacred meaning. Among the Inuit, for example, the polar bear figures prominently in many ivory and soapstone sculptures. According to Inuit beliefs, the bear is a helping spirit.

Each creation was carefully thought out — no elements were left to chance because everything was believed to be connected. People chose colours to create visual effects and in reference to the natural forces that surrounded them. Among First Nations from the Plains, for example, yellow commonly represented the sun, blue was often sky or water, and red illustrated the earth. Since these essential elements of nature were also seen as having spiritual power, their associated colours carried the same symbolic meaning.

Taken in 1907, this photograph shows designs on tipis from the Blackfoot Confederacy. Sky and earth are represented by the geometrical designs at the top and bottom. Encircling the middle are symbols of personal guardian spirits as revealed in visions to the tipi owner. These designs belonged to the owner, although they could be passed to others through ceremony. Research other Blackfoot tipi designs and compare the symbolism used with the tipis of other cultures.

Indians are not all tipi and rock painters. My ancestors created everything they made with the mind of an engineer and a heart of an artist. Everything from a fishhook to a pipe bag is art and commands honour and respect. Today we devalue all our possessions — we buy "stuff," use it for a little while, then throw it away."

— Kim Mclain, Cold Lake First Nation, *Seven Lifetimes: Yesterday, Today, and Tomorrow*

ENVIRONMENT

In the past, materials and inspiration for creative works were found in the surrounding environment. Stones, wood, and animal parts, such as teeth, bone, sinew, horns, and claws, formed the basis for many cultural objects. Natural dyes, pigments, quills, feathers, grass, hair, and shells served as adornments.

The kind of environment a group lived in was directly related to the kind of traditional creative work they pursued. This relationship was partly due to the supply of resources. In heavily wooded regions, for example, birchbark was used for everything from canoes and water vessels to cradles. In the Pacific Northwest, massive cedar trees provided material for carvings and dugout canoes.

Although First Nations depended upon the resources of their immediate surroundings, they were not limited by them. For example, trade with other groups meant that Blackfoot nations could acquire porcupine quills from First Nations living in woodland areas and Woodland Cree artists could trade for caribou hair, which was softer and easier to work with than moose hair.

The relationship between creative work and the environment was also practical. On the Plains, for example, the Siksika First Nation decorated their clothing with feathers and fringes. This type of decoration would have been impractical for a Woodland Cree hunter tracking game through thick forest. Hanging decorations would

CONNECTING CREATIVITY AND THE LAND

How is an Aboriginal group's relationship to the land and environment related to its traditional styles of creative work?

WHAT TO DO

1. Aboriginal peoples in North America are diverse in all cultural characteristics. In a small group, choose a specific First Nation, Métis, or Inuit community and research the group's culture and way of life to provide a background for their creative practices. You will likely want to learn about their environment, clothing, oral tradition, food, and so on.

2. Learn as much as you can about the forms of creative expression used by your group. Focus on symbols related to the group's environment, types of objects created, materials used, and any overall style.

3. Prepare a report to hand in to the teacher or, if you prefer, give an oral presentation to the class.

4. With your teacher's help, invite someone from the community who practices a traditional art form to demonstrate his or her work to the class.

quickly become tangled or torn. The Woodland Cree hunter's clothing decoration was close to the body, made of quills and beads. Likewise, a large Haida dugout carved of wood made sense in the ocean's heavy waves, but would be a burden during a Subarctic portage.

For Plains First Nations, one animal, the buffalo, fulfilled nearly all basic needs. The buffalo also provided the materials for cultural expression. Hides were painted to portray visions and great achievements, untanned buffalo skins — called rawhide — were stretched over wooden forms to make drums, and bones were carved into delicate flutes and whistles. For northern Alberta First Nations, the moose fulfilled a similar role.

The music and dance of First Nations and Inuit peoples also reflected reverence and appreciation for the land, as did storytelling, another form of creative work. The themes of songs and chants often addressed the Earth, sky, water, planting and harvesting cycles, and animal spirits.

Certain stories, songs, and dances were part of seasonal ceremonies or events, in harmony with the natural world's time frame.

IDENTITY

Music from drums and flutes brings people together. For many groups, the drum is of particular importance; its pulsating rhythm represents Mother Earth's heartbeat. Traditional dances, which could last for hours or days, connected people physically, emotionally, and spiritually with this same heartbeat and with each other.

Some forms of creative expression traditionally helped reinforce cultural and social identity. Many designs were unique to particular nations or clans. Use of them helped to enhance a common bond. For example, the salmon instantly speaks to First Nations from the Pacific Northwest, the polar bear to the Arctic Inuit, and the buffalo to the Plains First Nations and Métis peoples.

Traditionally, some significant designs were restricted to particular individuals, who were then responsible for passing on the design to the next generation. This practice ensured the integrity of symbols and designs from one generation to the next.

Creation stories and cycles of renewal were popular themes represented in artwork, reinforcing the importance of creation stories in traditional societies. Such affirmations are one of the elements that make First Nations and Inuit worldviews unique. Contemporary artists continue to use the cyclical theme in their work. Circles, cycles, and interconnection are all concepts represented in visual and performing art by First Nations, Métis, and Inuit peoples from past and present.

REPATRIATING CULTURAL OBJECTS

Imagine that something very private and sacred to you could be found on public display in a museum. What would be your reaction? For many First Nations and Inuit peoples, this is an all too familiar situation.

For hundreds of years, cultural objects, knowledge about the environment, and human remains that belong to their communities were used or taken without community consent. For some groups, the only way to see community treasures was to visit a museum.

Since the early 1970s, many First Nations and Inuit peoples have actively worked to **repatriate** cultural property. For example, in 1998, the Mookakin Foundation formed by the Kainai First Nation signed an agreement with the Glenbow Museum in Calgary for the repatriation of several sacred medicine bundles. Many communities view the repatriation of such articles as an important step in the preservation of their cultural heritage.

On October 17, 2003, members of the Haida First Nation danced with audience members in a ceremony at the Field Museum in Chicago. The First Nation delegates returned home with the human remains of 150 of their ancestors. Upon reaching the Queen Charlotte Islands, the remains were returned to an ancestral burial ground.

Your Project

1. Investigate a local effort to repatriate cultural property or human remains. How long do such projects take and what kinds of protocols must be followed? What issues prevent the immediate return of articles and human remains?

2. Expand your understanding about the kinds of items and knowledge that are considered sacred by a local First Nation. If possible, ask an Elder to attend your class to speak about this issue. Check with your teacher first to be sure you use proper protocol to issue this invitation.

3. After finding out about a local effort, investigate similar projects by indigenous peoples in other countries.

4. Once you understand the issues at stake, create a poster that brings awareness to the general public about the importance of repatriating cultural property. To make this poster effective and eye-catching, follow some general rules of advertising:
   - Write a creative, catchy message.
   - Have a strong visual.
   - Keep your poster clean and simple.

If you prefer, express your ideas and feelings about the issue in a work of visual art or performance.

TRADITIONAL ART FORMS

People in traditional societies had few belongings, but those they had were highly functional. These belongings were often decorated using many kinds of natural materials.

Each traditional art form was passed down from generation to generation. Some forms of expression, such as the designs on tipis, were only transferred to another individual through ceremony. Techniques like tufting, birchbark biting, and fish scale art, in contrast, were communal and learned by observation and careful practise.

Quillwork

One of the oldest and most widespread First Nations decorative styles uses porcupine quills in intricate designs. Preparing the quills was a delicate process. First the quills were sorted according to length — the shortest quills are found along the animal's underbelly, while the longest grow on its tail. The quills were then softened, traditionally using saliva. Next they were coloured, using natural vegetable and mineral dyes. Red and yellow, for example, were obtained from iron ore found in rocks. Other colours were mixed from materials such as crushed berries, bull rushes, and soot.

Once the quills were sorted, softened, and dyed, they were flattened and sewn onto a leather surface.

Beadwork

Like language and other aspects of culture, artistic techniques are often adapted to suit new circumstances. For example, beadwork is now considered a traditional form of First Nations, Métis, and Inuit artwork, even though it was adopted after European contact.

Accustomed to adapting to new technologies, First Nations, Métis, and Inuit women recognized that beads were easier to use than traditional materials such as porcupine quills. They quickly adopted beads as part of their decorative practice.

Tufting

Moose or caribou hair tufting is primarily practiced by Dene and Woodland Cree people. It is a another example of a traditional First Nations art form that incorporates new European technology.

While the use of moose and caribou hair to decorate clothing and other objects long predates European contact, tufting was developed in the late 1910s by Madeleine Lafferte, a Métis woman from Fort Providence, Northwest Territories. Lafferte was inspired by European wool punch work that she observed on the bishop's chair in Fort Providence. The punchwork

This caribou hair tufted picture was made by Arabella Creighton of the Kainai First Nation in 1985. She learned caribou hair tufting through a crafts program at the Northern Lakes College in Grouard, Alberta. She used caribou hair for the flowers and moose hair for the embroidered stems.

I believe birchbark biting has many teachings: patience, respect, kindness, creativity, medicine, imagination, and sharing. Birchbark bitings are like people. No two are the same and every one is special and beautiful in its own way. I strongly believe that Aboriginal people should strive to maintain their traditional art forms.

— Pat Bruderer Half Moon,
Mosakahiken Cree Nation, Manitoba

had been done by a Grey Nun, Sister St. Gregory, around 1912. Lafferte applied the wool punch technique to familiar materials, creating a new and highly original art form.

Tufting involves twisting thread around small bundles of about twenty short, dyed hairs. Each bundle is sewn tightly onto a hide or cloth background, often of black velveteen, then clipped to form the desired shape.

Birchbark Biting

One of the most labour intensive art forms is called birchbark biting. Also known as transparencies, the works are created by repeatedly biting into folded sheets of specially prepared birchbark. The folds allow the artist to create symmetrical designs that can be seen once the sheet is unfolded and held flat up to

Pat Bruderer Half Moon, who created this birchbark biting, learned the technique from her mother. Bruderer Half Moon goes through ten or more stages to finish one work and says birchbark biters get the design they want by visualizing it as they bite.

GHOST DANCE

Many First Nations forms of expression and celebration have been misunderstood and misinterpreted by Europeans. This lack of understanding has at times led to fear, which has in turn led to repression and legislation to forbid traditional practices.

In the 1870s, First Nations in the United States were experiencing problems similar to those in Canada. Communities suffered from the effects of disease, malnutrition or starvation, inadequate reserves, and failed treaty promises. A movement called the Ghost Dance swept through many Plains communities, particularly among the Dakota. In the face of the devastating changes faced by their peoples, First Nations looked for hope.

The prophecy of the Ghost Dance told that in the following spring, Earth would rejuvenate itself with new soil. With this rejuvenation, all newcomers to North America would be gone and only First Nations and their friends and relatives in the spirit world would remain. The dancers participated in this ceremony to show their belief in and support of this prophecy.

United States Indian agents misunderstood the dance and grew increasingly nervous. They feared the gatherings signalled aggressive feelings towards communities surrounding reserves. Their fears led to tragedy.

In a now infamous incident, what started off as a way of reuniting First Nations peoples ended as one of the largest massacres in North American history. On December 29, 1890, approximately 350 Dakota men, women, and children were killed at a Ghost Dance gathering by American Cavalry at Wounded Knee Creek, at the Pine Ridge Reservation in South Dakota.

◼ REFLECTION

Research the history surrounding the massacre at Wounded Knee Creek. Write a newspaper article or editorial as if you are a reporter working for a First Nations newspaper sent to cover the incident.

the light. Infused with sunlight, the tiny perforations made by the artist's eyeteeth reveal intricate designs of flowers, insects, and birds.

Fish Scale Art

Fish scale artwork involves creating designs out of individually placed fish scales, bones, and vertebrae. It is delicate work that takes great patience and care. In northern Alberta, First Nations use white fish — called *atihkamek* in Cree — which have larger scales than other fish. This makes them easier to work with.

The scales are carefully washed, cleaned, and sorted in a process that takes up to two days. Then they are normally dyed a variety of colours and glued onto a hide or cloth backing. Fish scale designs are not normally used for clothing decoration because they can be easily damaged.

Inuit Sculpture

Although contemporary Inuit artists use many different art forms, Inuit peoples are famous for their carving skills. Most Arctic communities began Inuit-owned cooperatives in the 1950s and 1960s to market and sell their work. Inuit sculpture today has an international reputation as an important contemporary art form.

Most traditional carvings were made from ivory. Contemporary carvers most often use stone. The word *soapstone* is often used to describe all Inuit sculpture, but this is misleading. Soapstone is quite soft and many carvers prefer harder

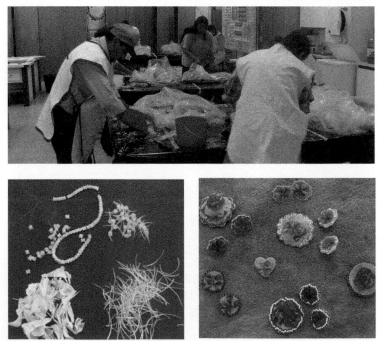

Students at Northern Lakes College in Grouard, Alberta, work to prepare fish scales and their final projects. Students in the program glue the fish scales to their surface and then glaze the surface of their work to protect it. Left to right: Ralph Davis from Kinuso, Josephine Didizena from Assumption, and Brenda Sound from Kinuso. All are participants in the 2003–2004 Aboriginal Clothing Design Program.

> At one time, when I was younger, I was shy, almost embarrassed to carve. If a woman was a carver it was a very unusual thing. People would see it as man's work, but today the woman has to be recognized more. Women are homemakers and mothers, but also women are carvers now. I want women to be strong, to try and use their talents.
>
> — Ovilu Tunnille, Andrew Gordon Bay, Baffin Island

material, such as serpentine or quartz. Some carvings are made with caribou antlers or ancient whale-bone, or a combination of materials.

Many contemporary carvings portray traditional subjects, such as animals, hunting, and family life scenes. However, spiritual images and figures from Inuit oral tradition also appear frequently. Different communities across the Arctic have unique styles of carving, as do individual artists.

Performing Arts

Storytelling, music, and dance were important forms of communication for traditional communities, as they continue to be today. Songs, music, dance, and drumming bring people together for ceremony and celebration. As with other art forms, some sacred songs can only be passed down by certain clans, societies, or families. Others, such as those sung at powwows, are universal and are shared among many different nations and cultures.

As you learned on pages 148–149, Métis peoples have many innovative traditional art forms. Community traditions such as the Red River jig, while incorporating aspects of European cultures, maintained the First Nations tradition of community bonding through song and dance. Métis people also have many other forms of traditional dance including the reel of four, the reel of eight, and drops of brandy.

Evi Mark (left) and Emma Grey, throat singers from Nunavik in northern Quebec, are performing here at the Yukon Storytelling Festival. Throat singing is a form of Inuit song that is usually performed by two women standing face to face. Each singer repeats a low- or high-pitched sound in a rhythm that sometimes sounds like birds and animals. Sometimes throat singing is used as a contest, with the winner being the person who can sing the longest. Many contests end with both contestants laughing.

Indigenous Knowledge

Using proper protocol, invite artists from your community to attend your class to talk about and demonstrate their work.

Dale Auger's paintings once focused on First Nations history, but now they portray more spiritual aspects of life, including a love of the land. Research some of Auger's paintings and information about his life.

Alex Janvier was born in 1935 on the Cold Lake First Nation. His Dene Sųłiné heritage is an important part of his work and he is regarded as one of Canada's top contemporary artists. He still lives and works near Cold Lake, Alberta.

CONTEMPORARY ARTISTS

Art takes many forms in contemporary society and First Nations, Métis, and Inuit peoples contribute to all of them. As accomplished musicians, storytellers, dancers, performers, architects, painters, sculptors, designers, choreographers, directors, actors, and filmmakers, Aboriginal artists have a significant place in Canadian and international arts and culture.

Some contemporary Aboriginal artists choose to continue the artistic practices of their ancestors, such as sculpting from stone, wood, and antler. Many combine modern ideas and techniques with old symbols and themes. Others adopt radically new types of art, such as those that use computer technology. The artists discussed on pages 222–224 are just a sample of the many Aboriginal people today making significant contributions in the fields of arts and culture.

Douglas Cardinal

Drawing upon his Kainai heritage, architect Douglas Cardinal creates buildings that reflect the traditional

The most powerful part of [my educational] journey was something that was with me the whole time. And that was the power to create. The power to access my visions. Then to bring them to life. The Creator has taken me full circle. He had given me the power to create and then sent me on my way to learn. And then he brought me back, which is where I am today.

— Dale Auger, Bigstone Cree Nation, *In Their Footsteps: Contributions of First Nations People in Alberta*

philosophies of his ancestors. His designs are not square and rigid, but are curved, natural shapes that reflect the environment.

Cardinal's goal is to create buildings that become part of the land, not structures that overpower it. In 1972, Cardinal was hired to design Grande Prairie Regional College. The building he created was completely different from any other structure in Canada. It established Cardinal as one of the country's leading architects.

Cardinal has always been interested in technological advances in his field. In the 1970s, his office was a test site in the development of CADD (Computer Assisted Drafting and Design), a software program now standard in architecture and other fields. In the same decade, he became one of the first architects in North America to completely computerize his architectural firm.

Early in his career, Cardinal sought the guidance of Elders and asked their advice on his architectural practice. They advised him to consider how people would be using the spaces he designed and they told him to think of his buildings as living beings. Cardinal's work is internationally recognized and he is a recipient of the nation's highest honour, the Order of Canada.

Tantoo Cardinal

When Métis actor Tantoo Cardinal left the northern Alberta town of Anzac in 1965, she had no plans beyond attending high school in Edmonton. Thanks to a teacher who believed in her and a bursary from Northland School Division, she left home at age fifteen so that she could complete her education.

Many years later, she decided that acting would help her do what she loved best — telling Aboriginal people's stories. At first, she had very few roles to choose from. Today she is one of the best-known Aboriginal actors in the film industry. Cardinal has had roles in major Hollywood films, such as *Dances with Wolves* and *Legends of the Fall*, as well as many roles in television and theatre.

Cardinal selects roles that she hopes will make Aboriginal people feel good about themselves. She is not afraid to ask for a part to be rewritten if she feels it presents a dishonest picture of Aboriginal peoples.

After receiving a National Aboriginal Achievement Award in 1998, Cardinal said she hoped to begin writing and developing projects that would help tell more Aboriginal stories.

Tomson Highway

The first language Tomson Highway learned was Cree, while being raised on his father's trapline on a reserve in northwestern Manitoba. His traditional upbringing is a major influence on the artworks he produces. Two of his plays, *The Rez Sisters* and *Dry Lips Oughta Move to Kapuskasing*, deal with life on a reserve and what it means to be a First Nations person in contemporary society. In the next section of this textbook, you can read more about his interpretation of this life. Highway describes his plays as a combination of "Indian reality, classical structure, and artistic language." Like Douglas Cardinal, Highway is also a recipient of the Order of Canada.

Architect Douglas Cardinal designed Grande Prairie Regional College, which was built in 1973. This photo features the north wing. What distinctive feature of his design reflects the architect's First Nations heritage?

Tantoo Cardinal, shown here in a television role on "North of 60," wants her work to help Aboriginal people tell their own stories in their own way. This goal is echoed by many other Aboriginal writers, actors, and filmmakers. Why do you think they feel this is so important?

Scriptwriter Paul Apak Angilirq (left) with director Zacharias Kunuk on the set of Atanarjuat *in 1998. June Kunuk, standing behind them, is Zacharias's daughter.* Atanarjuat *is the first feature film entirely in Inuktitut. What effects might this film have on non-Aboriginal audiences?*

This production of The Rez Sisters *took place at Cornell University's Schwartz Center for the Performing Arts in October 2001. Playwright Tomson Highway left his career as a classical pianist to write plays because he felt that theatre was closer to the First Nations cultural experience. What aspects of theatre do you think attracted him?*

Zacharias Kunuk

Zacharias Kunuk, with assistance from people in his northern community of Igloolik, has been creating films and videos from an Inuit perspective since 1981.

The irony in his use of this medium is that television was not allowed in Kunuk's community until 1983 for fear that its programming would disrupt traditional Inuit ways of life.

Kunuk's film *Atanarjuat*, which is Inuktitut for "fast runner," is Canada's first Aboriginal-language feature-length film that is written, produced, directed, and acted by Inuit people. The film has been critically acclaimed both nationally and internationally. It tells a story from Inuit oral tradition about love, courage, murder, and revenge in a small Inuit community. All aspects of the film, from the costumes and props to the production methods, were in careful accordance with Inuit cultural customs.

LOOKING BACK

Create a profile of one contemporary Aboriginal artist and present your information to the class. You might choose a visual or performing artist, including singers, dancers, painters, sculptors, and so on. If you prefer, profile a person from your own community, whether they are known outside the community or not. For suggestions on visual artists, visit *http://collections.ic.gc.ca/ artists/artists.html*. For a wider variety of artists, musicians, and other performers, visit the Web site of the National Aboriginal Achievement Awards at *www.naaf.ca/naaa.html*. Include biographical information, examples of the artist's work (photographs, video, or recordings) and your assessment of traditional influences on their work.

Literature

Although First Nations, Métis, and Inuit literature is diverse, dependent on such factors as region, linguistic group, and culture, certain themes and issues tend to appear over and over again. This is likely because similar experiences abound in Aboriginal peoples' lives as they navigate Canada's political, social, and cultural landscape.

Age is also an important factor in the kinds of experiences writers have and wish to recount in their work. As government policies and attitudes towards Aboriginal peoples have changed through time, so have the experiences of Aboriginal people in Canada. Different generations of Aboriginal writers reflect this evolution in their work as they relate their own experiences.

Anishinabé author George Copway was the first Aboriginal writer in Canada to publish a book in English. His autobiography, *The Life, History, and Travels of Ka-ge-gah-bowh*, was published in 1847. Copway, like other Aboriginal peoples who were among the first to learn English well enough to write books, was taught by European missionaries. Copway eventually converted to Christianity and became a Methodist minister. While he praised his ancestors for their extensive knowledge of the environment, he regarded Anishinabé spirituality as inferior to Christianity. Today most contemporary First

AS YOU READ

Aboriginal literature is as diverse as any other aspect of Aboriginal culture. Yet Aboriginal authors in Canada often share common concerns and approaches with each other and with indigenous writers from around the world. These common threads include a strong sense of connection to their ancestral lands and a cultural history of European colonization. This is often expressed as a sense of spiritual, physical, and cultural displacement. However, although Aboriginal literature once stressed themes of displacement most prominently, today it also reflects a growing sense of empowerment for future generations.

Make a list of the writer's names you encounter as you read pages 225–232, along with a brief note about their work or background. You will read the works of one of them for a project on page 233.

Nations and Inuit writers celebrate their peoples' spirituality.

INUIT LITERATURE

Because of their geographic isolation from most of the European people who settled in North America, Inuit cultures in general suffered less disruption than First Nations and Métis communities in southern Canada. The problems Inuit peoples experienced came later in history. Many contemporary Inuit writers celebrate the continuation of their traditions and question how to combine their traditions with modern cultural influences.

Much contemporary Inuit literature shows a political consciousness and an adept use of the English language. Journalism is often a popular format. For example, Tagak Curley, who was the first president of the Inuit Tapirisat of Canada,

(now the Inuit Tapiriit Kanatami) wrote the following passage for *Maclean's* magazine in 1986:

> Our land has never been conquered. If it was, we would be wiped out of our culture. The minute we step out of our community we are in our historical environment. But not down south. Indian people have to cope with that. They were deprived of their wildlife, their land. But we have something that helped our people. Our environment is harsh. Who would want to live here?

Today Tagak Curley is a Member of the Legislative Assembly in Nunavut, representing Rankin Inlet north. His written work, along with that of other contemporary writers, such as Alootook Ipellie, are today building an eloquent tradition of Inuit writing in English.

My people will sleep for one hundred years, but when they awake, it will be the artists who give them their spirit back.

— Louis Riel, 1885

RECLAIMING STORIES

First Nations and Métis authors write from a distinctly different perspective. After suffering generations of cultural disruption, many write to reclaim their cultural heritage and the right to tell their own stories in their own way.

Métis writer Maria Campbell is one such writer. In 1973, she published the groundbreaking book *Halfbreed*, which chronicled her life as a Métis woman in Canada. This work was significant because it was the first book that honestly depicted the reality of being Métis.

The first chapter describes the history of Métis people from a Métis perspective. For example, she describes how Métis people did not receive land the Canadian government promised them in the Manitoba Act of 1870. It is now widely known that Métis peoples were often cheated of their land by unscrupulous individuals and an indifferent government. Although this idea is now accepted as historical fact, it was revolutionary in 1973.

Campbell states in her preface that she wrote her life story for people outside Aboriginal cultures, so they could see what it was like to be Métis. Campbell writes "A close friend of mine said, 'Maria, make it a happy book. It couldn't have been so bad. We know we are guilty so don't be too harsh.' I am not bitter. I have passed that stage. I only want to say: this is what it was like; this is what it is still like."

Halfbreed is also significant because it inspired many other Aboriginal people to tell their own stories. Autobiography remains an important genre in Aboriginal literature. Many writers share their stories — good and bad — in an effort to help other Aboriginal people and to communicate their experiences to non-Aboriginal audiences.

SPEAKING OUT, SPEAKING BACK

When writers share works that come from their personal experiences, the most powerful are often those that are shared experiences. Many narratives speak out against the social problems that Aboriginal peoples often experience in Canada, as well as the causes of these problems.

Margo Kane's play *Moonlodge* deals with the abduction of children from their homes and cultures. This topic appears in many works because so many people experienced this form of displacement, whether at residential schools, through forced adoptions, or other family break-ups. According to Statistics Canada's 2001 Aboriginal People's Survey, for example, 44 per cent of First Nations people over the age of fifteen report at least one relative who attended a residential school. This number would likely be much higher if First Nations people living on reserves were included in the statistics.

Although residential schools and other policies that disrupted family life are gone, the effects of the policies linger in many communities.

As was discussed on pages 77–78, humour is a characteristically Aboriginal way of dealing with serious issues. For example, in *The Rez Sisters*, Tomson Highway reveals the lives of seven women living on a fictional reserve in Ontario — Wasaychigan Hill. Expressed in the play's dialogue is the women's frustration with the lack of work for their sons and husbands, the absence of paved roads on their reserve, the hopelessness that breeds alcoholism, and the Roman Catholic church's historic exploitation of their community.

A turning point in the play is when the women decide that they have had enough and one character announces "All us Wasy women, we'll march up the hill, burn the church hall down, scare the priest to death, and then we'll march all the way to Espanola, where the bingos are bigger and better."

Many Aboriginal writers use their work to speak back to institutions that have tried to take away their peoples' power. Marilyn Dumont's poem "Letter to Sir John A. Macdonald" speaks back to the long-dead prime minister to let him know that the Métis Nation has outlasted the railway that helped displace them from their land.

Maria Campbell's autobiography, Halfbreed, *does not begin with her own birth in 1940, but instead in the 1800s with the history of the Métis people. What does this beginning say about her sense of identity?*

Rita Joe started writing in her thirties to try to balance the negative images of Aboriginal peoples her children were learning in school.

IDENTITY

Perhaps the most common issue that Aboriginal writers explore is that of identity — what it means to be a First Nations, Métis, or Inuit person. Some write about how to maintain traditions and culture in the modern world. Others write about searching for self-identity after suffering family or community breakdown.

Mi'kmaq poet Rita Joe illustrates some of these points in "I lost my talk."

I lost my talk

The talk you took away.
When I was a little girl
At Schubenacadie school.

You snatched it away:
I speak like you
I think like you
I create like you
The scrambled ballad, about my
    word.
Two ways I talk
Both ways I say,
Your way is more powerful.

So gently I offer my hand and ask,
Let me find my talk
So I can teach you about me.

Her poem recounts her experience at the Schubenacadie residential school. She describes losing her First Nations language, but not being taught English very well, either. She, like many others of her generation, were left on the margins of two cultures, belonging fully to neither. Her sense of identity is a "scrambled ballad."

Richard Wagamese is an award-winning author of Anishinabé ancestry. In his autobiographical writings, he describes his early life of alcoholism and years spent on the streets and in prison. His fictional work reflects his personal experiences.

In *Keeper 'n Me*, Wagamese writes about Garnet Raven, a twenty-year-old man who returns to the First Nation he never knew. Garnet is disconnected from his culture and ashamed of his cultural heritage. He often poses as Hawaiian, African American, or Mexican — anything as long as he does not have to admit he is First Nations. Many Aboriginal people who grew up in homes or communities outside their culture share the same experience.

Since he cannot face who he is, Garnet wanders and, like Wagamese himself, ends up on the streets of a big city. In search of answers, he travels to the First Nation where he was born and meets Keeper, an old man from the community, who possesses much cultural knowledge.

In one passage, Keeper explains the significance of the hand drum "In our way we believe that the drum holds the heartbeat of the people. The songs you sing with it are very sacred. Nothin' to be played around with. When you sing you're joinin' the heartbeat of the people with the heartbeat of the universe. It's a blessing. You're blessing the land and the water and the air with the pure, clear spirit of the people."

Through his relationship with Keeper, Garnet finds some of the beauty and strength in his culture's traditions. At last Garnet begins to come to terms with his cultural heritage and identity.

Garnet's ability to pretend to be someone of many different cultures alludes to the difficulty many non-Aboriginal people have in seeing and understanding the diversity of Aboriginal cultures and peoples. Nipissing writer Wayne Keon's poem "Heritage" squishes the names of First Nations together into one uniform, tidy box. All distinctions are lost. As seen in the following excerpt from his poem, names are broken to suit the shape of the box and ordered alphabetically to suit the order of the English language.

heritage

AlgonkinAssiniboineAthapaskanB
eaverBellaCoolaBeothukBlackfoo
tCarrierCaughnawayaCayugaChilk
atChilcotinChipewyanCreeCrowDe
lewareDogribEskimoFlatheadFoxG
rosVentreHaidaHareHuronIllinoi
sIroquoisKickapooKitwancoolKoo
tneyKoskimoKutchinKwakiutlLake
LillloetMaleciteMalouinMenomine
eMétisMiamiMicmacMississaugaMo
hawkMohicanMontagnaisMuskogeeN
ahaniNaskapiNeutralNicolaNipis
singNootkaOjibwayOkanaganOneid
aOnondagOttawaPequotPetunPieg
anPotawatomieSalishSarceeSaukS
aulteauxSekaniSenecaShawneeSho
shoniShushwapSiouxSlaveStoneySu
squehannaTagishTalhltanThompson
TlinkitTsetsautTsimshianTuscar
oraWinnebagoWyandotYellowknife

Some writers express a heightened difficulty establishing a Métis identity. For many years, Métis peoples were not recognized as distinct from Euro-Canadian and First Nations peoples. Many Métis found that they did not fit with either group.

Drew Hayden Taylor explores stereotypes about how a First Nations person should look in his essay "Pretty Like a White Boy: the Adventures of a Blue-Eyed Ojibway" and his book *Funny, You Don't Look Like One*. His work, like the works of many other Aboriginal writers, deals with stereotypes about Aboriginal peoples and their cultures. He reports being turned down for many acting jobs to play First Nations people because he doesn't look like mainstream expectations of a First Nations person.

Other authors wrestle with issues of how First Nations or Métis they are. After a lifetime of searching, Métis poet Gregory Scofield writes that he did not feel he was truly Métis until he visited Batoche — a place with historical significance for the Métis Nation. He writes "The importance that I had once placed

Drew Hayden Taylor is a prolific writer, journalist, playwright, actor, and humourist. He also directed a documentary about Aboriginal humour for the National Film Board of Canada called Redskins, Tricksters, and Puppy Stew. Read a story, play, or article by Taylor and write your response in a two-page review.

Indigenous Knowledge

Most contemporary literature stresses strength and renewal, rather than loss and victimization. Look through collections of poetry or anthologies of literature by Aboriginal people to find a poem, short story, or other writing that stresses renewal and strength. How does the author convey this message? Write an essay describing your ideas and the evidence you find in support of your interpretation.

on being Cree — a true and pure Indian — seemed to disappear with the sinking sun. Suddenly, the colour of my eyes, hair, and skin seemed to belong to me, perfectly matching the prairie landscape that held such a dignified history… never again would I search for a place of belonging."

ORAL TRADITIONS IN LITERATURE

Aboriginal literature has been called both very old and very new. It is new in the sense that there are less than 150 years of written works in its tradition. Before this time, the oral tradition was the primary method of expression and record.

PROFILE

Louise Halfe

LOUISE HALFE
Saddle Lake First Nation

Cree poet Louise Bernice Halfe speaks for a generation of Aboriginal women. She leads readers into their deepest thoughts as buffalo herds disappear, epidemics decimate families, and bands are confined to reservations.

The voices in her poetry are stark, unforgiving, and evoke powerful emotion. "I have had people walk out of my readings, burn my books, or buy them from me only to give them back," Halfe says.

Born in 1953 to parents "traumatized by residential school dynamics," Halfe fought her own demons. While raising her children, she began to dream of her grandfather and grandmother, and wanted to explore the cryptic messages they offered.

"Sometimes I didn't know the meaning of what I dreamt for a long time. Then it would come, and I would write. For years, I was looking in dictionaries to find the words I needed. I was always asking my husband the meaning of words. I basically taught myself to write," she explains.

Much of Halfe's work is derived from meditations in which she asks her grandmothers to guide her pen. Other inspiration comes from her personal life, such as when she ate rabbit stew as a child or while she spends time as an adult at the ceremonial gathering place of Kootenay Plains.

In her book *Blue Marrow*, Halfe longs for the time when women "drummed, danced, lifted their dreams." Her references to past times and ancient ceremony are heavy with cultural symbolism, which she will explain "only if you come with respect and follow protocol," she instructs. "If I see you are sincere, and not just curious, I will assist you to dissect my dialogue."

▮ REFLECTION

Author Louise Halfe writes from her heart. Whether she is influenced by childhood memories or in meditation with her grandmother, cultural symbolism is central to her writing. Think carefully about your life thus far and relate a defining experience that you feel is characteristic of your cultural or personal identity.

It is old in the sense that contemporary Aboriginal literature continues to be influenced by the oral tradition. Stories, prayers, and songs that are translated into English and written down make up a significant part of Aboriginal literature. In addition, many of the techniques and symbolism used by authors reflect upon the techniques of the oral tradition.

For example, many poets repeat the traditional rhythms of their ancestors' songs and dances. Beth Cuthand, a Cree poet who grew up in Saskatchewan and Alberta, begins "Four Songs for the Fifth Generation" with

Drums, chants, and rattles
pounded earth and
heartbeats
heartbeats

These lines are repeated three times, as such lines might have been repeated in an ancient song. The "pounded earth" reflects the rhythms of buffalo hoofs running across the prairie.

Many authors use Aboriginal languages in their work. This both affirms the words of the oral tradition and maintains the use of their ancestral languages. Louise Halfe affirms her Cree culture and its traditions in her first collection, *Bear Bones & Feathers*. She writes of Pahkahkos — "Flying Skeleton" — a Cree spirit, and Nohkom Atayohkan — "Grandmother of the Legends." She also uses Cree words throughout her work, even in titles where the English word might have sufficed, such as Nicimos (girlfriend/boyfriend) and Nitotem (my relative). Her book provides a glossary with translations of Cree words.

Allusion is another literary tool used frequently by Aboriginal writers. An **allusion** is a brief reference to a person, object, event, or place — real or fictitious. Allusions may be drawn from history, geography, literature, or religion.

When writers use an allusion, they assume that you share the same cultural experiences and will understand their references. Allusions help draw a circle of understanding around the audience and speaker, author, or storyteller. It is also a common technique used in oral traditions.

The circle has neither beginning nor ending. It has always been. The circle represents the journey of human existence. It connects us to our past and to our future. Within the periphery of the circle lies the key to all Native philosophy, values, and traditions. All things living depend upon its equilibrium. If it is unbalanced, the effects on our physical, mental, and emotional health can be devastating. Native peoples have experienced continuous change in the last two hundred and fifty years, and the circle has suffered stresses beyond imagination. Yet, it remains intact like the original people of this land. The women are the keepers of the circle. They have the power to nurture and to replenish life forces. Through our writing, we are maintaining our Nativeness in the fast-paced, often foreign contemporary society. The written word has given us our voice, and we have begun the healing process. We are writing the circle.

— Robin Melting Tallow,
Writing the Circle: Native Women of Western Canada

Nineteen-year-old Helen Betty Osborne, from Norway House First Nation in Manitoba, was murdered in 1971, but it took sixteen years for one of the four men who allegedly took part in her murder to be charged and convicted of the crime. The case has made many non-Aboriginal peoples aware of the racism present in institutions, such as the justice system. It has also prompted many Aboriginal peoples to speak out about their own experiences and to work to improve the relations between Aboriginal peoples and the justice system.

For example, in her poem "Helen Betty Osborne," Marilyn Dumont alludes to the murder of a Cree teenager.

> Betty, if I set out to write this poem
>   about you
> it might turn out instead,
> to be about me
> or any one of
> my female relatives,
> it might turn out to be
> about this young Native girl
> growing up in rural Alberta
> in a town with fewer Indians
> than ideas about Indians,
> in a town just south of the
>   "Aryan Nations."

Dumont's allusion to Helen Betty Osborne draws not only one event, but a history of violence and racism into her poem using just a few words.

An allusion is also an indirect method of making a point, which is also characteristic of the oral tradition. Aboriginal authors, like storytellers, often leave the teaching in their work up to the reader or audience to figure out, or infer, for themselves.

Inference is a conclusion based on reasoning rather than on a direct or explicit statement. It requires that the readers engage with the story and make a decision about what it means for themselves. It allows individuals to apply their own experiences and understandings to the writer's topic.

For example, the main character in Piikani writer Emma Lee Warrior's short story, "Compatriots," is a First Nations woman. At no point in the story does Warrior actually describe her main character, Lucy, as First Nations. Instead, readers infer from the events of the story that she is.

It is a powerful tool, especially for combatting stereotypes. Readers slowly gain an understanding of who Lucy is and what she stands for by learning about her as a person. They are not given the opportunity to begin an understanding of her with preconceived ideas or stereotypes.

As in other traditional and contemporary art forms, symbolism is often used by Aboriginal authors. Many of the symbols they employ are traditional and can be found in the oral tradition — various Teacher-Creator characters, buffalo, raven, eagle, spider, and countless other images from nature.

Other symbols have a more contemporary point of reference. For example, in her poem "Now That the Buffalo Are Gone," Buffy Sainte-Marie ends with the line "Now that the buffalo are gone." The disappearance of the buffalo is a symbol of the lost traditions and lifestyle of her people.

WRITING WHAT YOU KNOW

How do authors' life experiences and backgrounds affect their work?

WHAT TO DO

1. Select a First Nations, Métis, or Inuit author from Canada that you would like to learn more about. Choose any of the authors mentioned in this chapter or consider one of the following:

    > Jeannette Armstrong, Shirley Bear, Joan Crate, Pauline Johnson, Lenore Keeshig-Tobias, Verna Kirkness, Brian Maracle, Lee Maracle, Teresa Marshall, Rita Mestokosho, Daniel David Moses, Eden Robinson, Armand Ruffo, Lorne Simon, Ruby Slipperjack, Richard van Camp.

2. Using the Internet and other sources, find biographical information about the author.

3. Read a minimum of two works or story excerpts by the writer. The more you read, the better your project will be.

4. Create a profile of your author. Include the biographical information you researched and answer the following questions:

    - How has the author been influenced by his or her life experiences or those of family or community members?

    - What literary techniques and symbols does the author use?

    - How is the human experience portrayed in the author's writing?

    - How is a specifically Aboriginal experience portrayed in the author's work?

    - What beliefs and values are evident in the author's work?

    - What purpose or message does the author's work have?

- In your opinion, what is the contribution of the author to Aboriginal writing and Canadian writing?

Your profile can be the form of a poster, written report, oral presentation, Web site, PowerPoint™ presentation, or another format that you clear with your teacher.

Thinking About Your Project

As a class, discuss any works or authors that your classmates liked the most.

LOOKING BACK

Before finishing this section, be sure you can answer the following questions: How do Aboriginal writers express their life experiences in their work? Are there qualities of Aboriginal writing that are unique and different from the work of writers who have other cultural backgrounds? Do you think written literature builds community and preserves cultural history (as oral literatures once did)? Explain your answer with specific examples.

Chapter Seven Review

Check Your Understanding

1. How was the environment important to traditional creative practices?

2. Explain how art was a holistic part of traditional communities. Contrast this with the place of art in contemporary society.

3. Explain the connections between spirituality and traditional forms of creative expression.

4. Give two examples of how forms of creative expression adapted to the influence of another culture.

5. Why do people use symbols? How are symbols used in traditional artwork by Aboriginal peoples?

6. Give an example of a symbol found in different forms of Aboriginal creative expression and explain its significance.

7. Describe how dance, music, and performance helped build community in traditional societies. How does this compare to their role today?

8. Name at least four contemporary Aboriginal musicians, actors, or performers and give an example of their work.

9. Give an example of an allusion used by an Aboriginal author and describe why he or she uses it.

10. In what ways does contemporary Aboriginal literature draw upon oral traditions?

11. What are common themes in Aboriginal literature? Explain each in a sentence or two.

12. Describe at least four traditional forms of creative expression.

Reading and Writing

13. Read the statement on page 235 by Kakisketa, the narrator of a book called *The Art of the Nehiyawak*. Explain in a paragraph how her statement relates traditional forms of expression to First Nations spirituality.

14. Choose an Aboriginal artist and write a biography outlining his or her life and work. If you prefer, write a letter to the artist that explains what you appreciate about their work and ask questions about aspects that puzzle you. (You can write the letter even if the artist is deceased. If the artist is alive, you can decide for yourself whether to mail the letter.)

Viewing and Representing

15. Write a review of a film telling Aboriginal peoples' stories that is written by, starring, or directed by Aboriginal people.

16. In a group, create a documentary film (maximum 20 minutes in length) that expresses some aspect of your life experiences as teenagers attending your high school.

    Create a plan for your documentary before you start and agree upon whether the film will involve interviews, dramatizations, action, or group discussions. To keep your documentary on target, write a theme or main idea that your film will convey and be sure that each part of your plan reinforces the theme. Clear your plan with your teacher before you begin filming.

    Using a video camera, film your documentary, but keep in mind that only students in your class or other individuals who agree to be in the film may be part of your video.

    Hold a world premiere for your class's films and invite a V.I.P. list of teachers, family, and friends to attend.

17. Many writers are inspired by historical events. Investigate the inspiration behind Marilyn Dumont's poem "Helen Betty Osborne." Find out what happened in this case. Research other key issues in Aboriginal peoples' history that have inspired works of art, and prepare a profile of one event and the artwork it inspired. Create your own work of art in response to the same issue.

Speaking and Listening

18. Give a talk about an Aboriginal musician or musical group to your class. Listen to a range of Aboriginal music, both traditional and contemporary, before selecting a musician or group to research. Play short selections of their work as part of your presentation and be sure to describe any cultural or other influences on their music.

Going Further

19. Locate an individual who practises some form of traditional artwork, such as beadwork, quillwork, or carving. Working with a partner, request an interview using proper community protocol. If possible, learn how to do a basic technique. Demonstrate what you learned for your class.

20. Attend an art gallery, museum, or performance that highlights Aboriginal creative work. Write about your experience in your journal.

21. Priscilla Morin, shown in the photograph on this page, is a winner of a 2004 Esquao Award. Visit the Institute for the Advancement of Aboriginal Women Web site at *www.iaaw.ca* to research the organization, the origin of the awards, and the names of past winners. Choose one of the winners to research and profile or nominate someone you think should be honoured in this way.

Priscilla Morin won a country music award at the Canadian Aboriginal Music Awards in 2000 and an Esquao Award in 2004 from the Institute for the Advancement of Aboriginal Women. She grew up at the Kikino Métis Settlement and attended high school in Lac La Biche, Alberta. In interviews, she states that her success as a musician comes from her musical father and her mother, who she describes as a "steadying force." Search the Internet for the Canadian Aboriginal Music Awards Web site to read about other significant musicians and groups.

A woman provides great prestige for her family by making beautiful things for them to wear. A woman can be very proud if she has found the time to do these things and take care of her family.

We live in a land filled with beauty and colour. We see the beauty of the Great Spirit all around us and we want to put this beauty into the things we make. The Great Spirit lives in each of us, and the Spirit speaks through us in the beautiful things we make.

— Kakisketa, narrator in
The Art of the Nehiyawak

LOOKING BACK

Look back to Marilyn Dumont's poem on pages 210–211. What have you learned in this chapter that adds to your understanding?

Now look back to the focus questions you first read on page 2 of this textbook. Compare your answers now to your first attempts when you started this course. Are you satisfied with what you have learned?

Glossary

The definitions provided here reflect the context of this textbook. In other contexts, some words and terms may have alternative meanings.

Aboriginal peoples: the original inhabitants of a land and their descendants. In 1982, the Canadian constitution recognized three groups of Aboriginal peoples — First Nations, Métis, and Inuit — each with diverse sets of communities with their own histories, languages, cultural practices, and spiritual beliefs.

Alliances: working partnerships in pursuit of common interests

Allusion: a brief reference to a person, object, event, or place

Animate: according to Western thinking, the quality of being organic, living, and breathing; e.g., people, animals, plants. According to traditional First Nations spirituality, some non-living objects (i.e., ceremonial pipe, certain landforms) are considered animate because they have a spiritual aspect.

Armed conflict: open, often prolonged fighting between groups equipped with weapons; a battle or war

Assimilation: the process of absorbing or being absorbed by a group or system. In Canada during the nineteenth and twentieth centuries, government policies of assimilation attempted to make Aboriginal peoples adopt non-Aboriginal culture.

Band council: the government of a territorially based group of First Nations people who share a common culture and ancestry; e.g., the Samson Cree Nation. Each band council includes one or more chiefs and several councillors.

Cairns: mounds of rocks built to show direction or mark significant or sacred spots on the landscape

Ceremonies: formal acts or sets of acts performed according to custom, law, or other authority; many Aboriginal ceremonies have symbolic meaning and a spiritual nature; e.g., the pipe ceremony, the Sundance

Circular seasonal time frame: a calendar system based on the cycles of nature through the four seasons and the repetitive changes — the migration of animals and birds and a changing food supply — that occur during those times. Traditionally, the activities, ceremonies, and rituals of First Nations and Inuit peoples centred on this sense of time.

Clans: related groups of people or families

Collective: belonging to a group of people. A collective inheritance is the knowledge and property handed down to a group of people by their ancestors. A collective government is a government with authority to deliberate on and make decisions about issues that affect many groups or individuals.

Colonial governance: the act of governing or the government itself within a colony or territory that is part of a colonial empire. Canada was subject to colonial governance by Britain, but also enacted colonial governance over Aboriginal peoples.

Colonization: the establishment of a colony or colonies involving one country taking political and economic control of another country or territory and attempting to change the existing culture, often by importing many people as settlers or administrators to encourage the social transformation. The colonized country is usually exploited for the benefit of the colonizing country.

Community initiative: an introductory program of action undertaken by a group of people with common identity living in the same local area

Confederacies: formal alliances of nations, states, organizations, or individuals

Consensus: a collectively held opinion

Constitution: the written or unwritten set of principles and institutions by which a nation governs itself

Council: a formal group that discusses and advises upon courses of action

Cultural environment: a geographic region that is home to groups of people sharing similar cultural characteristics. Much diversity can exist, however, even within a single cultural environment.

Cultural group: a number of racially or historically related people with a distinctive common culture

Cultural transmission: the process by which the standard behaviour patterns and values of the surrounding culture are passed on to and adopted by individuals as their own attitudes and beliefs

Culture: the collection of hereditary beliefs, values, and shared knowledge of a group of people that are embodied in customs, routines, roles, and rituals and that make that group of people distinct from others

Cycle of life: a repeating pattern of existence in which all living things pass through stages of growth and change until finally the end of life becomes a beginning for a new cycle

Discrimination: unequal treatment resulting from distinguishing one group of people as inferior to another, especially on the grounds of race, colour, or gender. Discrimination may be subtle — such as Aboriginal peoples experiencing greater difficulty than non-Aboriginal peoples in obtaining jobs — or blatant. Until 1985, the Indian Act blatantly discriminated against First Nations women by denying their legal status if they married men without status under the Indian Act.

Displacement: the state of people being forced to move from homelands as a result of war, abuse, disaster, or other conflict

Economic partnerships: relationships between individuals or groups that is characterized by mutual cooperation and responsibility towards a speoifio goal related to the production, development, and management of material wealth

Economic stability: the state of being strong and firmly established financially with the ability to withstand fluctuations in income and expenses

Elders: individuals recognized by their community as having spiritual and cultural wisdom

Entrepreneurs: individuals who establish a new businesses in which they take a financial risk in the hope that the business will succeed and be profitable

Evangelism: organized, zealous efforts to convert people to Christianity

Exploitation: taking advantage of something for one's own use or benefit, especially in an unethical manner

Extended family: a primary living group that includes adult siblings and their children, parents, and grandparents

Factor: the trader in charge of a trading post

First Nations: in Canada, the group of Aboriginal peoples formerly or alternately known as Indians (a disfavoured term; *see Indian*). First Nations refers to individuals — over 500 000 First Nations people live in Canada — and to communities (or reserves) and their governments (or band councils). The term, which arose in the 1980s, is politically significant because it implies possession of rights arising from historical occupation and use of territory. Though no Canadian legal definition of this term exists (the constitution refers to Indians), the United Nations considers the term synonymous with indigenous peoples.

Hierarchical: a system in which different groups are ranked one above the other, with those on the top having more influence and power than those on the bottom

Holistic: emphasizing the importance of the whole and the interdependence of its parts

Homeguard: First Nations people living more or less permanently around fur trading posts who established ongoing, reciprocal relationships with the trading companies, often lasting for generations

Inanimate: according to Western European thinking, the quality of being being inorganic, not living or breathing; e.g., rocks, rivers, wind, the sun. *See animate*

Indian Act: the law governing First Nations peoples (and the descendants of those people) that signed treaties or who were otherwise registered in the act's provisions, encompassing the governance of reserves and the rights and benefits of registered individuals. First passed in 1876 and amended many times since, the act designates federal government obligations towards registered individuals and regulates the management of reserve lands.

Indians: groups of Aboriginal peoples who generally prefer to be called First Nations. The term *Indian* is still commonly used by Canadian governments, including in the constitution. First Nations people generally disfavour the term because it originated from early European explorers' mistaken impression that they had landed in India. It also ignores the great diversity of history and cultures among various First Nations.

Indigenous peoples: the original inhabitants of a land and their descendants

Inference: a conclusion based on reasoning rather than on direct or explicit statement

Inherent rights: rights in existence prior to Canada becoming a nation and outside of Canada's constitution or any other government or legal authority. Aboriginal peoples claim an inherent right to self-government based on their position as indigenous peoples.

Institutions: recurrent, organized patterns of activity that facilitate a society's religious, legal, family, economic, political, government, social welfare, educational, and health care systems

Interdependent: when individuals or groups rely upon one another for some purpose

Interpersonal relationships: connections between people related to or having dealings with one another. One traditional purpose of the oral tradition was to teach culturally desired types of interpersonal relationships through example.

Inuit: the Aboriginal people of northern Canada, who live primarily in Nunavut, the Northwest Territories, Labrador, and northern Quebec. Inuit peoples also live in Greenland, Russia, and the American state of Alaska.

Kinship: a tie between related individuals, usually through blood, but also through adoption

Land claim: a demand for title to certain territories as legitimately owed to and deserved by specific groups of people. In Canada, comprehensive land claims involve land not covered by treaties and are generally based on rights stemming from historic use and occupancy of specific territories. Specific land claims involve areas covered by treaties where the terms of the treaties have not been met or land has been removed over the years without consent.

Linguistic group: a group of nations, racially or historically related, that have the same basic language. For example, First Nations who speak Cree are a linguistic group.

Matrilineal: a system of social organization that is based on kinship with the mother's line of descent

Métis: a group of Aboriginal peoples with First Nations and European ancestry. Métis people identify with Métis history and culture, which dates back to the fur trade era when First Nations women and European (mostly French or British) men married and had children. Métis people were for many years refused political recognition by the federal government, although they received recognition as Aboriginal people in the Constitution Act of 1982.

Métis Nation: Aboriginal people who identify themselves as Métis, who are distinct from First Nations and Inuit peoples, and who are descendants of Métis people living in the Red River area of Manitoba in the 1800s

Métis Settlements: land set aside by the Alberta government in 1938 for the use and occupancy of Métis people; similar to First Nations reserves

Middlemen: Aboriginal individuals who served as the link between trappers (producers of goods) and the North West or Hudson's Bay trading companies (the consumers)

Migration: the movement of a group of people from one region to another. Some traditional Aboriginal lifestyles followed regular patterns of movement based on seasonal cycles. *See circular seasonal time frame*

Missionaries: people conducting charitable religious work, often in a foreign country, who intend to convert others to their religion

Mutual support: a concept central to Aboriginal cultures in which relationships and activities benefit the whole rather than the individual

Nation: a community of people bound together by common traditions, culture, and usually language who have political independence and who occupy a distinct territory

Natural resources: materials existing in nature that are useful or necessary to people, such as forests, minerals, game animals, and water

Non-Status Indians: a term created by the Indian Act that refers to First Nations people who are not registered, for whatever reason, according to the act's requirements and therefore do not qualify for the rights and benefits given to people registered as Status Indians

Oral tradition: a practice in which the entire body of knowledge, history, language, and all other aspects of culture are passed from generation to generation through the spoken word

Origin: the point at which something began. For example, creation stories describe how the first people and the world came to exist.

Patrilineal: a system of social organization that is based on kinship with the father's line of descent

Personal autonomy: an individual's freedom and independence to determine his or her own course of action

Perspective: a particular way of seeing situations or topics, understanding relationships, and evaluating the significance of events; a point of view

Protocol: a set of formal rules, etiquette, or procedures for interactions between people that communicates respect and tradition

Racism: belief in the inferiority of a group of people solely because of race, skin colour, descent, or national or ethnic origin

Religions: institutionalized systems of attitudes, beliefs, and practices involving the worship of an acknowledged deity or god

Reciprocol: give and take; mutually beneficial exchange

Repatriate: to restore something to its rightful location, nation, or territory

Reserve: land set aside, or reserved, by the government during the colonization of Canada for the use of a First Nation. The federal government has jurisdiction over reserves and the people living there.

Rights: the authority to act or be treated in a particular way; e.g., the right to a fair trial. Most rights are recognized by law; many categories exist, such as human rights, Aboriginal rights, property rights, and women's rights.

Self-determination: the principle that people of a territory have the authority to establish their own political, economic, and cultural futures without external interference

Self-government: a community's right to make decisions about matters internal to the community

Self-identify: to regard one's self as belonging to a particular cultural group. For various economic, administrative, and political reasons, governments and Aboriginal political organizations create definitions for different groups of Aboriginal peoples, such as Status Indians, non-Status Indians, and Métis. These definitions include some people, but exclude others. How a person is identified by these governments and organizations can impact the rights and benefits a person has. The concept of self-identity acknowledges that an individual's identity is personal and cannot always be defined with a rigid set of criteria.

Self-sufficiency: to be capable of providing for one's own needs

Socialization: the lifelong process by which individuals learn and absorb the values and standards of their society

Sovereignty: the authorized right and ability of a governing individual (e.g., a president or monarch) or institution of a society (e.g., a government) to exert political control over a given territory or people. Aboriginal claims to sovereignty generally centre on the right of a nation to rule itself without external control or interference.

Spirituality: a set of beliefs relating to a higher power, such as the Creator, and incorporating high ideals, values, morals, and ethics. For traditional First Nations and Inuit peoples, spirituality is a part of daily life and personal identity. It involves honouring and respecting all things in existence and taking responsibility for maintaining harmonious relationships with them.

Standard of living: the level of material comforts (i.e., goods, services, and luxuries) available to an individual, group, or nation. The measurement of a particular group or nation's standard of living is generally used in comparison to the standard of living of other groups or nations. By itself, the measurement has no inherent significance. Standard of living is not the same as quality of life, which is an individual's own assessment of his or her life and their level of satisfaction with it. For example, people might live in a city where having an expensive car is common. A standard of living measurement might then assess people's living standard as lower than other people in the city if they do not have this kind of car. However, individuals might choose not to own a car for personal reasons, such as a concern for the environment. These individuals might assess their own quality of life as high because they feel good about not contributing to the world's environmental problems and enjoy the exercise they get while riding a bike or walking.

Status Indians: a term created by the Indian Act that refers to a First Nations person who is registered according to the act's requirements and therefore qualifies for certain rights and benefits

Stereotypes: rigid and inflexible mental images that portray all individuals of an ethnic, national, cultural, or other group as being without individual characteristics

Symbol: something that represents or stands for something else, generally a more complex idea, concept, or event. Symbolism is an integral part of traditional Aboriginal spirituality and is part of many cultural ceremonies; e.g., smoke from the ceremonial pipe symbolizes communication with the Great Spirit.

Technologies: tools or other applications of scientific and mechanical knowledge for practical purposes

Theories: plausible or scientifically acceptable explanations that have not been proven as fact

Trading captains: First Nations leaders identified by European traders as speaking for a group of people

Traditional: First Nations and Inuit ways of life that existed before contact with Europeans, as well as contemporary Aboriginal people or ways of life that are connected to the spiritual, social, and cultural teachings of this time period

Traditional territories: regions historically inhabited and used by a group of Aboriginal peoples. Land claims are often centred on traditional territories.

Treaties: legal agreements or contracts between two or more sovereign nations that set out obligations and responsibilities for both or all parties. Treaties signed between First Nations and the British or Canadian government provide specific rights regarding traditional territories.

Treaty rights: special rights to lands and other entitlements due to people recognized as Treaty Indians under negotiated treaties. These rights depend on the precise terms and conditions of the treaty. No two treaties are identical, but usually they provide rights such as entitlement to reserve lands, hunting and fishing rights, annuities (small annual payments) for members, and sometimes freedom from certain types of taxation.

Virgin soil epidemics: diseases that spread among populations that have little or no acquired immunity to the infection

Wampum: shell beads that some First Nations wove into belts or strings as a way of recording information or agreements

Worldview: the perspective from which a person perceives, understands, and reacts to the world around them. People from a common culture share many elements of the same worldview.

Suggested Resources for Further Reading and Research

Adams, Howard. 1989. *Prison of Grass: Canada from a Native Point of View.* Saskatoon: Fifth House Publishers.

Ahenakew, Freda and H. C. Wolfart. 1992. *Kôhkominawak Otâcimowiniwâwa (Our Grandmothers' Lives, As Told in Their Own Words.)* Saskatoon: Fifth House Publishers.

Anderson, Anne. 1997. *Dr. Anne Anderson's Metis Cree Dictionary.* Edmonton: Duval House Publishing.

Blondin, George. 1997. *Yamoria The Lawmaker: Stories of the Dene.* Edmonton: NeWest Press.

Bloomfield, Leonard. 1993. *Sacred Stories of the Sweet Grass Cree.* Ottawa: Fifth House Publishers.

Brant, Beth. 1988. *A Gathering of Spirit: A Collection by North American Indian Women.* Toronto: Women's Press.

Brizinski, Peggy. 1989. *Knots in a String: An Introduction to Native Studies in Canada.* Saskatoon: Division of Extension and Community Relations, University of Saskatchewan.

Campbell, Maria. 1979. *Halfbreed.* Edmonton: Alberta Education. Published as part of the Alberta Heritage Learning Resources project.

Cardinal, Harold. 1969. *The Unjust Society: The Tragedy of Canada's Indians.* Edmonton: Hurtig Publishers.

Cardinal, Harold and Walter Hildebrandt. 2000. *Treaty Elders of Saskatchewan: Our Dream Is that Our Peoples Will One Day Be Clearly Recognized as Nations.* Calgary: University of Calgary Press.

Cardinal, Phyllis. 1997. *The Cree People.* Edmonton: Duval House Publishing and Tribal Chiefs Institute of Treaty 6.

Coutu, Phillip R. and Lorraine Hoffman-Mercredi. 1999. *Inkonze: The Stones of Traditional Knowledge: A History of Northeastern Alberta.* Edmonton: Thunderwoman Ethnographics.

Dene Wodih Society. 1990. *Wolverine Myths and Visions: Dene Traditions from Northern Alberta.* Edmonton: University of Alberta Press.

Dickason, Olive Patricia. 2002. *Canada's First Nations: A History of Founding Peoples from Earliest Times.* 3rd ed. Toronto: Oxford University Press.

Dion, Joseph F. 1979. *My Tribe the Crees.* Calgary: Glenbow–Alberta Institute.

Fleury, Norman. 2000. *La Lawng: Michif Peekishkewewin (The Canadian Michif Language Dictionary) (Introductory Level.)* Manitoba: The Manitoba Métis Federation Michif Language Program.

Fox, Leo. 2001. *Kipaitapiiwahsinnooni (Alcohol and Drug Abuse Education Program).* Edmonton: Duval House Publishing.

Frantz, Donald G. and Norma Jean Russell. 2000. *Blackfoot Dictionary of Stems, Roots, and Affixes.* 2nd ed. Toronto: University of Toronto Press.

Garvin, Terry. 1992. *Bush Land People.* Calgary: Arctic Institute of North America.

Glenbow Museum. 2001. *Nitsitapiisinni (The Story of the Blackfoot People).* Toronto: Key Porter Books.

Harrison, Julia D. 1985. *Metis: People Between Two Worlds.* Vancouver: Glenbow–Alberta Institute in association with Douglas & McIntyre.

Hodgins, Ken J. 1988. *The Art of the Nehiyawak.* Edmonton: Plains Publishing.

Kulchyski, Peter, Don McCaskill, and David Newhouse (eds.) 1999. *In the Words of Elders: Aboriginal Cultures in Transition.* Toronto: University of Toronto Press.

Le Claire, Nancy and George Cardinal. 1998. *Alberta Elders' Cree Dictionary.* Edmonton: University of Alberta Press and Duval House Publishing.

MacEwan, Grant. 1981. *Métis Makers of History.* Saskatoon: Western Producer Prairie Books.

Meili, Dianne. 1991. *Those Who Know: Profiles of Alberta's Native Elders.* Edmonton: NeWest Press.

Minde, Emma. 1997. *kwayask ê-kî-pê-kiskinowâpahtihcik (Their Example Showed Me the Way).* Edmonton: University of Alberta Press.

Molloy, Tom. 2000. *The World Is Our Witness: The Historic Journey of the Nisga'a into Canada.* Calgary: Fifth House Publishers.

Moses, Daniel David and Terry Goldie. 1998. *An Anthology of Canadian Native Literature in English.* 2nd ed. Toronto: Oxford University Press.

Petrone, Penny. 1988. *Northern Voices: Inuit Writing in English.* Toronto: University of Toronto Press.

Price, Richart T. 1991. *Legacy: Indian Treaty Relationships.* Edmonton: Plains Publishing.

Price, Richard T. (ed.) 1999. *The Spirit of the Alberta Indian Treaties.* 3rd ed. Edmonton: University of Alberta Press.

Snow, Chief John. 1977. *These Mountains Are Our Sacred Places.* Toronto: Samuel-Stevens, Publishers.

Stonechild, Blair. 1997. *Loyal Till Death: Indians and the North-West Rebellion.* Calgary: Fifth House Publishers.

Tribal Chiefs Institute and Indian and Northern Affairs. 2001. *In Their Footsteps: Contributions of First Nations People in Alberta.* Edmonton: Duval House Publishing and Tribal Chiefs Institute.

Van Kirk, Sylvia. 1980. *Many Tender Ties: Women in Fur Trade Society, 1670–1870.* Norman: University of Oklahoma Press.

Waldman, Carol. 2000. *Atlas of the North American Indian.* New York: Checkmark Books.

York, Geoffrey. 1990. *The Dispossessed: Life and Death in Native Canada.* London: Vintage U.K.

Zaharia, Flora and Leo Fox. 1995. *Kitomahkitapiiminnooniksi: Stories from Our Elders. Vol. 1.* Edmonton: Donahue House Publishing.

Zaharia, Flora and Leo Fox. 1995. *Kitomahkitapiiminnooniksi: Stories from Our Elders. Vol. 2.* Edmonton: Donahue House Publishing.

Zaharia, Flora and Leo Fox. 1995. *Kitomahkitapiiminnooniksi: Stories from Our Elders. Vol. 3.* Edmonton: Donahue House Publishing.

Zaharia, Flora, Leo Fox, and Marvin Fox. 2003. *Kitomahkitapiiminnoonisksi: Stories from Our Elders. Vol. 4.* Edmonton: Duval House Publishing.

Index